Shining a Light

Creating Pathways to Equity, Safety, Healing, and Justice With People with Disabilities

Shirley Paceley

FOR MOM

CONTENTS

Shining a Light

Introduction

When I began my professional journey in 1973, working with people with disabilities who were being released from institutions in Illinois, I did not even recognize that I, too, had disabilities, related to scoliosis and years of childhood trauma. And yet, I always felt a kinship with people with developmental disabilities and their struggle to belong, feel safe, seek justice, find healing, source respect, and be free. To each of the people whose story is shared in this book, I am eternally thankful for our relationship and your courage. I am honored to have been a part of your life whether for a short time or for many years. We are bound together by an invisible thread created by our collective grieving, resiliency, shared joy, and our triumph over adversity. In 1973, this work was written in my heart, never to be erased.

I believe that stories can change hearts. I believe that stories can change minds. I believe that stories can change laws. I believe that stories can change the world. Each story in this book is the truth based on my best memory and my personal perspective. These stories portray the real lived experiences of each person through my lens. Permission has been granted for the sharing of any story bearing identifying information, and in other cases, names and other information has been changed to respect the identify of each individual. In some cases, even though permission was granted to share a story, the name was changed as agreed. I hope the stories are received with an open heart and bring you new ideas, inspiration, and a desire to join the movement for equity, safety, freedom, healing, and justice for people with disabilities.

This book is a collection of stories and lessons learned. This work has been my life's passion: emerged from my own internal struggles, anger, and questions that arose out of witnessing inequality, oppression, lack of access, horrific abuse, denial of services, and even hatred. The pathways to dignity, respect and access have had many twists and turns. I have had the honor of working with and beside people with disabilities and in some cases, their family members, law enforcement, prosecutors, victim services, disability organizations, schools, sexual assault forensic examiners, adult protective services, early childhood specialists, and others. After 48 years, there are still so many questions and so much work to be done. I wrote this book to shine a light on what I have observed and discovered and with the intention of expanding opportunities for others to discover what role they can play in this road to social justice for people with disabilities. I wonder, how can you show up? How can you use your light for good?

I am grateful that you have chosen to join me on this journey. This book can be used in a variety of ways. It is for you. Use it how it best fits with your job, your responsibilities, your interests, and your life. Sprinkled throughout the book are questions for the reader. These questions can be a personal journey in which the reader reflects on the questions to expand their understanding of themselves and humanity. The questions can be used as part of a study group or even as part of training within an organization. For the reader who only wants to read the stories and lessons learned, the questions can be skipped. For the readers who are curious and want to go deeper, reflect on the questions. My goal was to provide resources for personal and professional development for a variety of audiences. Flexibility is important for trainers and at heart, training is one of my callings. My hope is that some of the issues described in this book will soon become antiquated - that the painful stories are filed away and remembered as a part of history - because the movement makes major advancements in access, inclusion, respect, dignity, safety, and equality for people with disabilities. I encourage you to push the limits. Question the status quo. Dig deeper. Find new solutions. Listen deeply. Live boldly. Create access. Think creatively. Generate ideas with others. Join the movement to end violence against people who have been excluded. Be a change-maker. Be you.

A list of resources/references, by chapter, is included at the end of the book: denoted in text by a *

Content Warning: Some of the content in this book might be upsetting. Please take good care of yourself. Do what you can to feel safe. Know what people to contact if you need help. We care about you. We also know that painful stories need to be told so we can make changes…so less people are hurt…so more people can heal…so more people can be safe.

Shining a light - a poem

What seems
like a lifetime ago now
I walked in darkness
weighted down by acts of others
blinded by trauma
and unable to see
beyond the pain

Buried in darkness
I used to be obsessed
with survival
searching for light
 O u t   t h e r e
                somewhere

And then I noticed
some sparkles of light
  in the kindness of others
    in small acts of service
      in the joy of children
        in the fight for freedom

These sparkles grew and grew
as I nurtured myself
  opening my heart to love
  opening my mind to new ways
  opening my spirit to hopefulness

And as the light was uncovered
I began sharing it freely
   slowly at first

As my bravery grew
and my chosen family grew
and as I grew
so did my light

I know some days
It shines brighter
than other days
and now, most days
I own it boldly
I claim it totally
I share it freely

I think I have discovered
why I am here
   to shine my light
   and to see clearly
   the light in others
Perhaps, that is why
we are all here

Chapter 1

How it All Started

"Each of us has a unique part to play in the healing of the world." Marianne Williamson

"There is no greater gift you can give or receive than to honor your calling. It's why you are born, and how you become most truly alive". Oprah Winfrey

In the Beginning

I really did not know what to expect when I arrived for my first day of work at the "sheltered care home" at the age of 22, and I certainly didn't know that my whole life would be altered from the experience. The building was old, had previously been a hospital, and had been vacant for several years before becoming a 'home' for people with developmental disabilities. I had driven past it several times. It was my first job working with people with disabilities and I was hired at $1.60/hour, which was the minimum wage at the time. I was hired to be an aide to the 60 people who lived there. On that first day, I entered the building and was directed to a large room filled with tables piled high with clothes. I was told to "sort the clothes by size". I asked, "When is the rummage sale?" and was told by my supervisor the clothes were for the 'residents' and "if they are sorted by size, it will

9

make it easier for you and others to help people get dressed".   And then she was gone. I began sorting the masses of clothing wondering why people didn't have their own clothes. It was the first of many questions I would ask.

Approximately an hour later, she returned and gave me a tour of the facility. I asked her about the clothing and was told that 'residents' who had involved family members had their clothes in their bedroom closets. "It is important to take good care of theirs because the families get mad if things got lost". Again, I was confused. Didn't everyone deserve to have their own clothes and have them taken care of?

I was told the schedule including meals, meds, baths, and bedtime. I worked the 2pm to 10pm shift three days a week, and 6am to 2pm on the weekends. The most exciting part of that first day was meeting so many interesting people. I found that I really enjoyed meeting and connecting with the diverse tapestry of people who lived there. I was thinking maybe I would really like working here. That flow of positive energy came to an abrupt stop when bath time ruined my day!

There were two large bathrooms on the second floor - one on each end of the same hallway

- one for women and one for men. People lined up naked in a long line that extended through the bathroom and into the hall - each person waiting for their turn to get into the bathtub to use the same water as was used by those who had bathed previously. I was immediately sickened. I knew this was wrong!

Although it has been nearly 48 years since that first day, I still remember much of it vividly. I remember many of the faces and smiles and the warm welcome I received as a new person in the 'home'. I remember my confusion about some of the practices, and I deeply remember my nausea that turned to anger about the lack of dignity, respect, and equality. Over the next several months, many events deepened my anger and fed my passion to make a difference. Here are a few examples:

Donna

There was a fairly young woman, I will call Donna, who spent her days walking the halls, and although I had difficulty understanding her spoken word, it was obvious that she was sad much of the time. All of us Aides were told that if Donna wet in her pants, we were to give her a cold shower to teach her not to do that again. This seemed really cruel to me. I had several questions: Why would we

11

be mean to someone who was already so sad? Is there a medical reason that Donna cannot control her bladder? Are we assuming Donna does this on purpose? Are there kinder ways to prevent her from having accidents? How long have they been doing this to Donna? How does she respond when staff do this? Would any one of us want this to happen to us if we had an accident in our clothing? I was able to ask a couple of these questions and was told 'this is her behavior plan created by a professional'. The implications were—do what you're told, and you don't know about these things. I knew there was a lot I didn't know about people with disabilities, but I knew a lot about being kind. I never participated in the cold shower therapy. When possible, I would help Donna change into dry clothes before anyone else could see she was wet.

With a staff to resident ratio of two staff to 60 residents (evenings and weekends), I could not spend a lot of time with Donna, but I did try to spend a few minutes with her every shift I worked. I would walk with her as she paced the halls and would smile when she glanced at me - which happened more and more often over the months we were together. One day she began smiling back at me and I felt the power and gift of connection!

Food

At mealtime, I sat at the table with folks and ate whatever was being served, while helping those beside me who needed support. I started noticing a pattern about the quality of food. The early part of each month, the food was average; not fantastic but not horrible. Towards the end of the month, the food quality dropped drastically.

I understand that we all have some kind of relationship with food, so let me tell you about mine. I grew up in a home with amazing home -cooking! All the neighbors knew that my mom was the best cook in town. Nothing fancy, but always homemade and delicious! Once I moved away from home, I had some not so wonderful meals. There was the month when I basically lived on oatmeal (food commodities) - except for the one amazing, free breakfast at a small café. There were times I ate at missions for free, after sitting through a church service. There were a few times I had the free breakfast at a Salvation Army, after spending the night while traveling across country with almost no money. By the time I started this job, I could eat about anything. But there were days when I could not eat the food being served, and once or twice I could barely look at it. I also knew that I was privileged - I could go home at 10pm and cook some Ramen noodles and they would taste good. That wasn't true for the people who lived in this home. For many people, having tasty food based on our personal choices is one of life's pleasures that bring us joy. So, why not the people here? Again, I did not understand. Why were the opportunities for their lives so different, so limited?

Towards the end of my tenure, I was told that the cook received a personal bonus each month if she kept the food budget under a certain dollar amount. I also discovered that the company was a private, for-profit corporation so the cook helped keep the profits high by reducing expenses. I knew nothing about for profit and not-for-profit companies until that moment. Hmmm...maybe I was starting to understand something.

A few weeks after I left this job, there was this one food-related incident that haunted me for years. Two people who lived at the home, walked to a near-by grocery store, and stole a loaf of bread and some bologna. They were both arrested. One of them went to prison. No one asked why they were hungry in the first place.

Birth Control

ALL of the women at this 'home' received birth control pills without knowledge, consent, or genital examinations. I knew that my friends and I had a choice about birth control and received proper initial and ongoing medical exams. Why not the women who lived here? Again, I wondered why this was happening. Why was there no education, no choice, no health care?

Below Minimum

Some of the people who lived there worked to support the upkeep of the facility such as mowing the lawn, kitchen support, and cleaning. Their hard work took the place of employment positions, and they were paid way below minimum wage and saved the company hundreds of dollars every month. These hard-working residents had no idea they were being taken advantage of and had no life experience to compare with this work experience. They were simply grateful to receive a little bit of money, and nobody provided them education or choices about their situation, instead they took advantage of their lack of exposure and understanding. Why were they taken advantage of? Why weren't they at least paid minimum wage?

Teresa

One day, I arrived at the building a few minutes early and noticed two staff members on the stairs. They were whispering and frowning. As I got closer, I heard one of them say, "Tell Shirley. She'll do something." I asked what was going on and they told me to go to Teresa's room and I would find out.

Teresa was a delightful person! She loved people, enjoyed activities, and had a beautiful smile. When I arrived at her room, she was lying in bed and the housekeeper was folding linens at the end of the bed. I greeted Teresa and she began talking immediately, but I did not know what she was saying. I was shocked to see that she was paralyzed on one side and her speech was not understandable. There was fear in her eyes. None of these symptoms were present the day before. I tried to find out what was going on and was told the nurse was involved and the housekeeper had everything under control. I happened to see someone in the hall from an advocacy and monitoring organization and asked to her to step inside the bedroom. The two of us decided that Teresa needed to go to the hospital. I called an ambulance. Teresa was taken to the hospital a few minutes later.

I was called into the office to speak with someone in management. I was told that I had no business calling an ambulance and that if Teresa died, it would be my fault for having her moved. I was told that I was NOT a medical professional, which I already knew. I was asked to sign a paper that I would never go against management or any professional again. If I signed the paper, I could keep my job. I replied, "I cannot sign that. I will always do what I believe is best for the people who live here. As for today, everyone has a basic right to health care." And that was it, my job was over. I had no opportunity to tell anyone goodbye.

I was devastated. For a couple of minutes, I questioned myself. Did I do the right thing? Had my anger over the situation spurred me into wrong action? But after some soul-searching, I honestly believed that I had done what was right for Teresa. I was angry and sad at the same time. I had grown close to the people who lived there. We had smiled and laughed together. We had cried together. I loved their open hearts and they had touched mine in many ways. I missed them. I worried about them. I made a promise to each of them, although I could not tell them at the time, that I would find a way to make a positive difference in their lives. I was heading fast into a lifetime commitment…and that's when I got serious about getting a college education.

By the way, when Teresa arrived at the hospital it was determined that she had had a stroke. She was in the hospital for 21 days and then returned to the sheltered care home to continue her life.

For many years, when someone asked me how I got started in working with people with disabilities, I would point to this first job experience. But now I know there was a foundation laid before this - some other factors that combined with this job to set me on the path I have taken.

Questions for the reader:

1. Can you relate to any of the author's early job experiences?
2. What were some early jobs that you had? How did these jobs influence your career path?
3. Have you ever experienced a gross injustice toward other humans? How did you feel about those injustices? What did you do or not do, and why?

4. Have you defined your purpose or purposes in life? Does that purpose or purposes make your heart smile? Are you fulfilled with those choices?

The Foundation

As with everyone, my experiences during childhood played an important role in the development of my personality and values. For purposes of this book, I will share the major experiences that I believe led me to a life of service and advocacy.

My mother, Alice (Rose) White was an amazing woman who left quite a legacy. She taught us to be kind, to help others, to follow our hearts, to be of service, to be flexible, to be independent, to work hard, and to be strong. She was a Registered Nurse and was often called on by neighbors for assistance with injuries, ailments, and for medical advice. She was an incredible cook (which I am not) and shared this talent with many others. She was a 'church woman' with very strong values and standards. Looking back, I can only remember a couple times when she outwardly judged someone negatively. She taught us to love everyone - through her words and example. She gave birth to four children that survived, as well as twins who were born too early to live longer than a few minutes. I was the third living child out of the four biological children.

When I was 13, mom began a process to become a foster parent. Our home soon included a four-month-old baby who had been neglected and physically abused early in her life. When she arrived at our home, she had a shaved head with four bandages covering her scars from brain surgery, and her eyes rolled around in her head. These injuries resulted from extreme abuse and trauma. My sisters and I became incredibly involved in her care, including her physical therapy exercises. The story of her first few weeks of life broke my heart and I was desperate to help, as were my two sisters, Linda, and Carol. Mom always said, "That child never had a diaper rash! One of my girls had their hand under her diaper constantly, waiting for their turn to change her." That may have been an exaggeration, but we did argue about whose turn it was to change her diaper.

Since we were spoiling the baby so badly, mom decided she needed another baby so we could spread out the attention. And it blossomed from there. Mom adopted that first baby, and we had a permanent sister (Reneta) join our family. Over the years, mom had approximately 26 foster children of all different ages. Everyone who joined our family, whether for four months or 10 years, had a history. We heard lots of sad stories and watched my mom love and advocate for each child. You might think that all these children would make me feel grateful for my life blessings, but that was not my experience. I was mad that the world was so cruel. I was sad for the children and youth that had to endure such neglectful and abusive circumstances. I was on fire to change the world! When I moved away from home after I graduated from high school, I occasionally met a teenager in a bad situation, called my mom, and she figured out how to legally bring them into her home and into her life. I was grateful that she had the tenacity and the willingness to open her home and her heart to so many. I found some folks who needed a good home, but mom did all the work.

Because we shared our home with so many children and youth, and because my mom was so open-hearted and loving, seeds of service and compassion were planted deep in my soul. This was the strong foundation that prepared me and beckoned me to live a life of service. It was my job to determine what that service was meant to be. Thank you, Mom!

****

The second influence from my early years was the childhood sexual abuse committed against me by a close family member. These experiences impacted who I became and my adult life choices. The sexual abuse began before the age of three and continued to age nine. These repeated incidents of abuse left me feeling broken, less-than, angry, alone, and very depressed. It remained buried for decades.

The effects of child sexual abuse committed against me exacerbated during my teen years. I was impulsive, experienced episodes of feeling rage, did not trust anyone, was suicidal on several occasions…and I knew I was very alone in all of this. My ways of coping included writing poetry and taking long walks down country roads. But there were two things that kept me alive during this difficult, lonely time: a tiny spark deep inside of me that let me know I was here for a greater purpose ("Hang in there, Shirley. There are good days to come.") and a Junior High teacher, Fern Westerman, who saw my whole person and treated me with love (a smile, a gentle touch on my shoulder, the way she said my name and stood up for me when I was laughed at by peers). Fern transitioned many years ago, before I was able to thank her for her importance in my survival and my realization that the influence of one person can really save a life,

In high school, the anger about the abuse I endured, manifested in my standing up for students who were being bullied. I befriended the classmates who were identified as 'underdogs' and mistreated. I was not very good at speaking up for myself but was great at standing up for others. It is interesting that five, 10 and 15 years after high school graduation, I received phone calls from some of my previous classmates whom I had defended in school with this question: "Shirley, are you going to the high school reunion? I will go if you are, otherwise, I would not feel safe." It is very real how emotional abuse and bullying can cut so deeply into our being.

As for the history of sexual abuse, I believe my painful past led me to work with others who experienced pain and were viewed as different and having less value. **I wanted to turn my pain into purpose**. I did not want others to experience what I had experienced. For people with trauma histories, I wanted them to know it was not their fault. I wanted to support them to break the silence and move into recovery; I wanted them to find safety, joy, connection, and meaning. And those are things I wanted too.

Years later, I discovered that I could heal from the trauma I endured as a child. At the same time, I knew I could never "unfeel" what it was like emotionally to experience it. Those two things would become my strengths in this work: compassion for each person's experience and hope for their healing.

****

The third influence is harder for me to articulate. My brother Bill was born four years before me. Four years difference in age can be a lot when you are growing up and have other siblings who are closer in age. I was closer to my sisters, and yet, as far as my career path is concerned, my brother had a great influence in my life. After he moved out of the house and left for college, I saw him grow into a person who cared very deeply about social justice. Then I saw him build a career in mental health and addiction services. He was super busy, defining his passion and building his impact in the lives of people with addictions and the organizations designed to help them. When he was home, I hung onto every word. He was smart, savvy, witty, grounded in real work with real people, and determined to make changes. He gave me hope. Even though I was pretty messed up and felt worthless at the time, his example made me believe that maybe, just maybe, I could make a difference in this world too! Maybe, just maybe, I could turn my hurt into helping. Thanks, Bill, for providing a lifeboat to your little sister.

Questions for the reader:

1. What early experiences did you have that influenced the choices you made in your life?
2. Did you have any painful experiences that impacted how you treated others? Your career paths? Your parenting styles?
3. When you were growing up, who did something kind that made you feel important and worthy?
4. Is there someone from your childhood or teen years that you would like to thank? Can you find a way to thank them?

Chapter 2

Inequality

"Our lives begin to end the day we become
silent about things that matter."
Martin Luther King, Jr.

"We cannot all succeed when half of us are
held back." Malala Yousafzai

Anna Teaches Us About Freedom

When Anna was born, she did not look like the other babies and the doctors advised her parents to put her in an institution where she could be taken care of properly. "They'll know what to do and you can get on with your life" was the message often given to parents.

A few days after her birth, Anna was moved to an institution for people with disabilities. She never met anyone in her biological family. She was there when she took her first steps and said her first words. She was there when most children her age started kindergarten and played games outside with others in the neighborhood. Anna was there: missing birthday parties, family holidays, graduations, and dances. Her sense of self and ability to visualize and define a path for her life were completely limited by the walls of the institution.

As an adult, Anna loved children and often went to the units with the small children so she could help with their care. Yes, Anna lived in the institution until her early 50s when she was moved to a nursing home in another city.

Anna, who was perfectly healthy and physically active, lived in a nursing home. She lived with lots of other people who required skilled nursing services and a few people with developmental disabilities. Anna was among the youngest people in the home.

A couple years later, Anna moved to a 4-bedroom house in an old, yet desirable neighborhood with three other women who had also lived in nursing homes following years of institutional living. She invited me to come see her new home and we scheduled a time for my visit.

I knocked on the door, and almost immediately, Anna opened the door and said excitedly, "I get to open the door!" She invited me in and walked towards the kitchen. She stopped short of the threshold between the living room and the kitchen. Slowly, she stepped over the threshold and proudly announced, "I get to be in the room where the food is made!" She showed me the pantry, the cabinets, the refrigerator, the table, the silverware drawer and said, "I get to help!" For the first time in Anna's life, she got to be in the kitchen, in the home where she lived.

After the kitchen tour, Anna took my hand and led me down the hall to her bedroom. "Look! It's my room! My bed!" Then she stood in front of the closet and proudly told me, "My clothes!" shaking her head 'no', she added, "No key! No staff!" and then smiling and pointing to her chest, she added, "Mine!" For the first time in Anna's life, she got to choose her own clothes and was able to keep them in her own private room!

Anna then took my hand one last time and led me down the hall. She stopped by a light switch and said, "Look what I can do!" And then Anna turned the hall light on and then off again. She looked at me and smiled with great joy.

I was happy for Anna. She was happy. But I could not understand, why we had locked her up when she was a newborn. Why had she been denied freedom all of those years? She noticed the tears in my eyes, and we sat on her couch and talked. I told her I was sorry that she didn't grow up in a home with a family. I was sorry that her clothes were locked up and she wasn't allowed in the kitchen. Anna patted my hand and said, "It's okay, Shirley. I am here now."

Anna and I saw each other regularly, but I never thanked her for being one of my greatest teachers... because at the time, I did not realize it. Anna passed away several years ago. Thanks Anna, for being such a wonderful person and teacher. Thank you for teaching me what strength and resilience look like. Thank you for sharing your joy in new opportunities so I can remember to do the same. Thank you for showing me that we can be grateful for freedom even when it takes decades to arrive.

Let's think about Anna's life.

When I ask audiences why they think Anna was sent to an institution as an infant, the most common answers that are given include:

Ignorance: People didn't know what to do; didn't have information on supporting a baby with disabilities.

Fear: Fear of doing harm; Fear of stigma; Cultural fear that the parents are being punished (in some cultures, when a baby was born with disabilities, there was a belief that

32

the parents were being punished for their sins); Fear of going against the medical professionals.

Prejudice/Ableism: Society does not like people who are viewed as different than the norm. (Some parents have shared that when their babies were born with severe disabilities, they were asked if they wanted the baby's life to be ended. Each time, the parent(s) went on to share what a gift their baby's life has been and shared grief over being asked the question about terminating their child's life.)

I believe that Anna was separated from her family after birth because she was different than most of the other babies. **Let's face it: We don't do different very well.** We judge, label, separate, mistreat, profile, oppress, deny basic rights, and on and on. So, as a new baby, Anna was sent to an institution. That was the norm at the time she was born. I hope we never return to that oppressive practice.

Anna only got to move from the institution to a smaller place with more freedom because some people became outraged. Some families, some people with disabilities, and some professionals, created a movement - a movement to end the institutional segregation and oppression of people with disabilities. Anna was a benefactor of that movement. First when she left the institution and then again when she left the nursing home. It felt like too little too late, but she did get there…and she brought with her that incredible wisdom, forgiveness, and positive self. It was wonderful to see her living with more freedom and at the same time, you do wonder how her life might have been different if she had not experienced so many years of injustice and oppression.

I want to be clear…Anna did not spend most of her life in an institution because she had a disability…she spent most of her life in an institution because we had a **system of exclusion for people who looked different and maybe acted differently.** Once we create those systems; they are difficult to dissolve. The United States continues to have institutions that house and segregate people with developmental disabilities from their rightful communities.

Questions for the reader:

1. As you read Anna's journey to freedom, what thoughts and feelings did you experience?
2. Many times, history repeats itself, what actions can be taken to assure that people with disabilities can live equally and freely in their communities going forward?
3. What other minority groups have painful and traumatic histories? What steps can you take as an individual, or as a group, to work towards equality and freedom for people who have been denied their human rights?
4. As you read the small part of Anna's story that was presented, are there any lessons for you about how to live your life?

James Teaches Us About Privacy

James had an energy and a spirit that was electric and contagious -well, to some people. Some people judged James as bossy or aggressive. You see, James knew what he wanted in life. He wanted to be treated with dignity and respect. He wanted to decide how he spent his time and who he wanted to hang out with. He wanted to say NO to things he didn't want or like, without being criticized or punished. He wanted people to slow down and listen when he spoke. He wanted to have fun! James wanted to organize others with disabilities to change the entire system of services and supports. James had a vision!

James, too, had spent many years in an institution and then in a nursing home before moving to a group home in his community of origin. James had spastic cerebral palsy, with control over one leg, his eyes, and parts of his face. James communicated through facial expression and by moving his leg in certain directions for yes and for no. He also had with a board at the end of his wheelchair that contained letters, small words, and pictures: he pointed to each item with his foot, often spelling out the things he wanted to say. James had a lot to say. Unfortunately, most people would walk past him without taking time to listen. It was easy to ignore James, because no one could hear James speaking since he spoke with his body and not his voice.

James and I visited regularly. He expressed a lot of frustration about people not seeing him - instead only seeing his disability. James also shared with me when he observed a staff member not treating him or one of his friends with respect.

For example, he shared with me when staff would make people stop eating even though they were not finished with their meal or would make people eat things they did not like. He also shared his joys and dreams. One day James asked to speak with me in my office. From experience, I knew this meant it was something very important.

When we got settled in the office, I grabbed a notebook and a pen, ready to record the letters that he pointed to with his toes. Several moments later, I read out loud the words I had recorded.

"I've been seen naked by hundreds of people, and no one has ever asked permission."

As James indicated 'yes, this was correct', I was shocked and temporarily silenced. I thought back to my early days of providing direct support, and said, "Oh my God! I've done that! I am so sorry! What shall we do? How can I help?"

We created a plan and held an emergency meeting with the supervisors that week. Together, we told the supervisors:

1. From now on, before anyone supports someone with going to the bathroom, dressing, taking a bath or shower, or any personal care need, the staff member shall

ask the person for permission and wait for a response.

2. If a person does not respond when asked, after waiting several seconds, the staff member may begin the process and watch for signs that the person is indicating 'no' through their body language.

3. If at any time during a personal care activity, the person says "no", "stop", or resists, the staff member is to stop what they are doing and try to discover what the problem is.

Later we added:

4. Inform family members of these procedures so they are aware of them and can implement them too.

Many of the supervisors were surprised and not happy by this directive. We heard things like, "Everybody will say no! Everyone will be filthy dirty! People are going to stink! If they can say no to a bath, they will start saying no to everything. We will lose all control."

James assured them that most people liked to be clean and if someone says no, they have a good reason. I told them to try it for a week and then we would get back together. In the meantime, if someone said no, the staff could call me at home, and I would come and talk with the parties involved. During the week 'trial', I only received one call. The person who had said no, explained to me in private that they wanted a bath, but the staff person who was going to help them, was not very good with lifting. She was concerned that the staff was going to drop her. I asked if she wanted to train the staff how to work with her and offered to be with her during the training if she thought that would be helpful. Her response was, "I don't want her (the staff) mad at me. Can you help with that?" After exploring her concerns about the staff, she said she wanted to train the staff with me present. After that training, there were no further concerns.

When James and I had the follow-up meeting with the supervisors, everything went well. James thanked the supervisors for helping him feel safer and respected. We discussed ways that staff could assure privacy during personal care activities and ideas for making this approach to respect and privacy a part of the ongoing practices. After a few weeks, we created this objective for all employees who provided support with personal care activities:

<u>Objective:</u> Before helping anyone with personal care activities (going to the bathroom, dressing, or changing clothes, taking a shower or bath, etc.) I shall ask for permission and wait for an answer.

This practice became part of each of those employee's performance evaluations. A few months later, a supervisor told me that this was one of the few performance objectives related to how staff treated the persons they provided supports to - most were about training requirements, being to work on time, taking CPR classes, completing paperwork, etc. What we measure tells our employees what is most important.

Let's talk more about what James taught so many about privacy. I hope you too were shocked by what James told me that day in my office. As humans, we need privacy in our lives. We need private time and space away from others, for our own mental health. We need privacy for private activities and for private conversations. We have the right to our private thoughts that we choose not to share with anyone else. For people with disabilities who live in group settings, privacy can be a rare commodity.

For those of you who think that James being seen naked "by hundreds of people" was an exaggeration, consider this: James lived in an institution for three decades. That's three shifts a day,365 days a year with various people helping James go to the bathroom, take a bath, and change clothes. Consider staff turnover. Consider his time in a nursing home and then in a group home. Do the math. In James' time in the institution alone, there were over 10,000 days of support, three shifts per day.

Kelly Teaches Us the Power of Respect

Kelly received 24-hour services and supports from a progressive agency with policies, procedures, training, and employee evaluations related to respecting the privacy of the people they supported. Kelly was a pleasant woman who loved flowers, friendships, music, family, one-on-one conversations, and taking walks. Her family was an important part of her life, they visited her at her home and at the workshop she attended. But she had not been in her family's home for some time because the entrance had steps and Kelly used a wheelchair to get around.

I received a phone call from her family asking if there was any way we could get Kelly to a family gathering at their home. I spoke with Kelly, and she was excited to see her visiting family from out of state and to be in her family home again. I asked her if we could get some staff that could carry her up the steps, would that work for her? She said 'yes' with a big smile.

So, on the day of the planned reunion, Kelly made it to the party along with everyone else. Staff dropped her off and we had a time scheduled to pick her up a few hours later. She was only gone an hour or so, when I received a call from her sister who said, "What have you done to Kelly? She slapped her aunt. She's never done anything like that before!"

I agreed that it did not sound like Kelly and asked for more details. Her sister explained, "Aunt Marie and I were taking her to the bathroom, because you know it takes two of us, and she slapped her aunt!"

Now I understood. I told the sister about the new privacy procedures for personal care activities. I apologized for the fact that the family had not been informed when these procedures had changed. Kelly had experienced being treated with respect and now when she was not asked permission while being supported to transfer to the toilet, she reacted with a slap. I cannot say for sure, but it appeared that the sudden touching and movement scared her, and the slap was a startle response to that sudden movement. What I became excited about was the fact that because Kelly had been treated with respect and choices related to her privacy, she expected that. It was her routine. And now when she was not asked permission before touching, she reacted. It seems that this respectful privacy practice made her safer against unwanted touching. I did feel bad for the aunt and the family because they should have known about the change, and we failed to include them in this respectful practice...but I must admit, I did a happy dance at what Kelly had demonstrated. It was clear to me that Kelly was now safer from unwanted touching than she was before she was treated consistently with dignity and respect for her privacy.

Cathy Questions My Actions

My work with James happened in 1990. Twenty years later, this happened. A team working to address sexual violence against people with disabilities organized a gathering of people with disabilities and educators at sexual assault centers across the state. On the first day, a woman I knew named Cathy asked if she could write a poem about the experiences of the event and share it at the closing. I told her that would be wonderful!

The next afternoon, it was time to bring the gathering to a close. Cathy came to the front of the room to share her poem and I asked if I could put the microphone on her jacket. She said, "What?" and I repeated, "Can I put this microphone on your jacket?" She nodded 'yes' and proceeded to read her poem, *A Catalyst of Peace.* The two-day gathering ended with her powerful words and a standing ovation for her spoken words.

A couple weeks later, I received a phone call from Cathy. Here is the part I want to share with you:

"I've been worried about something that happened at the training. I want to talk with you about it." Cathy said.

"Okay. What happened?" I wondered.

Cathy then shared, "Well, at the end, you asked if you could put the microphone on me. I don't know why you did that. How could they hear me if I didn't use the microphone?"

I responded, "Cathy, I don't touch people without their permission."

And she said with great feeling, "Is that a thing?"

I smiled, "I hope it's a thing. People have a right to say 'yes' and 'no' to touch by others."

"Really? Even my PAs (personal assistants)?"

"Yes, even your personal assistants, your family, friends - everyone."

"Can I tell people about this? Can I tell the people who live in my building? Can I tell my PAs?"

"Cathy, yes. Please tell as many people as you can and want. That would be great!"

Cathy and I have had several conversations about this over the years. We recently spoke at a conference together and we both laughed when I asked if I could put the microphone on her jacket. I am very grateful for the ongoing relationship I have with Cathy. She has been a colleague, a friend, a muse, a gift, a student, and a teacher.

Let me expand. Cathy never lived in a nursing home or an institution and yet, she still had the experience of people touching her (and seeing her) during personal care activities. Permission was never asked or granted. This lack of respect and privacy in the lives of people with disabilities seems to be one of those "It's the way it's always been" things. In working with one agency about privacy I was told, "Well, I can see that for some of 'our people' but not for Joan - she doesn't care!!" My first instinct was to shout, "THEY ARE NOT YOUR PEOPLE!" but I had done enough recovery work to respond calmly…well, most of the time. The main point I wanted to communicate in that moment was this: "The fact that she doesn't care is a big problem. We want her to care when she is not treated with respect, when people touch her without her permission. Let's work together so Joan can learn what privacy and respect feel like."

Questions for the Reader:

1. What are your thoughts about asking for permission before touching someone? Is this a practice you have done?
2. What other steps can be taken to assure that people who need support in personal care can have privacy?
3. Do you agree that Kelly was safer from unwanted touch after being asked permission

for touch in a consistent manner? Why or why not?
4. What other performance objectives could be focused on respecting privacy and treating people with respect?

Bathrooms

When I think about discrimination and abuse of power, my mind turns to bathrooms. We (society) have used access to bathrooms to separate and oppress people who are not like the majority. People who are marginalized have had separate bathrooms throughout much of history. This is also true for people with disabilities, throughout history and even today. The message of separate bathrooms is loud and clear: "YOU ARE NOT GOOD ENOUGH TO USE OUR BATHROOM. WE DON'T WANT TO CATCH WHAT YOU HAVE!"

In 1992, the organization I worked with moved into a building designed and built to house services and supports for people with disabilities. A few of us advocated for integrated bathrooms and that value was included into the design - a small but important win for equality. A few weeks after we moved into the new facility, this happened:

I was in a stall in the women's bathroom when I heard a voice in the stall next to mine.

"I'm sorry, but I had to go really bad. I don't want to get in trouble." The person said nervously.

I replied, "It's okay. You are welcome to use this bathroom anytime you want."

"I'm not getting in trouble?"

"No, you are not getting in trouble. I promise, it is ok."

I left the bathroom before the person came out of the stall. I did not know who it was, and I never met them. But I knew something about their history. I knew that they had a lifetime of experiencing separate bathrooms for staff and people receiving services. I knew they had been criticized and punished for using spaces that were designed for employees only. Or perhaps they had learned the bathroom segregation rules by watching others with disabilities getting criticized and punished. This person had learned who had power over them - even when it came to using the bathroom.

Over the next several months, I watched with joy as the bathrooms were used equally by everyone. I spent many years after that encouraging other organizations to consider the value of stopping their patterns of segregating bathrooms between people with disabilities, employees, and guests.

Making this kind of change within an organization can lead to resistance. Some employees will voice very loudly their negative opinions about such changes. One I have heard repeatedly is "I don't want to have to work when I go to the bathroom. If they are in there, I will have to help some of them." Hmmmm.... Did you notice the use of the words 'they' and 'them'? I observed support between all parties in the 'new and improved' bathrooms; not just staff supporting people who came to the agency for supports, but support in both directions. Staff were just as likely to ask someone receiving services for something as the other way around. When this became the norm, the power differential seemed to melt away. Well, at least in the bathroom. It is a beautiful thing when we naturally support each other when support is needed.

One of the agency's that I consulted with over the years, had a 'Staff Break Room'. This room had cabinets, a countertop with a sink and coffee pot, a refrigerator, a couple of tables with chairs, a few vending machines, and a one-person bathroom. From my observations, this had always been a space for staff only. I was working at this agency one day and went in to get a cup of coffee and noticed that something had changed. I did not hear "You have to leave. This room is for staff." No one was knocking on the door for permission to speak to a staff member. Everyone now had access to this room and the sense of comfort and equality seared through me.

I was so thrilled, I asked to speak with the administrator, Dina Donohue-Chase. I asked her how she had made this change happen and this savvy administrator said, "I changed the sign on the door. I have found that sometimes, that's all you have to do. It happened naturally after that." I will add that this was an organization that was very clear about their values and lived their mission every day. Thanks Dina, for your insight and action!

I still see some organizations with bathroom signs indicating staff only, but from my experience it has become less common. Another way of segregating bathroom use by some people with disabilities, is by not having bathrooms that are physically accessible to all people. The Americans with Disabilities Act of 1990 includes the right to access public facilities and provides guidance on standards for an accessible bathroom. Yes, I know we have made progress. But there are still so many places that do not have an accessible bathroom. I encourage you to become aware of this if you haven't already. I have gone out to eat and noticed accessible parking, accessible entrances, accessible space to dine and then go to the bathroom and it is so small, many adults without disabilities would find it hard to even enter the stall. That's when I speak to someone in management. When you call ahead to check on accessibility, they usually say yes, it is. Throwing a bar on the side of a bathroom stall does not make it accessible if you cannot get into the stall door…or if the toilet is low to the floor, or if there is no space to turn your chair around in the stall…there are so many important things to consider!

I want to share a personal experience. One of my sisters lives in a nursing home, a few hours drive from my home. When I arrive for a visit, I usually have to pee. There are two bathrooms in the lobby and they both have what appears to me to be a child-size toilet. I tried them both and my only choice was to pee standing up. Not an easy task for someone without a penis. After that, I went to the front desk to find out where the accessible bathrooms were and discovered there were none. I could not believe what I discovered: Here was a nursing home - filled with people who use canes, walkers, and wheelchairs to get around, and there is NO accessible bathroom!

Let's face it, we are not always inclusive in building design and renovations. Join the choir and help make these changes!

Questions for the reader:

1. What do you think of the historical practice of having separate bathrooms (and other spaces) for employees and people with disabilities?
2. What other minority groups have been denied access to bathrooms or had separate bathrooms?
3. Have you or anyone you know had any difficulties in accessing or using a bathroom? How could this difficulty have been avoided?
4. What action can you take, big or small, to improve bathroom accessibility?

Application of the Lessons Learned

When I think about James and Cathy and Kelly and many others who need daily supports for personal care, the lack of privacy sends rage throughout my body. I am furious that this lack of respect for privacy continues when the rate of sexual assault experienced by people with disabilities is outrageous. We need to establish very strict boundaries and limit non-consensual visual exposure to naked bodies to the degree possible.

Here are some recommendations related to providing personal supports:

If you are a person who needs support in your personal care

- Speak up for what you need.
- When hiring staff, consider talking about personal care, privacy, and boundaries in your screening interview.
- Share with others the importance of asking permission before performing personal care activities.
- You can create the rules that you want for your body and share them with others who provide you with support.

- Be prepared to speak up if someone breaks one of your rules.
- Consider what action you want to take if someone does break a rule.

If you are a person who supports someone with personal care needs (including family members)

- Ask permission and get consent before you begin and at each step of the process.
- Ask the person how they want to be supported
- Pay attention and listen closely, with your eyes and ears and heart.
- Partner with the person to find ways to create more privacy while you support the person (For example, drape a towel over the person's lap while they sit on the toilet).
- Spread the word to others who do this work.

If you supervise people who provide personal care to others

- Consider how they can be trained to ensure privacy and respect.
- Engage people receiving care to co-train during employee training to share the value of privacy.

- Ask employees to share what it might feel like if they had no privacy in the bathroom (remember when your children were young, and you couldn't go to the bathroom alone).
- Provide opportunities for each person receiving care to directly train their individual support staff about their own needs, wants, and the best ways to support them.
- Consider incorporating privacy into employee screening, orientation, training, evaluations, etc.
- Gather input from persons who receive supports in crafting policies and procedures related to privacy.

If you are a manager at an organization that works with people who need personal care supports

- Establish a culture of privacy, including; privacy during personal care supports, privacy during conversations and phone calls, receipt of unopened/uncensored mail, privacy in interactions and relationships, privacy in personal space and belongings. Be sure to obtain input from stakeholders, the people receiving support, when developing privacy standards.

- Establish clear policies and procedures on what is expected in relation to all kinds of privacy.
- Consider ways to screen potential employees about their values around respect and privacy.
- Establish training programs and evaluation methods to emphasize the skills that reinforce rights, choice, dignity, respect, and privacy.
- Clearly establish how specific breeches of privacy will result in disciplinary actions, up to and including termination.

Questions for the reader:

1. Think about privacy in your own life. What do you cherish the most? Are there parts of your life in which you would like to have more privacy?
2. Why do you think people with disabilities are not always given the privacy they deserve?
3. What suggestions do you have to improve privacy practices for people who need help with personal care?
4. How could an organization build a 'culture of privacy' in lieu of attitudes that "we have always done it this way"?

Cipher in the Snow

I do not recall where or when I first saw the movie *"Cipher in the Snow"*, but I do recall the impact this story had on my spirit and in my life. This short story was written by Jean Mizer and made into a short film by Brigham Young University in 1973. The movie demonstrates the values of belonging, attention, and love in our lives. In the movie, a middle school student dies suddenly in the snow outside of the school bus. As the school explores who this student really was, it is determined that he was a cipher, a 'zero', a person who had been gradually erased. He died of loneliness and a broken heart.

As I began working with agencies that provide services and supports to people with disabilities, I often wondered, "Who are the ciphers? Who are the people who go along quietly with whatever is happening and are basically ignored? Like in any setting where there are many people, there are the people who are the shining lights, and the people whose personality and actions demand lots of attention, and then there are the people in the middle. Some of the folks in the middle are ciphers.

How do we create cultures in which every person is valued and honored? Of course, the best answer is that adults with disabilities should not be crammed into day services or other large group settings. True equality demands that we create a world which embraces and respects all people to live safely and meaningfully in their communities. In the meantime, we must pay attention to people who are 'in the middle'... people who may just go along with the crowd...so they are not erased.

In 1992, I was working at a not-for-profit agency which served over 800 people with disabilities every year. Approximately 300 adults were enrolled in adult day services with ages ranging from 18 to 92. Under the direction of Kay Scrogin, we were able to hire two full-time employees whose job was to focus on community integration. The process involved taking one - three people out of the agency building and into the community for exposure, experience, and access to the larger community. We intentionally decided that it was important that the people involved had the opportunity to access new experiences, decide what things they enjoyed and preferred, and build relationships with people outside of the agency based on common interests. Those persons identified with the greatest need participated in this intentional community interaction on an ongoing basis.

I really want to share a story about someone whom I believe was a cipher in the system of services for people with intellectual and developmental disabilities. Ray was a man who had been institutionalized at a young age. He was 'released' to the community as an adult during the de-institutionalization movement. When I met Ray, he lived in a home with 15 other adults with intellectual and developmental disabilities. According to his chart and the staff who knew him best, Ray was described as quiet, compliant, non-verbal, and 'no problem'. Wow…really? Besides food, no one seemed to know what he liked or disliked. Seemed to me, Ray had already been partly erased by the system designed to support him. Because we did not know his preferences or dreams, the community integration specialist began taking Ray to a variety of places in the community. There would be one-on-one engagement with the staff person and exposure to a variety of activities. Over time, Ray and the staff person established a close relationship. I will never forget the day when Neda Jenkins came to my office to excitedly tell me; "You will never believe what happened today! Ray and I went to the airport, and we were outside hoping to see a plane take off or land when Ray suddenly got excited, pointed to an airplane, and said, 'airplane!' I did not know he could talk! It was amazing! It made me so happy, and I told him thank you and how happy I was!" This may seem like a small thing, but it is a big thing. Ray was no longer a cipher. He now had a relationship with someone who believed in him, saw his value, and knew what he liked.

I often wondered what the world looked like through Ray's eyes. He saw everything that was going on without his presence making any direct influence. I would love to read the book he could write about living inside a system of segregation, benevolence, oppression, and othering.

A Trail of Taco Salad

I was working in a rather large building with three wings that were connected by a large open area and a cafeteria. One day at noon, I walked to the cafeteria to pick up some lunch. As I walked, I greeted people I passed along the way. The special for the day was taco salad - one of my favorite things they made there, and I placed my order. As I was leaving the cafeteria with my taco salad and utensils, I kept the plate with the taco salad near my body to help me balance my load. I am not very graceful, and this seemed like a good idea. Soon, I had some taco meat and sauce on my shirt, so I pulled the plate away from my body a little bit and some fell on the floor. I had no way to clean it up so continued on my way. By the time I got to the office, there was a trail of taco meat, salsa, cheese, and lettuce throughout the halls. I picked up some paper towels and began the trip back to clean up my mess…and the evidence of my clumsiness. As I was cleaning the floor, Roger approached me and asked, "What you doing?" I said, "I made a mess, and I am cleaning it up." Roger looked at me kind of confused and then asked in all sincerity. "Staff make mistakes?" He was stunned! I noticed the look on his face and said, "Yes, Roger, staff make mistakes. I make mistakes every day. We all make mistakes."

He sat quietly for a few seconds and said, "I didn't know that."

I could not stop thinking about Roger and what he said. I began to look at myself and the messages my words and behavior communicated to people I worked with. Self-awareness can hurt sometimes, but the freedom it offers us can lead to beautiful changes. The trail of taco salad was over 30 years ago, but I carry with me today the memory of Roger's words and the look on his face. The gap between 'us' and 'them' was so huge that he did not know that everyone makes mistakes.

Questions for the Reader:

1. What gaps have you observed between 'us' and 'them' in your life?
2. What factors may have contributed to Roger believing that 'staff' do not make mistakes?
3. Was it important for Roger to know that all people make mistakes? If so, why?
4. Is there someone in your life that might benefit from knowing you are not perfect and make mistakes? If so, how would you share that with them?

Never a Congratulations

"After the birth of my third child, the doctor told me, 'I am sorry, but your baby has a disability.' I was given a notebook and a pen. The doctor told me to write some things down. The first list was all the things my child would never be able to do: he would never walk or talk or drive or have a job or get married or have children or live independently. The second list was all the things I would need to make sure my child received: early intervention, speech therapy, physical therapy, occupational therapy, neurological services, and special education. I was shocked and not ready for any of this information. I took it seriously though. I worked really hard to make sure my child got everything he needed…whatever the experts told me to do, I did. I was the super mom of the 'special' kid. And over time, I learned a few things. My child could walk, and my child could talk. My child could learn, and I began believing that he could do anything anyone else did - only he learned differently, and sometimes it took longer to learn and that was okay! I learned that the so-called experts were not really very knowledgeable about MY CHILD! Most importantly, I learned that MY CHILD DID NOT NEED TO BE FIXED! I talked with other parents, and they said the doctors' predictions about their children were wrong too. Hmmmm…so I let that all go and let my child lead the way. But there is one thing leftover I want to share - I still grieve the fact that on the day my son was born, no one ever said, 'Congratulations, you have a beautiful baby boy!'"

This story is a compilation of stories I have heard over the years from parents. A couple of parents shared with me that their doctors had actually asked them if they wanted to keep their infants alive because of their medical conditions and a poor prognosis for any 'normal kind of life'. In addition, two adults with disabilities in different locations told me the same story: "When I was born, my parents were asked to sign my birth certificate and my death certificate…at the same time. I think that was cruel. You can see that I lived." These stories are heartbreaking and demonstrate the lack of value that society has had when it comes to people with disabilities. I dream of a world in which all parents are told 'congratulations' when they give birth to a living child.

It's All About Power

At this point you may have noticed that the people in these stories had a lot less power in their lives than you and most of the adults that you know. Here's the deal. When society perceives someone as being different than the norm, they assume they have less value. In the case of people with disabilities, there has been an historical assumption that people without disabilities need to be in power because they know more and can make better decisions. In many cases, people without disabilities want to protect people with disabilities from harm. In thinking about adult relationships, most of us want to be in equal relationships - a relationship where power is shared. That can be a rare experience for many people with disabilities.

When I have taught adults with intellectual and developmental disabilities about power and relationships, we discuss three kinds of power:

Power Inside

Equal Power

Power Over

Power Inside. I believe that we are all born with personal power inside of us which includes our ability to express our feelings, hopes, dreams, preferences, and desires. This is a power that needs opportunity to flourish. If people are denied the opportunity to use this personal power and are maybe even punished when they use this power, it can become a squashed and forgotten spark.

Equal Power. Equal power is when two people share power. They both have opportunities to make decisions and know how to take turns.

They have fun together and respect each other. They consider themselves as having equal value in the world.

Power Over. Power over is exactly what it sounds like. One person has power over the other person. This person makes all the decisions in the relationship. This person thinks they know what is best for the other person. This person denies the other person the opportunity to make independent decisions. The person with power over another person views the other person as 'less than' and as an 'other'. There is a quality of "I know what is best for this person".

I have known many people who have only experienced 'power over' relationships - other people have had power over them in every aspect of their lives. When your experiences are based on others being in charge and you have little or no opportunity to use and experience your personal power, you may not know you have any power. It's like having muscles but not being able to use them…they shrink and fade.

I think it is important to understand this if you care about people who are part of an oppressed community, including people with disabilities. So, how can you tell if someone does not know about or access their personal power?

- If you ask them a question, they look at their parent, staff, boss, etc.
- They ask others what to do in multiple situations.
- If you ask their opinion, they may be shocked or hesitant, or ask you what you think.
- They tend to go along with the group.

From my experience, one of the best ways to help someone recall their personal power is by providing opportunities for sharing power (equal power). Healing occurs through relationships. Since the personal power was erased as a result of 'power over' relationships, the personal power can be restored through equal relationships. Within equal relationships, there are opportunities for both parties to blossom - space for both people to feel strong and confident.

As I write this, I am reminded of a dinner I had in Chicago several years ago while doing a few days of training. Some people I know were also visiting the city and asked if I wanted to meet them for dinner. I was delighted to reconnect with them and thrilled to be invited to share a meal. As I recall, there were five people from central Illinois with one support staff. We were a chatty group, and everyone was sharing stories about their adventures in the big city. When the food arrived, everyone closed their eyes and folded their hands for a prayer. The support staff offered a prayer which included…"and thank you for this opportunity to teach social skills…" WHAT? REALLY? So, we cannot even have a nice meal and celebrate relationships without making a point that one person is there to teach, and others are there to learn…that one person has more power? Can't we just enjoy our food and our time together? What felt like equal power was suddenly ruined. I did not blame the staff member for this. This sense of "I know best" and "My job is to teach THEM" is widespread in the human services field…and common in society.

I share this story in hopes that we can transcend 'us' and 'them' thinking. I hope that we can transcend 'programming' and consider equal relationships as a radical act of social justice, in hopes that we can be IN relationship WITH people as it brings value to all of our lives.

In 2004, I had the opportunity to interview almost 100 adults with intellectual and developmental disabilities about personal power. Lots of the people I listened to had a strong sense of their personal power due to their involvement in the self-advocacy movement (i.e., civil rights movement for people with disabilities).

When I asked people what they wanted to be changed in their lives, the common thread was this:

- for people to listen to me when I speak
- my parents to respect what I say I want in my life
- my staff to ask me what I want and listen to me
- for me to be in charge of my life
- to make my own decisions

So, I began to wonder, how could we make that happen? I engaged others in conversations in which we imagined what it would be like for the people who are supported by service agencies to have equal power with the staff members who provide support. We imagined agencies being operated with the ideas and influence of the people who were receiving services represented on committees and boards. We imagined people leading their own service planning meetings. We wrote a grant with these ideas and received funding, one year at a time, for five years. During that time, the vision grew as we worked with people with intellectual and developmental disabilities and the Illinois agencies that supported them in an attempt to shift the power dynamics and create cultures of equal power. We made changes at the state and the organizational level.

At the state level, people who were supported with state funds had regular opportunities to express their needs and wants to the state leaders in several ways including:

- Input on state rules, standards, and forms
- Input on job titles of the people who provided their supports
- Input on what was working and not working in their services
- Their ideas on needed changes in the state system
- Serving on statewide committees and task forces
- Regular, ongoing contact with the top leader for developmental disability services
- Opportunities to ask for accountability from state leaders

Some lasting changes were made. Some changes were made and later unmade.

At the organizational level, people most impacted by the organization's work - people with disabilities - were engaged in the hiring, training, and evaluation of support staff. They were members of committees and the Board of Directors. People were engaged in the development of policies and procedures. Policies and procedures were modified to be easier to understand. Some people led their own meetings and set the agendas. We created picture-based tools to support these activities. We changed some laws, job titles, forms, and lots of practices. After five years, the funding ended. Eleven years later, some agencies reversed many of the positive changes when new leadership took over, but some changes that were made have been sustained.

Systems of power are resistant to change. It is heartbreaking to see things go backwards. That is one of the reasons I am writing this book. To show what is possible when we listen to the real experts - people who live with disabilities. We have witnessed what is possible when people with intellectual and developmental disabilities are respected as having equal value. We know what is possible when those most effected by decisions are at the table with power to influence those decisions.

So far, we have discussed the value of recognizing personal power within every human being and we have discussed the value of being aware of 'power over' in our relationships with people with disabilities. I strongly encourage the reader to practice shared power and equal power in relationships with people with disabilities (and other people as well).

There is one more power issue I want to address. When an adult hires another adult to help them with something, the person doing the hiring has some power over the person they are hiring. For example, if you hire someone to mow your lawn or clean your house, you get to set the rules and decide how it is to be done - what is included in the job and any specifics that are important to you. You get to ask the person who is helping you to perform these tasks a certain way. You get to decide if the job is done to meet your standards. So, when someone is hired to help a person with disabilities, the person needing the help is the only person who knows if the job was done the way they want it done. The person with the disability has 'power over' in these circumstances. That person can set the standards for privacy, touch, communication, quality and quantity of work, and work ethic (being on time, personal calls, personal visits, etc.). From my many years of experience, this does not happen very often. Sigh. We need to do better!

If you are feeling resistance to this last paragraph, take a breath and sit with this idea for a while. How would it be in your life? If you had to hire someone to help you after surgery, what expectations would you have for this person? Who would you want to be in charge of the care of your body and your living space?

Questions for the reader:

1. Think about a relationship you have had as an adult where someone else had power over you. What effect did this person have in your life?
2. In what ways do you use your personal power?
3. Do you have a relationship in which you have power over another person? What can you do to make sure you treat the other person with respect?
4. What is your experience with relationships of equal power? What feelings come to mind when you think about those relationships?

Chapter 3

Connections

"Out of the fires of desperation burn hope and solidarity."   Sharan Burrow

"I define connection as the energy that exists between people when they feel seen, heard, and valued; when they can give and receive without judgment; and when they derive sustenance and strength from the relationship." Brené Brown

Connecting with Amy Walker

I first met Amy Walker at a Statewide Advisory Council meeting. This was a meeting sponsored by the Division of Developmental Disabilities to gather input from and share information with people with developmental disabilities, family members, and service providers. Each region of the state had three voting members who served on the Council - a person with developmental disabilities, a family member, and a disability service provider. The Council members and the developmental disabilities state representatives, including the Director, all sat at tables that made a huge square in the middle of the room. The tables had table-top microphones that were used whenever anyone spoke. On both sides of the tables, chairs were set up for additional interested parties to attend. There was a standing microphone on each side of the room for those who wanted to speak about the topics being discussed. One of my jobs was to support people with developmental disabilities to attend this meeting and speak out about what was important in their lives. This was a unique opportunity for people to come right up to a microphone and be heard as they expressed their concerns, experiences, and dreams, within a forum that could influence the quality of their lives.

At my first meeting, the larger group of interested attendees was primarily composed of service provider representatives and parents; noticeably absent were the people who actually received and participated in services. At one point during the meeting, the Director of the Division shared a state rule about services and asked for input from the Council members. Several parents and provider representatives made comments. And then it happened. Amy Walker, a Council member representing her region, asked for a turn to speak. She held the rule in one hand and stated: "This is too complicated to understand. If you want our input, you need to write in simple words." She slammed the document on the table and added, "If this is **about us,** it should be written **for us**!" The room was silent for several seconds.

After the meeting, I introduced myself to Amy and asked her if she would like a job where she could be paid for her contributions. Her job would be supporting others to speak out and to work with the Division of Developmental Disabilities to make changes. This was a life-changing day for me and many others in Illinois! Amy and I met a few days later and she began work soon after that.

Amy is one of the most creative people I have ever met! She writes poetry and short stories; creates beautiful power point presentations; creates games with a social justice theme; does presentations with humor and passion; reviews blues musicians and has a flair for theatrics! Amy dreams big! When we first got to know each other, she was learning to play chess and wanted to learn to speak Russian. Amy and I worked together for five years and by the time we finished our work together, she had become a fantastic Russian speaking chess player!

Amy and I traveled the state teaching various groups of people about self-advocacy, power dynamics, systems change, needed legislation, and sexual assault prevention, intervention, and recovery. Amy and others with developmental disabilities created a movement to **require** disability history and awareness training in all public schools. They wanted children and youth to learn about people with disabilities and to recognize the humanity in all of us. People with developmental disabilities met with legislators, the Board of Education, Principals Association, and others. Several people testified before the Illinois house and the senate. Amy created and distributed a list of no-cost resources that could be used in schools. The Bill became Public Law 096-0191 in the School Code on August 10, 2009. We celebrated this landmark achievement, not only for the obvious success of the day but for the long-range impact it could have on the children and youth of Illinois.

Here is another example of the power of self-advocacy in action. Illinois received a Department of Justice federal grant to address sexual violence against people with all kinds of disabilities. The team consisted of a variety of professionals who held state-wide positions related to the issue being addressed, including representatives from, the Division of Human Services Bureau of Sexual Assault and Domestic Violence, the Division of Developmental Disabilities, the Division of Mental Health, the Division of Rehabilitation Services, the Illinois Coalition Against Sexual Assault, the Department of Aging, the Family Violence

Coordinating Council and Blue Tower Training. I would say it was a rather intimidating group for someone who was not used to meeting with what Amy would call 'a bunch of bureaucrats'. The team clearly lacked the representation of people with disabilities and Amy was invited to come to a meeting and see if she wanted to be on the team. At this first meeting, Amy introduced herself by reciting a poem she had written titled, "The ABCs of Living with My Disability." The poem had 26 nuggets of personal information about Amy and her life.

The ABC's of Living with My Disability

By Amy Walker (shared with permission)

A is for AMAZING. It was amazing that I even survived as a premature baby.

B is for BRACES. Leg braces, that is! I wore two of them for most of my life.

C is for CEREBRAL PALSY. That's what kind of disability I have.

D is for DETERMINATION. I've had to have a lot of that during my 26 years.

E is for EMPLOYMENT. It was hard for me to find a job but I love mine now!

F is for FAILURE. I flunked out of college – twice - but that didn't stop me.

G is for GLAD. I'm glad to be alive (and that no one makes me lift hay bales!)

H is for HUMOR. Laughing has helped me get through life's ups and downs.

I is for IMAGE. I worry more than most, I think, about others' opinions of me.

J is for JUDGMENTAL. I try not to be this way, as some have been toward me.

K is for KISS. I've had my 1st (and 2nd) but not with the man I'll marry. Yet.

L is for LANGUAGE. I speak English and Spanish and working on Russian!

M is for MISTAKES. I've made a lot, but I've always tried to learn from them.

N is for NORMAL. Almost no one in "normal society" thinks I am, but I do!!

O is for fantastic OPPORTUNITIES I've had in life. I think I'm very lucky.

P is for PATRONIZING PEOPLE. Please don't treat me like I'm "dumb". I'm not.

Q is for QUESTIONS. I have far, FAR more of these than I do answers in life!

R is for RETARDED. I got called this by one kid at school almost every day.

S is for SEXUALITY. I'm human, and I'm human in THAT way too. Don't judge!

T is for THOUSANDS. I am one of thousands with disabilities. We want to be heard.

U is for UNDERSTAND that all of us are people with value, just like all of you.

V is for VICTORY. If we work together, we can conquer scorn and prejudice.

W is for WIN, It's what we have to do to defeat our enemy of oppression.

X is for XENOPHOBIA. We must fight this "fear of anyone who is different."

Y is for YES! Yes! We can fight for our rights, and our hopes and dreams.

Z is for ZOOMING into a future with no hatred for who we are, or what we do!

Amy challenged all of us to write an ABCs poem about ourselves and bring it to the next meeting. And everyone did! This one courageous act on Amy's part moved this team from formal, polite interchanges to opening our hearts to each other and our collective work. We learned quickly to be honest and to respect and trust each other. Doing this hard work requires a team with good relationships. Amy led the way and we all joined in. Here is my ABCs poem from that time.

THE ABC'S OF LIVING WITH MYSELF
By Shirley Paceley
2-8-07

A is for acceptance…it took many, many years before I could accept myself as a worthwhile person.

B is for bravery…it took a lot of bravery to survive my childhood and adolescent years.

C is for can…Can't used to fill my head but now I embrace the words "I CAN!"

D is for daring and disclosure…it was a daring moment when I disclosed my sexual abuse and again when I confronted my offender.

E is for example. I hope to be a good example of recovery and hope.

F is for feelings. I used to stuff them but now they flow-- mostly.

G is for gratitude. I am a grateful student of this life's journey.

H is for hopeful. I am hopeful that together we <u>can</u> make a difference.

I is for imagination. I imagine a world of love and peace for everyone.

J is for job. I have the best one in the world…for me.

K is for kindness. I want to extend my heart more to others.

L is for light…that's how I feel inside my mind and my heart now.

M is for meditation. I love to meditate and connect with spirit.

N is for "no! … a word that was hard for me to learn.

O is for Orieda - one of my greatest mentors, friends and allies.

P is for passion, power and purpose. I know my heart and follow my passion. There is power in our purpose.

Q is for queen. Recovery has led me to feel like a queen!

R is for rights. We all have the right to be safe from sexual abuse.

S is for spiritual. I am.

T is for talent - something I see in every person I

have ever met who happens to have a developmental disability.

U is for unity - one of my great hopes for humankind.

V is for vines. I love plants and nature.

W is for willy worms. I grew up in the country and that's how we predict the winter weather.

X is for X...x-victim; x-perfectionist; x-enabler!

Y is for YES!! Yes, we can change the world!! Never give up!!

Z is for zany...I have the freedom now to be zany, zany, zany!!

Amy invited all of us to look at and share ourselves broadly, from A to Z. This enabled us to deepen as individuals, grow as a team, and enhance the quality of our collaborative work.

After working with Amy for a couple of years, she came to my office one day and wanted to talk. She asked me a question that I had never been asked before. A question that had a compelling influence on my life and my work.

She asked: "What do you see when you look at me?"

I took a few seconds to think and then responded with, "I see a poet and an artist, a creative person with no bounds…a smart and capable woman…a lover of music and chess and challenges…a brave woman…a strong self-advocate…a colleague and friend…someone with a sense of humor…a great story-teller."

Amy replied, "Really? All most people see is that I walk and talk funny."

This is when it hit me so strongly that what we see when we look at someone makes all the difference in the world. And the person can usually tell what we see. Our attitudes and beliefs about someone come out when we look at them; interact with them. If we think someone is 'less than' us, it shows in how we look at people and how we act. The person knows that! Having been in relationship with hundreds of people with disabilities, I have learned this: You can't fake the funk. Even if you try and cover up your true feelings, the person can usually tell what you really think and feel about them. If we want people to be their best, it helps if we see that power within them. It is a powerful practice to be aware of what you see when you look at someone else. Become aware of the messages your body, eyes and tone communicate when you look a child, family member, partner, co-worker, and others in your life. This awareness may lead to some positive changes as well as some surprising realities. Remember to be gentle with yourself. We are all a work in progress.

It is also important what we see when we look at ourselves in the mirror! On those days when I know it will be difficult to stay present and grounded with someone who is in pain, I try to look closely at myself in the mirror. I want my eyes and my presence to give a message of love and compassion and hope. I try to ask myself this when I look in the mirror:

Do I see in myself someone who can sit with someone else's pain and just be present?

Do I see in myself someone who can hold space for another person's healing?

Do I see in myself someone who can make a difference in the world?

And I would practice seeing those qualities within myself. This is a practice that you can do too! So, to take a lesson from Amy, what do you see when you look at yourself?

Amy taught me in a very deep way that WORDS MATTER! For example, we were in a meeting together and someone said that people with disabilities were vulnerable to sexual violence. Amy very passionately expressed her feelings about the word vulnerable being used to describe people with disabilities. She did not want to be referred to as vulnerable and thought it was wrong to describe an entire group of people as vulnerable (as if everyone in that group was the same). After the meeting we had a long discussion about the word vulnerable and together, we added these concerns: the word vulnerable as a descriptor indicated that nothing could be done to solve this social issue; the word vulnerable was a form of victim-blaming; and that the word vulnerable actually increased their risk for sexual assault. This makes lots of sense. When we focus on weaknesses instead of strengths, people are at greater risk for "Power Over" relationships and systems. Power Over relationships lead to abuse.

Another word that Amy questioned in a meeting was population. When someone said something like "this population of people." Amy said, "What? I thought population was the number of people who lived in a town." Amy questioned every acronym and word that had multiple meanings. She taught us all to do the same. Two important things happened to our team because of Amy:

1. We were able to establish an 'acronym free zone' and

2. We created a culture where it was the norm to question anything that was not understood.

This was one meeting where no one left wondering what something meant. It was a beautiful thing to be a part of. Plain language and authentic connections were developed. (See the Illinois Imagines section later in this book for more information about the outcomes of this team's work.)

Amy and I worked together for five years. When I asked Amy recently, what memory stood out for her, she said "all the road trips, travels and training sessions we did together". Amy and I co-trained throughout Illinois and in several additional states. Recently, Amy reminded me of something that happened in the women's restroom after a session we had completed.

I was washing my hands and a woman nearby said, "I was in your session. It was really good. Where does Amy live?"

I replied, "You will have to ask her. She will be out in a minute."

Amy came out of the stall and the woman approached her and said, "Hi Amy. You speak really well. Where do you live?"

"Thanks. I live in Decatur." Amy replied.

The woman shook her head and said, "Oh that's not what I meant. What kind of place do you live?"

Amy said, "In an apartment."

The woman, looking very frustrated, asked, "No, I mean, who do you live with?"

To which, Amy said, "With my cat."

Clearly this woman assumed that Amy lived in a group home or a facility for people with disabilities and had trouble accepting Amy's responses of living a typical life in the community. Sigh. Because of the long history of people with disabilities being segregated from mainstream society, this woman had probably not been exposed to many people with disabilities. Sometimes just being present in spaces where you once were not allowed, is a form of social change and resistance.

Amy brought many gifts and talents to the self-advocacy movement in Illinois. She also trained nationally and personally met several dreams of her own. Amy and I had many deep and profound conversations which informed and deepened my understanding of equality, power, respect, and healing in the lives of people with disabilities. Thank you, Amy!

Questions for the Reader:

1. Do you serve on any committees, boards or teams that lack the representation of people who are impacted by the group's work? It could be people with disabilities, brown or black people, cultural or religious communities, LGBTQ+ community members, immigrants, etc.   If so, what steps can you take to increase membership by underrepresented communities?
2. What talents do you have that can be of service to your family, neighborhood, workplace, etc.?
3. What do you see when you look at yourself in the mirror?
4. Would you be willing to write an ABCs poem about yourself and share it with someone you trust?

Brenda - We Laughed, We Cried

When you first see Brenda, you notice her long, thick hair and her beautiful smile. She has a softness about her, a quiet voice, and a sweet manner. Like most of us, there is a lot more to Brenda than you might think during that first interaction.

Brenda grew up in a small mid-western town in a family of seven.   Brenda was born with cerebral palsy and was abused by her mother on a regular basis-both physically and emotionally. None of the other children were treated that way, only Brenda. Brenda often wondered why her mother abused her but none of the other children. She told me, "I think it was because I had disabilities and she didn't know what to do." At 21, Brenda moved to a group home in her town, happy to be out of her family home. Brenda's relationship with her mother was always strained. "It is still hard to think about it...the things she said and did to me, I will probably never get over it." Brenda moved to her own apartment before the age of 30.

In 2000, we were testing a sexual abuse prevention curriculum with people with intellectual and developmental disabilities in several pilot sites across Illinois. I remember the day I met Brenda very clearly. We had driven over three hours to meet with the 8 people who had been in the classes. We wanted to evaluate their experiences with the material and the teachers. Brenda initially appeared to be shy and then she spoke…slowly, deliberately, powerfully. "I never knew I could say no. But now I can say no. This [the training] changes my life."

After that day, I began to see Brenda once or twice a year as we continued to implement and evaluate the curriculum. Brenda was one of the first persons with disabilities to co-train the curriculum. Beginning in 2005, Brenda and I began traveling and co-presenting at conferences and other training events. Before that, Brenda had never been outside of her small town. Brenda and I became close friends and traveled/trained together in several states - including Illinois, Pennsylvania, Indiana. Massachusetts, North Carolina, Minnesota, and Washington. In the true nature of friendship, Brenda and I shared deep discussions, comfortable silences, grieving tears, and uncontrollable belly laughs. Traveling with Brenda was a true joy as she had a way of engaging strangers in airports, hotels, and restaurants - a great companion for an introvert like myself. As Brenda and I grew older and our physical needs increased, we could no longer travel and train out of state together. But our connection continues as we keep in touch by phone, text, letter, and are occasionally able to visit in person.

I learned a lot from my time with Brenda. The first lesson I learned was to 'never pretend you understand someone if you don't.' Brenda's speech was difficult to understand at times and especially if you did not know her well. She had a way of telling if people were pretending and would call them out on it. She would flat out ask you - "Can you understand me?" and if the person said yes, she'd ask: "Then what did I say?" She helped me to understand that sometimes people pretend to understand because they feel uncomfortable and think they are being kind - but pretending is a lie and is disrespectful. On the other hand, if I took the time to try and understand her, she knew I cared about her. How much better it is to be honest and tell someone I do not understand? This allows for the two people to work together and figure out the best way to communicate, patiently working on it in unison.

I will never forget the time we were co-training in Boston on *Communicating with people with intellectual and developmental disabilities*. She was telling the audience something and looked to me to help translate and I did not know what she was saying either. Brenda and I went through our usual process with no help and then she said, "I will spell it". She spelled out the key words and then I knew what she was saying. Together, we figured it out. Later, one of the participants asked if we had done that on purpose to show the audience what to do. Nope. It was real. None of us are perfect at communication. Brenda taught me that caring enough to try really hard is a sign of respect. And it is up to the person speaking when they decide to quit trying.

Brenda also taught me a lot about courage. Brenda was shy when I met her and compliant with those in positions of authority. Over the years as her confidence grew, she became very brave. Her focus was on doing what was right. If she observed something that was unfair or wrong, she would report the concern and watch for changes to be made. When the agency where Brenda received services changed their smoking policies, she noticed that the staff did not always follow the new rules, but the individuals they supported were made to comply. Brenda not only made her concerns known to management, but she also reported the Administrator, who smoked in the building, to the national accrediting organization during the agency's survey process. Brenda knows what equity looks like and speaks up when it is not present. That takes courage.

When I read Brenda my original draft of this section for her approval and ideas, she said, "What about the time they took my crutches away? Can you put that in there?" So, here is that story. The first out of state trip we took together, was to speak at a national sexual assault convention in Pittsburgh. Brenda, Randy (another co-trainer), Randy's support staff, Joe, and I flew to Pittsburgh. We all had dinner together and then returned to the hotel. A couple hours later Brenda noticed her crutches were not in our hotel room. It seemed they had been accidentally taken to the other hotel room where Randy and his support person were staying. Brenda called their room and said, "Why did you take my crutches? I can't walk. Bring me my crutches." Randy had taken advantage of the night life in Pittsburgh and was out dancing until after midnight. So, Brenda figured out how to walk to and from the bathroom with my support. Early the next morning, the crutches arrived along with sincere apologies. Brenda's ability to adapt and problem solve is amazing and it enhanced my life to witness her creative solutions to life's challenges.

Brenda was the first person who taught me how exhausting it can be to travel if you have disabilities. It was a common experience to have service staff address **me** when they had a question for **her** - "What does she want to eat?" "Is she checking any luggage?" "Does she want a wakeup call?" Really? How do I know what she wants to order for dinner or if she wants to check a suitcase or if she needs a wakeup call? She is right here - ASK HER! It was angering, but I knew the person was doing what society had trained them to do....and so I would say things in a neutral tone of voice like, "You will have to ask her what she wants." Then the conversation shifted.

And then there are the spaces that are not very accessible. We still laugh about the attached hotel rooms we had in Asheville, North Carolina where we worked for three days. The hotel rooms were very nice, and the bathrooms were perfect to accommodate our needs. However, the bed was higher than normal. This did not work well for Brenda, but in her usual approach to life, she made it fun. At that time, Brenda used metal forearm crutches to support her walking. I hope you can picture this scenario in your mind: She backed up across the room and walked as fast as she could with her crutches to try and leap onto the bed.

Nope, didn't work. Then she decided that maybe she could use her suitcase as a step. So, we placed it next to the bed. Nope. That didn't work either. She kept trying. Finally, she was able to get her upper body partly on the bed and asked me to lift her lower body. Success! By this time, we were laughing so hard, we could not stop. I know some of you who are reading this are asking why we did not call the front desk for help, or you are thinking of some other solution - please keep in mind whose life we are talking about. Brenda got to decide how she wanted to solve this problem. Not me, not you...Brenda. And she smiled and had fun figuring it out!

Brenda learned quickly that I am a bit of a workaholic. After our first couple of long-distance trips, Brenda began asking what we were going to do for fun during our trip. We would review the work schedule and she would insist that we carve out time for some adventure. Thanks to Brenda, we visited the space needle in Seattle, took a 'duck tour' in Boston, and drove through the mountains in Asheville, North Carolina. Brenda's thinking was: If you are going somewhere for the first time, you should see more than the training room and the hotel room. Training is fun and so are adventures in new cities! Thanks to Brenda, I learned to appreciate both!

On a not so fun note, we were flying back after four days of work in Spokane and the Seattle area when an amazing trip turned sour. We landed at a small-town regional airport in Illinois and would be deboarding outside. Despite what Brenda said, the flight staff decided that Brenda needed to be strapped onto an aisle chair and began barking directions at her and physically 'helping' her transfer from her plane seat to the chair. This was a difficult process for everyone. The straps were not working, and everyone was frustrated. I asked Brenda what she wanted to do, and she told them firmly, "I can walk down the stairs. I need a person in front of me and a person behind me. I can do it." Lo and behold, Brenda knew exactly what she needed. I positioned myself in front of her, she placed her hands on my shoulders and we proceeded to leave the plane. At the bottom of the steps, there was a wheelchair ready for her trip to enter the airport. As we entered the building, we heard this announcement over the airport intercom: "Your suitcases will be at baggage claim soon. We apologize for the delay, we had to help the handicapped." Brenda and I looked at each other - frustrated and exhausted. I raised an eyebrow and

Brenda said, "Not tonight. We can call them tomorrow. Let's get out of here." Again, the people who thought they knew what was best for Brenda because of her disabilities, made things harder. When we respect and listen to the experts, life goes much smoother.

Today, Brenda lives in her own place in her town where she was born. She has a motorized scooter that she takes to the store and about town. There is a colorful flag rising high from her scooter which seems to announce that someone fun is out for a ride. She is in a long-term, committed relationship and lives with her snuggly, fluffy cat, Angel. There was no resolution between Brenda and her mother before her mother passed away. At the end of her life, Benda's mother experienced disabilities of her own and was in a lot of physical pain. Brenda understands that we do not all get an apology when a family member has abused us. She also understands that one can live a good life without an apology. She is thankful for the many people she has met and the places she has been. She is most proud of "making it every day on my own." She feels that she has been able to live the life that she dreamed of because of the many people who listen, care, and encourage her…and she added, "practice…practice is important".

Questions for the Reader:

1. From this brief description of Brenda, how would you describe her abilities and talents?
2. How do you feel about the "don't pretend you understand me when you don't" advice from Brenda? Have you ever pretended you understood someone when you didn't? What might happen if you took Brenda's advice?
3. What thoughts do you have about the way Brenda was treated when it was time to get off the plane?
4. What is a skill or trait that you have that takes practice?

Stephanie, Bold and Brave

Stephanie and I first met at a rally with self-advocates (i.e., people with people with intellectual and developmental disabilities who want to speak up for themselves, their lives, and the movement for people with disabilities to have freedom and equality). I was immediately impressed with this gutsy and honest woman. She listened carefully to others and had no problem disagreeing with people or stating her own opinions. After the rally was over, she pushed herself up from her wheelchair, held onto the table and helped clean the room. She gathered papers and generally helped to make the room presentable so we could all leave. When I thanked her, she said something like, "We are supposed to help each other. Don't thank me."

After that, I saw Stephanie at several self-advocacy events. She was bold and passionate. She spoke her mind and didn't seem to care who disagreed with her. She loved deeply and was loyal to her beliefs and to her friends and family. She was also funny and liked to have a good time with those she trusted. The agency where she received services had made a commitment to self-advocacy and dedicated a staff member to support and organize events and training with their self-advocacy group. Leanne Mull was the support person, and although she is no longer with that agency, she continues her commitment to self-advocacy as I write these words.

One of the best memories I have of Stephanie and Leanne occurred at the Crowne Plaza hotel in Springfield, IL. Stephanie and I co-presented a half-day session for the Adult Protective Services supervisors. Adult Protective Services is an Illinois agency that handles abuse, neglect, and exploitation of older adults. The Adult Protective Services in Illinois was just beginning to work with adults with disabilities in the community and I had helped them with policies, procedures, and training. This day, Stephanie and I presented on "The Disability Experience" and compared and contrasted age-related disabilities and lifelong disabilities as well as several other topics.

The training took place on the second floor of the hotel, and we took the elevator to the training space. After the training, we met Leanne outside the training room, who was ready to take Stephanie back home a few hours away. Stephanie made a remark about riding the escalator down and Leanne said, "Come on!" Stephanie smiled and began to push herself up from her wheelchair. Leanne put her arm around Stephanie and stabilized her. They rode the escalator up and down a few times. I took the elevator down to take photos. I don't do escalators. People stopped and watched. Leanne and Stephanie smiled and laughed. After this day, anytime Stephanie and Leanne were in Springfield, they would stop by the Crowne Plaza and ride the escalator.

This story is very important. Let me explain. For many people with disabilities, if they want to do something, they must have the prerequisite skills. So, programs for people with disabilities have traditionally had prevocational classes and "Pre-Life classes"! There is a slogan in the self-advocacy movement called "PRE MEANS NEVER". Many people are told, when you can do X, then you can do Y. In this example, it might have been, 'When you can walk independently with balance, then you can ride an escalator.' If Leanne believed that, Stephanie would never have ridden an escalator. "Pre Means Never" is an obstacle for many people to try new things or to reach for their dreams. So many people die before they get to do some very simple things they would like to do. Instead of asking, 'do they have the prerequisite skills?' What if we asked, 'How can we make that happen?' That is what Leanne did that day, and together they made it happen! I co-trained with Stephanie a few years later and she shared a picture of her escalator ride and told the audience that it was among the top five experiences in her life.

Adults with disabilities are frequently told they are 'not ready' for something they desire. This is another form of "Pre Means Never". One man I know who lived in a group home was told, "You aren't ready to get your own apartment. When you make your bed every day for one year, then we will help you get an apartment." Really? I have asked audiences of professionals many times, "How many of you make your bed every morning?" A few hands go up, but the majority of people just laugh. If you don't live in a residential services facility/home, you get to choose whether or not you make your bed. This is another form of inequality and oppression. Stephanie knew this. She saw inequalities on a regular basis and spoke up for people with disabilities to have freedom and choice.

Another great memory of Stephanie occurred at a statewide conference for developmental disability service providers. This conference had always been exclusively for staff members from agencies that provided services. This year, for the first time, we supported at least 10 people with developmental disabilities to attend and many of them presented workshops. During an open session for all participants, the presenter was summarizing the key points from the two-day conference when Stephanie raised her hand. She leaned against the table as she stood up and said, "I want to know why the staff have to cook our popcorn at the workshop? I can burn my own popcorn as good as the staff." What a great question! Stephanie was serious and the audience roared! A few days later, Stephanie and Leanne placed bags of microwave popcorn in all the staff mailboxes at the workshop with Stephanie's quote on the bag. Some people thought

Stephanie was a troublemaker. I saw her as a shero!

I will never forget the trip with Stephanie and Leanne to Boston. Leanne would provide personal care support for Stephanie and 'voice' for her when needed. Voicing means that Leanne would repeat what Stephanie said to ensure the audience understood the message. As I arrived at Leanne's home where we were meeting to head to the airport, I saw Stephanie's wheelchair on the front porch. There was a handwritten sign on the chair which said: "Property of Stephanie Campbell. DO NOT TOUCH!" More on this later.

As I entered the home, Stephanie waved me over to the couch to sit next to her. She looked very serious, and I wondered what was going on.

She said, "I need to tell you something". As she pointed her finger near my face she added, "You have to promise not to cry."

I knew she would not continue until I promised, so I swallowed slowly and said, "I promise."

And then with a tear in one eye, she continued, "I have breast cancer. I just found out. I don't feel like going, but I promised you I would speak, and I will. I keep my promises."

Then she added, "Remember, you promised." And then we hugged.

It was important to Stephanie that we not talk about the cancer while we were gone. She was a very private person, and I knew that about her. However, something changed while we were in Boston. On our very first day of training, before the first break, Stephanie told the audience about her cancer.

At break time, we were walking in the hall and a very tall, muscular law enforcement officer, bent down, and asked Stephanie, "Can I share something with you?" She said "yes." And he proceeded to pull his shirt collar down and show Stephanie a long scar on his neck. "We have something in common. I had cancer too. I beat it and I believe you will too." Stephanie looked my way and shook her head no; reminding me not to cry. It was such a powerful show of compassion and connection, and I did have a tear in my eye. I sucked it in and held myself together.

That night at the hotel, none of us wanted to leave the room so we ordered room service (something that is very rare because of the added expense). We shared fun memories and prepared for the next day's work.

The next day was a much larger group and in an auditorium. Before lunch, Stephanie was exhausted and took a break during the session. When she came back, she told the audience members about her cancer and apologized for her break.

At one point during the day, she shared her wheelchair story. At the workshop where Stephanie spent her weekdays, she chose to transfer from her wheelchair to a regular chair while she worked. She discovered that some of the staff would have other folks sit in her wheelchair during these times. When Stephanie told the staff that it was her chair and she didn't want anyone else sitting in it, she was told, "Well you aren't using it." And she was called "Selfish". The Director of Adult Protective Services in Massachusetts, Nancy Alterio, told Stephanie that in Massachusetts, the staff member's actions would have been totally unacceptable and might have been considered an abusive act. After that, Stephanie was reenergized. At the end of the training day, Nancy stayed with us while we waited for our ride back to the hotel. I will always remember

Nancy's kindness. If you are not familiar with Nancy's work in Massachusetts, check it out: Disabled Persons Protective Commission. * She is a real visionary!

Stephanie chose not to have chemotherapy as she did not want to lose the physical strength she had worked so hard to maintain. She had surgery on the breast with the cancer and did okay for a while. Then the cancer returned. She had three goals during these last few months. One was to be surrounded with family; another was to write a book of her life; and lastly, she wanted to attend the annual Speak Up Speak Out Summit. She moved in with her sister and saw family members every day. Leanne Mull sat with Stephanie for hours to support the writing process and then Leanne raised the money to print her book, *My Journey Through Life* by Stephanie Campbell. Stephanie was able to see her book and share it with others. Over 1500 have been distributed.

By the time of the Speak Up Speak Out Summit, Stephanie was on continuous oxygen and on major pain medication. Again, Leanne found a way to help Stephanie with her final dream. Speak Up Speak Out: Here We Come! Although she was very tired, Stephanie said goodbye to her friends, passed out heart cookies to her favorite people and even worked the exhibit with me on sexual assault. In the evenings, we shared memories curled up on the couch. We laughed and we cried. Yes, it was finally okay for me to cry in front of Stephanie. We knew we might never see each other again. It was time to share our gratitude and feelings openly.

Stephanie's greatest vision was for young people with disabilities to know their value and their power. She was always saying, "We got to start with the young people." Related to that, she had a message for parents who had family members with disabilities. She often said, "I love my mother, but she was overprotective." She wanted to tell parents to give their children with disabilities chances to make mistakes and to learn to speak up for themselves. During the last years of her life, she had the opportunity to speak to parents as well as to young people. Stephanie's presence, words, and actions left quite a legacy with all who met her or heard her speak.

Questions for the reader:

1. Consider times in your life when a "Pre Means Never" attitude was an obstacle to meeting a dream or goal. What was your experience?
2. What ideas do you have about balancing risk with dignity, when someone wants to try something that might not be successful? How do you do this in your own life?
3. Do you think that parents with children who have disabilities are more protective than other parents? What are your thoughts about that?
4. Why do you think Stephanie went from being a private person to sharing freely with the audiences in Boston?

A Friendship with Lester

Lester Pritchard was a disability rights activist with a smile that lit up a room. Sometimes his smile was so big it made you wonder what kind of good trouble he was planning. He worked at the local, state, and national level to change laws, systems, practices, and attitudes about people with disabilities. He was a visionary who loved direct action, and absolutely nothing could keep Lester away from a protest or demonstration. He was generous and kind and mischievous. He co-founded the Campaign for Real Choice in Urbana, IL with the mission of gaining full inclusion for people with disabilities. Lester received many awards for his advocacy including the American Bar Association Paul G. Hearne Award for Disability Rights; Lester was only the second non-lawyer to receive this award! Lester took this work very seriously and he also believed that activism needed to be fun. Lester recognized his privilege as a white, cis man with financial means and told me once that he felt indebted to people with intellectual and developmental disabilities.

I remember Lester speaking at a gathering of around 100 people with intellectual and developmental disabilities and he told them that when he was two-years old, his mother took him to the doctor to see if he was okay. He was not doing what other two-year-old children were doing. His mother told him that the doctor put a small hammer to his knees and then told his mom, "Your child will never amount to anything". But his mom did not believe that, so she took him home and continued to treat him with love and over time, she became an advocate for her son. Lester told the people in the audience not to pay attention to people who don't believe in them. He made sure everyone knew they had value and that "We all believe in you." The people there were in awe of Lester and hung onto every word he said - as respoken by his wife, Barb. I will never forget that day. But how did this all begin?

I think it was 2005 when I received a phone call from Jennifer Knapp with the Campaign for Real Choice. She called to schedule a meeting with Lester Pritchard, the founder and leader of the Campaign. I had heard of Lester but had never met him. I knew he was a disability activist. I knew he was a person who made things happen. But I had no idea what a truly amazing person he was and how much influence he would have in my life.

Our first meeting was at an Applebee's Restaurant. At first, Lester interviewed me. He asked a question, Jennifer translated (repeated his words), and I answered. On occasion, Jennifer would ask a question. Before long, there was a shift and it felt more like a deep, philosophical conversation. The kind of conversations you have with like-minded friends about the meaning of life and how to change the world.

Lester was 'bigger than life' in many ways. He had an infectious smile, an amazing sense of humor, an enormous heart, and a passion for direct action to **'free his people'**. Shortly after the first meeting, we began meeting regularly at Lester's home or my office. His wife and co-founder of the Campaign, Barb, participated in the meetings. While Lester was a shining star, Barb had a bright flame as well. Lester and Barb spoke at some of the rallies we organized. In 2008, we began collaborating on a vision about ways to bring people with intellectual and developmental disabilities together to speak up for freedom. There were still several state institutions in Illinois. People in group homes shared stories of control and oppression. We formed a committee and began monthly meetings and organized what we called 'Freedom Quest'. In May 2009, three caravans began across the state: Southern, Northern and Northwest. Each caravan consisted of several vans filled with people with intellectual and developmental disabilities and their support people. Each caravan stopped in several different towns with a rally that self-advocates facilitated. Every participant wore a t-shirt that said: **FREEDOM QUEST: People with disabilities calling for real freedom in Illinois.** There was a buzz all around as newspapers covered the events in the various towns. There were speeches and songs and skits and lots of energy! The event was organized so that all three caravans arrived in

Springfield (the state capitol) on the same night. The next day, we had arranged for a police escort as the many vehicles drove from the hotel east of town to the state capitol. We had reserved a long line of parking spaces near the capitol. We had invited the media as well as legislators and senators. One by one, people with intellectual and developmental disabilities raised their voices and told the government what they wanted and needed. Lester's heart filled with joy and hope as he listened to the speeches. Lester (and others) raised his fist in solidarity with hundreds of people calling for freedom. It was invigorating and exhausting, and Lester organized a debriefing meeting soon afterwards. There was still much work to do, and Lester did not slow down…until…

In October, Lester was in the hospital with Barb at his side. Facts were gathered and decisions were made. I'll never forget the phone call from Jennifer Knapp. "Lester is in the hospital and only has a few hours to live. He would like you to drive over if you can. He wants to have a party." I jumped in my car and drove to the hospital an hour away. I was greeted by Jennifer who told me the rules Lester wanted everyone to understand. "He wants to hear stories and memories. No crying is allowed in his room. If you have to cry, you need to step out.

He wants us to laugh together." We all respected his desires. People who loved Lester floated in and out of his room for hours, sharing stories and love and laughter. We had the party he wanted. We pledged to keep his vision alive, to continue our work so that people with disabilities could live independent lives that had meaning and purpose. We said thank you and goodbye. Lester directed his death with beauty and generosity, just as he had directed his life.

A short time later in November 2009, hundreds gathered at the Annual Speak Up Speak Out Summit. Lester was the original visionary for this event and people gathered to honor him and grieve the huge hole in our community. Of course, the biggest hole was left in Barb's life, and she graciously accepted condolences, stories, and hugs from many attendees. Karen Donovan performed a song she had written to honor Lester.

The lyrics are here: (recording available on YouTube)

"*Real Choice*" * by Karen Donovan
Recorded at Speak Up Speak Out; November 5, 2009

I don't want to be what you think I should be
And I don't want to see what you think I should see

And I want to be me
And I want to be free

I want a real choice, yeah
I want a real voice
Give me a real choice
And let, let me be me

You must see the me that I know I can be
You must hope and free these chains holding me

And you, can make it all change
And you, must make it all change

I want a real choice, yeah
I want a real voice
Give me a real choice
And let, let me be me

We are here to make a stand as one
And we are here to shape what we have begun

And we, come to speak up
And we, come to speak out

I want a real choice, yeah
I want a real voice
Give me a real choice
I want a real voice
Give me a real choice
I want a real voice
Give me a real choice

And here are some words I wrote for Lester's celebration of life:

What I learned from Lester Pritchard:

- ♥ That freedom is the most precious human gift
- ♥ That passion can carry us beyond our wildest dreams
- ♥ That pizza is a food group
- ♥ That the next voice added may be the one that gets the job done
- ♥ That civil disobedience is sometimes the best option
- ♥ That humor connects us all
- ♥ That friction and conflict can move us to a better place
- ♥ To never give up on equality for all
- ♥ That greatness and humility can co-exist
- ♥ That activism can be fun

♥ That it is possible to die with as much love,
  control, and dignity as one lives
♥ That his spirit lives on in our actions for change

Barb continues the work that she and Lester had so tirelessly championed. They were a strong pair of activists. After years of publicly voicing for Lester so his words could be understood by all, I am sure that there are times when Barb is speaking, and she feels his presence and his words coming from her mouth. He will always be a part of her, but make no mistake, Barb has an inner power all her own that speaks up for justice and equality in the lives of people with disabilities. I am indebted to both Barb and Lester for welcoming me into their home, their lives, and their life's passion.

Questions for the reader:

1. As you read about Lester, what stands out most for you?
2. How can we all be actively involved in directing our end of life supports?
3. Are you aware of the direct action that people with disabilities took to get the Americans with Disabilities Act enacted? If not, take some

time to review the documentary *Lives Worth Living. **

4. How can direct action change unjust systems at a local or state level?
5. Activism is serious business and hard work. Why do you think Lester said that activism needs to be fun?

I am filled with gratitude to Amy, Stephanie, Brenda, and Lester who compassionately shared space with me as equal pioneers on this journey of seeking equality, safety, freedom, and justice.

Chapter 4

DREAMS

"If our legacy is not entitlement, it must be hope." Melissa Gilbert

"Never deprive someone of hope, it may be all they have." H. Jackson Brown

I think it was Dave Hingsburger who coined the phrase 'Mass Dreamicide". As a society we have killed the dreams of people with disabilities. We can take away freedom: lock people in institutions, separate them from their friends and families, sterilize them without their knowledge or permission, steal their money, deny them quality food and access to relationships…but **how can you take away an entire community's dreams?** We erase dreams by repeatedly telling people that their dreams don't matter; that they do not count in this world. We erase dreams by never even asking people about their dreams and by telling them that their dreams are not realistic! We erase dreams by 'doing for' and 'doing to' people instead of 'doing with' them. We erase dreams by focusing on what people can't do and not what they can do. Instead of empowering people to choose their goals based upon their own interests, desires, and delights, we erase dreams by having goals based on functional assessments and limiting labels. We abolish dreams by not listening and not validating people and also by deleting their very existence as fully human.

I think the more time I spent with other people with disabilities, especially those with intellectual/developmental disabilities, the more I understood the importance of dreams in all of our lives. When I was a young person with suicidal feelings, I believe it was my dream that kept me alive. There was a bright spark inside of me that encouraged me to believe that one day I might be able to make a difference in the lives of others. That dream was important to me! I believe that dreams are important to everyone.

Throughout the years, I heard story after story about dreams being denied. I remember asking Janis what her dreams were, and she said, "I'm not allowed to have dreams." A dream lives inside of us - sometimes very deep and quiet - how can others control that? Dreams are denied when others make you feel that you have no value; that you don't deserve to have more than you already have. Dreams are denied when a dream is shared and the person is told, "That will never happen" or "That's not realistic." When I asked Janis to 'tell me more about that', she said, "All my life, all I've heard is can't, can't, can't". She looked sad and depressed.

Sometimes when we tell others an important dream, we are given the message of NO WAY! This messaging occurs when children are born with disabilities, in schools, and in adult services. Some people are crushed by this response and give up on their dream. Some people become more passionate about the dream and take on a WATCH ME attitude. And some people may not really care what others think. For many people that I have worked with over the years, this dream crushing has been so subtle and so consistent and so pervasive, it really feels like dreams are impossible. Many people have tucked their dreams away deep inside. I discovered that with some encouragement and hope, people can uncover and share their dreams. For example, I told Janis, "Right here, it is okay to dream. Think about what your dreams are. We can talk about that in a few minutes if you want to." I worked with another person for a few minutes and when I turned around Janis had listed on a piece of paper 13 different dreams for her life!!

In 2006, the Illinois Council on Developmental Disabilities released a grant related to person-centered planning. We applied and received a six-year grant to support people with IDD to say/show their dreams. We created "Dare to Dream", a half-day training and scheduled them across the state.

We designed the training so that each person attending would be able to:

- Identify at least one dream for their life
- Have a person to support their dream
- Be able to tell or show their dream to others
- Brainstorm at least one step to take to get their dream
- Practice what to say/do if someone says 'no' to their dream
- Create a dream collage

At the end of every Dare to Dream event, each person showed and talked about their dream collage. When the person was finished, everyone else said, "WE BELIEVE IN YOUR DREAMS".

I remember fondly a Dare to Dream event a few hours from my home. Early in the day, when we were talking about what dreams are, some people were sharing a few dreams they had when one man said, "I have relatives in Minnesota, St. Louis and California that I never see." I asked, "Do you want to go visit them?" He pounded his hand on the table and said, rather loudly, "Don't you see my wheelchair? I can't fly!"

We never argue with people when they say things we disagree with because it can feel disrespectful and doesn't really help, so I said, "I see your wheelchair. You believe you cannot fly to visit your relatives because of your chair." He said, "yes" and we moved on. During the day, he quietly participated in all the activities. He listened closely to others. Towards the end of the day, each person was asked to make a dream collage. After everyone was done, each person showed and talked about their dream collage. When it was his turn, he presented his dream collage to the group. It was an aerial view of the United States with three places marked: St. Louis, Minnesota, and California. He pointed at each of the three places and said proudly, with a big smile on his face, "I'm going to fly to all three of them!" After the training, a person from another agency, shared information on ways to get financial supports for his desired travels. It was one of those days when I felt so much gratitude because I witnessed a person move from being stuck in the "It is impossible" to a place of hope, dreams, and possibilities. WOW!! We watched and listened as people who had never spoken in front of a group, shared their dreams with passion and clarity and confidence! The room was filled with joyful hearts and life doesn't get much better than that!

Over time, we heard stories about the dream collages being presented at person-centered planning meetings. A person-centered planning meeting is when a person and their services team get together and plan the person's future. (These are sometimes called: Individual Service Plans, Individual Treatment Plans, Individualized Education Programs, and others.) The team typically includes the person and other family and staff members, ideally chosen by the person. These meetings are required for people with intellectual and developmental disabilities who receive services paid for with public funds. It was exciting to hear that people were taking their dream collages to these meetings so the team could discuss what the person really wanted in their life and ways others could provide support.

We heard about dream collages being placed on bedroom walls and in case records. One high school student, with support from his mother, put together a power point and presented his dreams at his Individualized Education Program meeting at school. His mother beamed as she told us about her son leading his own meeting. She followed up with us as he met his initial dreams. This is a mom who believed in and knew how to support her son's dreams!!

Dreams Come in All Different Sizes.

When we first began our dreams work, we heard lots of resistance from family members and professionals. One concern was that the dreams would be so big, they would be impossible for the person to achieve. One parent asked, "What if they want to go to Hawaii? We can't afford that!" Another concern was that most of the dreams would be unrealistic for the person to do. Lots of professionals and families said, "I don't want to set the person up for failure. We need to make sure the dreams are realistic."

Let's chat. Many of us have dreams that seem unrealistic. Many of us have BIG dreams. Does that mean we should not be allowed to dream? To me, dreams represent hope - hope for something new and delicious. The simple act of dreaming can give meaning to our lives. When someone believes in us and our dreams, it is life-affirming. I know several people without disabilities who do not easily share their dreams because they are so precious that they don't want anyone to

131

question or criticize their dream. They hold these dreams very close to their hearts and only share them when they really trust someone. I personally have some dreams that will probably never come true, but those dreams still mean something. They still matter and make my life better. I think this is true for lots of people. And you know what? Sometimes unrealistic dreams do come true!

What we discovered is that dreams come in all different sizes, and they are important to the person no matter what size they are. Dreams give our life meaning and for some people, it is a dream that allows them to get up every morning and say, "I can do this one more day."

Having a dream champion is a positive experience - someone who listens to your dreams, asks questions so they understand what the dream means to you, and believes in you and your dream. A dream champion works in partnership with the dreamer to get as close to the dream as possible. A dream champion has no judgment about a person's dreams and does not discourage their dreams.

Here is a small list of dreams that people shared with us:

To never be called the R-word again

To fly in a hot air balloon

To be able to take a nap in my bedroom on the weekend (the door to this person's bedroom is locked during the day so they had no free access to their own bedroom)

To visit my girlfriend's grave (the girlfriend had died 2 years before and they had not attended the funeral or visited the grave)

To take the train with my boyfriend to Disney

To go to KFC

To volunteer with children

To work with animals

To drive a car

To have a real job

To decorate my bedroom

To choose what I eat

To spend time with family

To mow the lawn with the riding lawn mower

To take a class at the community college

To take a plane to visit family

To get a power chair

To have my own apartment

To grow tomatoes and share tomatoes with the neighbors

To have my mom listen to me

To have my staff listen to me

To join a self-advocacy group

To stay in my pajamas all day on the weekend

To stay home alone when my parents go out of town for the weekend

To work on a newsletter

To be a photographer

To stay in a hotel

To be in a movie!

To go to college

To ride the city bus

To go on a date

To go to the "Speak Up Speak Out Summit"

To deliver Meals on Wheels

To lift weights at the YMCA

To talk on the phone in private

To be safe

The participants in the Dare to Dream trainings challenged us to expand our reach. People wanted to feel listened to and supported by parents and other family members as well as professionals. We would hear things like, "My mom/dad won't like my dreams. They want to pick what I work on." And "When I tell my staff, they won't care. They want me to learn how to make my bed, not what I want to do." So, the original Dare to Dream events blossomed into the creation of more training, first for family members and then for disability professionals.

We had lots of time in a car (Krescene Beck, a colleague, called it windshield time) driving all around Illinois to meet with people about their dreams, and we began writing down what we learned about the value of dreams and how people wanted to be supported. Soon, we began training groups of parents/family members and then groups of service providers/teachers. When we went to a town to conduct Dare to Dream training, we began scheduling an additional workshop for staff and one for parents/family members. Our goal was that the people who had previously had their dreams squashed, could present their dream collages to their family and/or their staff members and would receive support, not roadblocks.

Bridging the Gap Between Dreams and Reality sessions for family members and for professionals had these components:

1. How to respond to someone who speaks or shows a dream
2. How to understand what the person means by their stated/drawn dream
3. Low-cost and no-cost tips and techniques that they can use to respect the dreams of the people they support
4. Ways to encourage the development of self-advocacy skills
5. Identifying barriers that prevent people from achieving their dreams
6. Strategies to support the person to share dreams with others during their Person-Centered Plan and Individualized Education Program meetings and other conversations

For the most part, families and professionals who attended these sessions left with open hearts and open minds. They were excited to see the dream collages and to support the person they cared about in a new way.

I recall one parent very clearly. I asked her what her son dreamed about for his future. I watched her face as she sat quietly, and a tear began to stream down her cheek. She said, "I don't know. No one has ever asked me that, but I'm sure going to find out." Other parents have shared gratitude for expanding their view of their child's possibilities in life. It was common for someone to say, "Thank you for helping me to understand my daughter based on what she dreams about. I've known about their diagnoses, programs and strategies, but never what was important to them."

Here is an example of the typical way someone had responded before the training:

"I want to drive a car."

"You can't get a driver's license. You can't read. No way you can drive!"

"Okay."

Here is an example of the new way someone responded to this same request:

"I want to drive a car."

"Tell me more about that."

"I want to pick the songs. The driver picks the songs. I don't like country music."

"Oh, I didn't know that. You can pick the music next time we get in the car."

In this situation, the person didn't want to drive a car. The person wanted to control the music/radio in the car. Before, an assumption was made about what the person wanted…which was totally inaccurate. This dream was super easy to accomplish!

It was amazing for families and professionals to discover a way to respond that was not critical or dismissing. To continue with the driving a car theme, here is another example:

"I want to drive a car."

"Tell me what that means to you."

"I want to be independent. I want to come and go when I want to."

"That sound really important. Would you like to go to the place that is in charge of people driving? I am happy to take you. We can find out what you would need to do."

"Yes. I would love to do that."

In this situation, the person was supported in learning what it takes to get a driver's license and to learn how to drive. The person did not know how to read, so that was a barrier in taking the written test. **The person decided** they wanted to learn how to read and began taking a class in the community with other adults who could not read. They were also offered the opportunity to learn how to take the city bus, so they had more independence traveling in town.

Another person who wanted to drive a car, had a parent who was extremely nervous about taking his daughter driving. He told this story. "I knew it was her biggest dream and I wanted to be her dream champion. First, we practiced driving on the beach front where I knew we couldn't crash into anything. Then we moved our practices to empty parking lots and eventually to the town streets. I want to tell you all that today, my daughter can park on a dime and is one of the best drivers I know. It has changed her life and our relationship! She always knew I loved her, and NOW SHE KNOWS HOW MUCH I BELIEVE IN HER."

In some agencies, staff found a new way of looking at things. Here is an example:

"Maybe Carol doesn't have to make her bed every morning 75% of the time before she can get her own apartment. That seems really restrictive and unfair. Lots of adults never make their beds. Let's find out what Carol's dream of living in her own apartment might look like. Let's see what supports she will need to achieve her dream of living on her own. Let's be her dream champion."

Another staff told us, "I thought I knew everything about Deja. I've known her for years and spent lots of time with her. But when we started talking about *her* dreams for *her* life, I discovered a whole new person! Opening that door - the conversation about dreams - has changed everything. It is so much fun to support her in reaching for her dreams." The relationship changed to one of respect, empowerment, and equality. The scales of power stretched to be in balance.

Remember the woman who told me she wasn't allowed to have dreams? One of the dreams on her list of 13 things, was to ride in a hot air balloon. Several months after that day, I received a notice from an agency that was scheduling hot air balloon rides for people with intellectual and developmental disabilities. They had space for some extra people and wondered if I knew anyone who might be interested. Why yes, I certainly did!! I phoned the agency where Janis received services and asked for her support person. I explained the opportunity and asked if I could speak with Janis. The support person said, "Well, that's not one of her dreams. I wonder if you are remembering someone else." When I assured the staff that it was Janis, she said she would go talk with Janis and call me right back. As it turns out, Janis had never told anyone else about this dream, believing it was impossible. Janis was thrilled about this opportunity and her support staff agreed she would drive her the four hours to and from the hot air balloon location.

I want to pause the story here and acknowledge this staff person and this organization. First of all, the staff member knew she could make this decision without getting permission because it was a person-centered decision and in line with the agency's mission. Secondly, the staff member was willing to take an entire day out of her busy schedule to support one person's dream. Kudos all around!

As it turns out, the weather was not suitable for hot air balloon rides during the scheduled time. Janis was very disappointed. The event was rescheduled in a few weeks. Again, it was too windy for safe hot air balloon rides. Janis again, was very disappointed. After five cancellations due to weather, Janis may have wondered if she would ever rise into the sky in a hot air balloon. But Janis' dream to ride a hot air balloon did come true. On the sixth scheduled date, the weather cooperated, Janis rose excitedly above the ground and experienced the feeling of freedom, and her support person shared her joy and knew she had done something that really elevated Janis' life. (No pun intended). Here are some of the words Janis used to describe her experience:

magical   floating   peaceful   safe   beautiful

peace and quiet

Nothing could hurt me up there

Months later, Janis said, "I didn't think it could happen. Now I know dreams can come true." Keep working on that long list Janis. We believe in you.

The Power of Dreams

By Shirley Paceley

The power of dreams is the power that you feel when you know in your heart what your dream is…and knowing that it can't be wrong because it is yours.

The power of dreams is the power you feel when you know 100% that someone else believes in you and your dreams, so you raise your head a little higher.

The power of dreams is the power in hoping for a new and improved life and the sense that it really might happen, no matter what has come before.

The power of dreams is the power that comes when you take that first step, and the fear and the joy get all mixed up inside and you know it is worth the risk.

The power of dreams is the power of your heart, combined with other hearts when you have support for what is important to you, and your heart almost bursts with delight.

The power of dreams is the power of several people coming together for one dream of living lives with freedom and equality.

The Power of Dreams is sometimes hard to measure and hard to express, but it is the power to change lives.

Questions for the Reader:

1. Think about a time when someone questioned, criticized, or dismissed a dream that you shared. What was your response?
2. What dreams do you have in your life?
3. Who is your dream champion? What does this person do to support your dreams?
4. How have your past experiences influenced how open you are in sharing your dreams? Do you have a dream you have never told anyone?
5. Is there someone for whom you are a dream champion? Describe that experience.

An Insightful Opportunity

Krescene Beck and I had been doing "Dare to Dream" workshops for a couple of years when I received an interesting phone call. The call was from an agency a few hours away and it went like this: "I hear that when you go out and do training, people with disabilities train with you. Well, we have a man here who wants to train other people with disabilities - it is his dream and is even in his annual plan. Any chance he could train with you?" I asked to speak with the man on the phone and a few minutes later, I was talking to Charles. We arranged to meet three months later when I was in his part of the state. We would meet one day, and if he wanted to, he would train with us the next day.

We arranged to meet at the place where Charles spent his days. Krescene and I waited in a small meeting room for Charles to join us. As soon as he entered the room, it filled with his energy. He had sparkling bright eyes, beautiful brown skin, and an authentic smile. His wisdom and decades of life experiences were immediately evident. His voice was gentle and considerate. We talked about dreams - both his and the value of dreams in the lives of people with disabilities. We talked about the training that would happen the following day and his payment for his work. He chose what parts of the training he wanted to facilitate.

We had been together for quite a while, when Charles said, "I've always wondered about something, but I never thought I could ask anyone about it. I think I can ask you. Is that ok?" Not knowing what he was going to ask, but ready for anything, we said, "Sure." And Charles replied, "I've been using a wheelchair since I was little. I've always wondered, what is it like to walk?" I will admit, this is a question no one had ever asked me/us before. Krescene said, "I never really thought about it. It's just something I could always do."

I said, "Well, walking is how I get from one place to another. Sometimes it is okay, sometimes it hurts. I think it is alright if we have different ways of moving around. "

We sat in silence a moment and then Charles said, "Thank you."

What a profound moment that was for all of us. Charles had the courage to ask a question that had been on his mind for most of his life, and we were invited to join him in the moment of deep honesty and vulnerability. Maybe finding the courage to ask his question was one of his dreams. We were honored and blessed to be a part of that moment.

After that, we were done with business and kept talking and enjoying each other's company. Spontaneously, one of us asked, "What was the best day of your life?" Charles stated, "When a group of us went to huge disability rights protest out of state. Lots of people with disabilities were there and we held signs about freedom and equality. It was great to be speaking up for our rights. I felt like I was part of something really big and really important."

Then he added, "Do you want to hear about the worst day of my life?"

We answered, "If you want to tell us."

And then we heard another part of his life story. "The worst day is more than one day, but here it is. I have personal assistants who come to my apartment every morning and get me out of bed and help me get ready for the day. And the person comes back in the evening and helps with dinner and bedtime preparations. One Friday night, my PA was getting ready to leave, and placed my phone on the side of the bed where I could reach it. That was unusual. The next morning, he did not come to help me. I could not reach him, so after several hours I called the police and explained what happened. No one came. There I laid. He did not come that evening. When Sunday morning arrived, I was certain he would be there to help me, but again, he did not come." A tear began slowly streaming down his cheek. "Again, I called the police. I needed help. No one came. On Monday, my PA came to help me. He told me he had a drug problem. I was so hurt. There I laid for two days with no way to get out of bed." By this time, we all had tears running down our faces. Krescene asked Charles, "May I wipe your tears?" and Charles nodded "yes". Krescene gently wiped his tears from his face. After a few moments of silence, Charles said, "Thank you both for today. And thank you for the opportunity to train tomorrow." We thanked him for meeting with us and for being so open.

We left with hearts deepened through Charles' open and honest sharing, and an increased awareness of the courage it takes to face the daily challenges of living alone and needing to rely upon support from others who may not be reliable. Charles' willingness to openly share his experience of the vulnerability of life was a gift; an invitation for us to live more softly, look and listen more deeply, and to remember his strength and courage as we continued with this work.

The next day, when Charles was presenting to a group of 20 or 25 people with disabilities about dreams, he shared this: "One of my dreams, was to present to a group of people like me. And here I am, my dream has come true. Another dream I have is to be at the ocean with my toes in the sand. Whatever your dream is, believe in it. Believe in yourself." After the training, Charles received sincere applause. He signed a voucher to be paid for his training/expertise and we waited for his ride to arrive. Hugs of gratitude were shared before we parted.

A few months later, we heard that Charles had died a peaceful death. Our first thought was a vision of Charles strolling on the beach with a smile on his face and his toes in the sand.

Question for the reader:

1. What does it feel like to walk?

Chapter 5

Sexual Assault

"I didn't know I could say no, and I sure didn't know it was against the law."
Survivor with a disability

"...the shared experience ends where marginalization begins."   Megan S. Paceley

I wrote this blog several years ago and thought it might be a good introduction to this part of the book.

This is Not Okay

It has been a frustrating few weeks. A woman was sexually assaulted. She is experiencing trauma. She happens to have an intellectual disability. She cannot access counseling services because she is "too low". That is discrimination.

I understand the concept of 'do no harm' in this situation. We should not further harm a victim of sexual assault through our interventions. But isn't it harmful to deny services to someone who desperately needs them? Isn't it harmful to tell the family "Your daughter is too low"? I believe that a very harmful assumption has been made in this situation. I wish I could tell you this is unusual, but it is not. It appears to be somewhat common practice to deny people who communicate in a non-traditional manner access to quality victim services. I am appalled and saddened by this.

Yes, it has been a frustrating few weeks. A different woman was sexually assaulted. She happens to have a developmental disability. The assault happened nearly three years ago. The family is fighting for justice in a criminal justice system that does not see this victim as credible. This, too, feels like discrimination.

I understand that this 'case' might take more time to collect evidence and to prosecute than in 'easier' cases. I believe that everyone communicates and that many people who communicate differently can testify in court. I also know that sometimes an evidence-based prosecution may be the best course of action, but do we even try that when the victim may not be able to testify in court? I do not understand when people whose job it is to protect the public do not even try. I understand very clearly that the message to perpetrators of sexual violence across the nation is this: sexually assault people with disabilities and nothing will happen to you. And unfortunately, the message to the victims with disabilities is often this: We do not care. I am appalled at these messages! We can do better!

Yes, it has been a frustrating few weeks. An excellent prosecuting attorney, who believes that the voice of every sexual assault victim should be heard in court, contacted me. A woman with developmental disabilities was sexually assaulted by staff at her group home. There was physical evidence. There was access. There was testimony. The jury voted not guilty. The defense attorney called the victim evil and referred to the victim as an object. The offender on the other hand was called a 'person with a family'. So, the victim (who has a disability) was painted as bad and the person who sexually assaulted her was painted as a person whose life has value. Apparently, the jury believed this hateful story. When will the public be outraged at this targeted violence against people with disabilities? When will the public see people with disabilities as having equal value with other human beings?

Yes, it has been a frustrating few weeks. A young student was sexually assaulted at school. The student attends special education classes and has had no prevention education. Other students in the same school receive education on bullying, respect, healthy relationships, and reporting abuse, ... but not the special education students. This feels like discrimination. And now I am not sure what I understand - why would we not educate the students who are at the greatest risk of experiencing bullying and other forms of violence?

Yes, I have felt a lot of frustration the past few weeks. So, what happens next? Well, those of us in this movement at the intersection of violence and people with disabilities channel our frustration into our passion to make changes. We walk or roll side by side with people with disabilities and speak up about the issues. We work with families and schools and victim services and criminal justice personnel and hospital personnel and others. We use our voices and our actions to say this is not okay - and we will not stop. I am grateful to all of you who are in this movement to stop sexual violence against people with disabilities. We are stronger together. Together we grieve. Together we speak out. Together we rise above the discrimination and create a world of equality and safety.

Questions for the Reader:

1. Every job has frustrations. What work frustrations have you experienced?

2. What strategies might be helpful to you and others when feelings of helplessness emerge in your life?
3. What are your thoughts and feeling about educating students in Special Ed classes about bullying, healthy relationships, and human sexuality?
4. What personal, social, and professional resources do you have to manage social injustices in your own life or the lives of others?

The Ultimate Mentor

I believe it was the Fall of 1992 that I attended a five-day Train the Trainer event in Northern Illinois. The participants had been chosen to become trainers on the prevention of sexual assault against people with developmental disabilities. Ten trainers came from across the country and each one presented for a half day on their area of expertise. During the evenings, the participants worked to create a curriculum from the lessons learned that day. Some of us stayed up late after the work was completed and talked into the night about our work and our dreams to change the world.

Among the trainers were Dave Hingsburger and Leslie Walker Hirsch. It was an amazing week! One morning we were introduced to the trainer Orieda Horn Anderson who filled the room with her passion and presentation style. I was mesmerized with her and felt so honored when she happened to sit by me at the lunch table that day. She invited me to an evening session that she was conducting later that week. I attended the session and stayed after to consult with her about a person I was working with who, for many years, had been sexually assaulted by a family member. I wanted to make sure I was doing everything possible to support this person. Orieda and I spoke for hours. We created a strong connection, and she became my mentor and good friend. It was because of her connection and influence that I transitioned from a clinical director position to creating a training division so I could do training/consulting full-time.

After Orieda retired from a full-time career as a chemist, she began another full-time career working with people with intellectual and developmental disabilities and their families as well as professionals in the area of human sexuality and sexual assault. Her husband Howard, also a retired chemist, drove her around the country, carried the heavy stuff and managed the audio-visual aspects of her presentations. They were quite a pair. Some of the 'heavy stuff' included lots of materials, including flaccid and erect penis models and anatomically correct human models. One time, when they were parked on a street in New York City, someone broke into their car. Orieda's biggest concern, and also a thought that made her giggle, was that the car burglar may have stolen her penis models! Fortunately, the fears were unfounded. Behold, the models were safe for another training event!

In addition to being on the road and training, Orieda spent lots of time with survivors of sexual assault, their family members, and professionals. By the time I met her, much of this counseling and consulting happened at her kitchen table. Her daughter, Judith, lived across the street. Orieda would meet with the person who had been harmed while the family and/or staff would go with Judith to her home. It was important that Orieda meet with the person without any undue influence from their family or support staff.

Orieda opened her home to these visitors, always offering coffee and homemade treats and offering a safe and comfortable environment for people as they did this difficult work. Judith set up a comfortable space as well. The family member or support staff were warmly greeted. Judith was friendly and accommodating - centering the time and space to meet the needs of each person.

When Orieda and the person were ready to invite the family and/or staff to join them, Judith would bring them back to Orieda's home. Orieda and the person would share, depending on what the person wanted shared. The person, with support from Orieda, would tell their family/staff what supports they needed to feel safe and to heal. The plan for moving forward was always on the agenda.

Typically, there was a lunch break at some point, as this process took several hours. No two experiences were the same. Sometimes, the person made lots of decisions about how the process went. Sometimes, Orieda had to be very stern with a family member or staff member. If there was a practice or relationship that harmed a person, she could be very bold and confident and 'in your face' if that was needed.

Over the years, Orieda and I consulted with one another on several occasions, and I was privileged to be involved in some of the "kitchen table therapy sessions" she facilitated with survivors with disabilities. For several years, Orieda organized an annual 3-day retreat style event in a beautiful part of the state. The event was centered on human sexuality, and she invited five survivors with developmental disabilities with whom she had worked to serve as co-trainers for the professionals who registered to participate. These gatherings were emotionally draining as well as up-lifting! The final half day focused on celebrations and healing.

Orieda helped me to clarify my values and moral stance when it came to working with victims/survivors. She taught me some amazing ways to work with survivors who may process information without speaking, without traditional communication. She taught me about healing from trauma. Orieda and I did not have the same style in creating therapeutic relationships or in working with families/professionals. We were different people. A good mentor respects who you are as a person and what you bring to the table.

Orieda was in my life when I became aware of my early childhood sexual abuse. She was a tremendous help in my healing process. She told me months after my initial disclosure to her, "I knew when I met you that you were a survivor of childhood sexual abuse. I was waiting for you to bring it up." And there we were, connected compassionately in yet another way.

The Universe was very generous in bringing Orieda and I together. It was generous again, in joining us before Orieda passed this earthly plane. I hadn't seen her for a few months. I was planning a work trip near her home and when I called to arrange a visit, I discovered she was in the hospital. Her daughter told me, "This will be the last time the two of you are together. She would love to see you." When I arrived in her hospital room, the family stepped out and told me to text them when I was ready to leave, and they would come back. Orieda waved me over to her and patted the bed. I sat next to her. Orieda said, "I am on hospice and my time is short. I am scared." She began crying. I asked if she was afraid to die. She said, "Heavens no! I'm not afraid of death. I'm afraid of not finishing what I promised people I would do." So, I got a pen and a piece of paper and began writing her list of promises. For each one, I asked her who she thought should complete that promise. After the list and assignments were completed, I laid down beside her and held her in my arms. I thanked her for her friendship and her mentorship and her love. I left that night with a long to do list, teary eyes, and a full heart.

Orieda died a few days later, in her home, as she directed. Her legacy lives in her family, the books she wrote, the lives of people who were better because she loved them, and in the many spaces where people continue to speak her name with fondness and respect.

Questions for the Reader:

1. In your opinion, what qualities does a good mentor possess?
2. Think about a mentor that you have had in your life. In what ways did this person impact your life?
3. Have you ever mentored someone to learn a skill or take over a project? What was that experience like for you?
4. When we reach the later years of our careers, why is it important to mentor others?

A Common and Painful Experience

I had been working with people with disabilities for several years before I realized the prevalence of sexual assault in their lives. It was an experience that began with what I thought would be a half day's work that turned into several weeks. By the time I completed this targeted consultation, my heart and mind had exploded with the reality that people with disabilities experience sexual assault at alarming rates.

It started with a phone call from a parent informing the agency that her adult child and a male staff member had been speaking on the phone during the evening. The mom wasn't sure what the phone call was about, she said it sounded friendly but didn't think staff should be calling people receiving services at home in the evening. I met with Taylor and slowly and gently tried to discover the details of their relationship with the staff member. A few hours later, Taylor said that this staff member had hurt them sexually. They (Taylor's pronouns are they/them) wanted to go to the hospital to get checked and wanted their mom to meet us there. Taylor made all of the choices that followed. It was a long and difficult day for Taylor and for mom. It was the beginning of a long and difficult several months for the entire family and for everyone involved.

As we were waiting to be seen at the hospital, I realized that this staff member had private access to many other people. I consulted with the agency Executive Director and prepared myself to meet with each person. I was trained in investigations and knew how to ask non-leading questions. Over the next three days, I met with each person to see if anyone else had been similarly hurt by this staff member. No one reported having been touched by the person who hurt Taylor. Yet, all but one person mentioned a history of sexual assault. One person mentioned an uncle; one person talked about a teacher; another a brother; the list of abusers continued. Some of the people I spoke with, had a long history with this agency. There was no mention in their files about sexual assault. Most of them had never spoken of this before. Maybe no one had told because they had never been in that type of conversation ... a conversation about hurtful and unsafe touch and their right to choose who touches them and what part of their body is touched. I knew that it was important to make some drastic changes in how people were supported. But first, Taylor and their family needed some supports; the community sexual assault center was contacted, and this young survivor and their family began receiving supportive counseling and victim advocacy. It was an exhausting week and I had to grieve my broken heart. I took the weekend off.

As Monday rolled around, my mind was spinning. First, we needed to recreate the system so that all people had opportunities to receive prevention education. We also needed to educate families and employees. We needed to create policies and procedures and make sure all employees understood them. We needed to work with the local sexual assault centers on education, advocacy, and counseling for people with developmental disabilities. We needed to collaborate with local law enforcement and with the emergency rooms. My biggest question at that time was how do we create safe spaces and practices that support the telling of these stories and ongoing healing for survivors of sexual assault in our service delivery systems and communities?

In 2020 on an interview on *The View*, Stacey Abrams, politician, lawyer, and author, said something that I have always known in my heart, but didn't know how to articulate. "When the system gets fixed, everything else falls into place." In the late 1980's when I first became aware of the appalling frequency of violence in the lives of people with disabilities, that's what I wanted to do but I wasn't sure how. Would I get clarity and a chance to help fix the systems? My mind was mingling with the possibilities.

Questions for the Reader:

1. Reflect on a time in your life when an experience was surprising and overwhelming. How did you handle the original surge of emotions?
2. What self-care strategies have you found helpful over the years?
3. When you think about social injustice and systems change, what thoughts and feelings come to your mind?
4. What suggestions do you have to change the system so people with disabilities have equal access to education, advocacy, and counseling when they experience sexual assault?

An Unexpected Turn of Events

It was 2004 and my first time in Hershey, Pennsylvania. I was pleasantly surprised to receive two Hershey candy bars when I checked into the hotel. It was a large conference hotel, and I was there to speak at the Everyday Lives Conference - with people from across Pennsylvania including people with intellectual and developmental disabilities, family members, and professionals.

When I do a breakout session on sexual assault at a conference with broad topics, I never know how many people will show up at the session. But this day, the room was so full that there were people sitting on the floor, standing in the doorway, and leaning up against the walls. Afterwards, I spoke with several parents, not knowing that one of those parents was about to have her life changed.

A couple of months later, on a Friday afternoon I received an urgent email. I will have to paraphrase it here as I cannot recall all of the details.

> "I attended your session at the Everyday Lives Conference in Hershey, PA. As you were describing the indicators of sexual abuse of people with disabilities, I was checking off the ones that my daughter exhibits. By the end of your session, I knew that she was being sexually abused and since have discovered it was by a family member. I took her to the doctor and have tried to protect her from the abuser. There is a court hearing next week and no one is helping us. Please help me. I am frantic!"

I sat with the reality of the email for a while. I wondered what I could do to help. There was no phone number, and it was after 5pm on the East Coast. I sent an email in response with my phone number and told the mother I would be available to talk with her over the phone when it was convenient for her.

I sat with the message some more. And I got really, really angry.

"Why should a parent have to call someone they heard speak at a conference several states away for help with her child who has been harmed and may be in danger of that harm continuing?" I asked myself this over and over. Sometimes there are no good answers.

I stayed near the phone Friday night and into Saturday and then at 2pm, the call came. This fierce mom shared the story of her daughter's situation in great detail. She shared every action she had taken on behalf of her daughter and every feeling she had experienced. It seems she talked for over an hour without taking a breath. She was relieved to be listened to and to have her feelings validated. We crafted some questions and some possible strategies. This was our first phone call. We talked regularly until her daughter was safe from the person who had hurt her. The person who assaulted her daughter was sentenced to nine years in prison.

In 2004, this young survivor was eight years old. In 2020 she had graduated from school and worked full time with toddlers. She continues therapy and still carries the abuse with her. She has fears about the offender showing up in their neighborhood. They moved once to avoid the offender and mom says, "…eventually we will move out of state."

There have been several situations like this over my time doing this work. I have been fortunate to work with several Child Advocacy Centers and Sexual Assault Centers in many states. The work they do for and with victims is extremely important. It is my belief that these victim service organizations can work effectively with ALL victims of violence - with and without disabilities. Because of the long history of oppression and segregation of people with disabilities, some advocates, educators, and counselors have had little exposure to people who may communicate in non-traditional ways. Several I have spoken with say, "I have no idea how to communicate with someone who does not speak. I would not want to do any additional harm." Some communities have set up "special" advocates or teams to work with children and/or adults who experience sexual assault.

Over the years, I have worked with many Child Advocacy Centers who are welcoming and affirming to children and youth with disabilities and do an excellent job with **ALL** children who experience child abuse. They are a model and a positive statement about what can be done to include all children in their valuable services.

Let's reflect on this story. A mom goes to a breakout session at a state conference. Something inside of her told her to attend a session on sexual abuse. She listened to her own inner guidance. She found out what she did not know before. She learned about the indicators of sexual abuse and noted that her child had many of the indicators. She took action. She talked with her daughter. She believed her daughter. She went to great lengths to find support for her daughter. She sought the accountability of the person who harmed her daughter. She has worked tirelessly to keep her daughter safe. She also worked to create more supports in her community for other children.

Questions for the Reader:

1. Have you ever had a feeling you should do something but didn't know why? Did you do it? Why or why not?
2. Think about a time when you were worried about a child's safety. Did you experience any feelings of helplessness? What did you do?
3. Do you see any similarities between this mom and how you feel about children in your life?
4. How do you think communities can make Child Advocacy Centers and sexual assault centers more open to children with disabilities?

One Mom's Phone Call

I worked with a young woman for a few years right after she graduated from high school. She was high energy, fun, enthusiastic, delightful, friendly, assertive, smart, hard-working and a lover of life! Her family always dreamed of living in the country away from city life. It was a bittersweet day when Nancy and her parents moved out of town. I was happy for the family and also knew many of us would miss Nancy's presence.

A couple years after they moved, I received a call from Nancy's mom. The call went something like this:

"I must tell you what happened. After we moved, we all adjusted well to living in the country. A van picked Nancy up during the week and took her to the workshop. Nancy made new friends and she liked the staff there. But after a while, Nancy changed. She became belligerent and would yell and throw things, at work and at home. We had several meetings to try and fix the problem. We used her music and activities as a reward for good behavior. Nothing seemed to help. She also began complaining of stomach pain. We took her to the doctor and no cause was discovered. We kept trying to modify her behavior by giving her what she likes when she was good and taking away what she likes when she was not (her behavior program).

One day I received a really nice phone call from Nancy's caseworker. She reported that Nancy was in a new class about relationships and wanted me to know how well she was doing. It was nice to get a call about something positive for a change.

The next morning as Nancy was waiting for the van to pick her up, I told her I had gotten a call from her caseworker. Nancy lowered her head and began crying. I told her it was a good call. I told her I was proud of her for doing so well in the new class. And then, Nancy told me what her dad had been doing to her. I was shocked and sad and angry ... and determined to keep her safe!"

Several things changed after the family moved to the country. The father lost his job resulting in a loss of self-esteem. He also had access to Nancy while mom was working. Based on these facts and Nancy's reports (and personality and behavior changes), it appears the abuse began after the family moved to the country. Mom said that she called so that others would be aware that people like her daughter can be sexually abused by someone whom they trust ... and the family trusts.

Over the next several months, many things happened.

- Nancy received apologies and support from her mom and her staff.

- Nancy received counseling from the local rape crisis center.
- All behavior programs were stopped. She now had free access to things that she liked.
- Dad was arrested and eventually sentenced to prison.
- The organization and the local rape crisis center collaborated on prevention education, advocacy, counseling services, and cross-training.
- Mom spoke out at community events about sexual assault against people with disabilities.
- The organization took time to evaluate its practices and made some positive changes for prevention and response to sexual assault.

I want to talk briefly about the tentacles of trauma in situations like this one. Nancy experienced the direct trauma of being repeatedly sexually assaulted by someone who had been a trusted person in her life. Mom experienced trauma because her daughter was harmed by mom's husband whom she had trusted and loved. Mom and many people at the organization experienced guilt because of the implementation of the behavior program they had designed for Nancy. Lots of healing needed to occur.

I want to acknowledge that Nancy was in a class to learn about healthy relationships, boundaries, and abuse prevention. I believe that this education planted the seeds for her to tell what was happening in her life. It is quite common, that when we provide education, people disclose abuse that has happened or is happening to them.

Here are some of the positive things that happened after Nancy bravely told her mom about her sexual assault:

Mom did something that was critically important. When Nancy told her what was happening, mom believed her. When someone first tells someone about sexual assault, the response they receive will either support them on a healing journey or add to the pain that has already occurred. It is critically important that we "**Start by Believing**". *

In addition to believing Nancy, mom did not judge or criticize or blame Nancy. She only blamed the person who caused the pain and broke the law.

Mom also took immediate steps to assure that Nancy was safe. Dad was no longer allowed in the house or near his daughter. Mom advocated for his arrest and accountability for his crime. The criminal justice system worked well on behalf of Nancy and other potential victims in their jurisdiction.

The disability agency and rape crisis center worked together to support Nancy and Mom. They worked together to assure that people served by the disability agency had access to education, advocacy, and counseling on an ongoing basis. The rape crisis center provided training for the disability agency on sexual assault and their available services. The disability organization provided training for the rape crisis center on working with people with disabilities and their available services. The two organizations continued working together to make sure that others in their geographic area who had disabilities were given education as well as advocacy and counseling when needed and desired.

If Nancy had not been in a class about sexual abuse and healthy boundaries, she may not have told her mom about the abuse. Her father may have continued to harm her. Instead, she found the courage to tell and as a result, found safety and a pathway to healing.

Questions for the Reader:

1. How common or unusual do you think it is for a family member to sexually abuse another family member?
2. What tactics might this perpetrator have used to keep the abuse hidden from his spouse and to keep Nancy from telling?
3. What role do you think the education class that Nancy was in may have had in her telling her mom what was happening to her?
4. What role did the collaboration between the disability agency and the rape crisis center play in Nancy and her mom's healing process?

Before I close this chapter, I want to talk about one of the quotes I selected for the chapter page. This is a quote by my daughter, Megan S. Paceley, who is a well-known scholar in the area of LGBTQ+ youth. "…the shared experience ends where marginalization begins." This is what the quote means to me as it relates to people with disabilities. Lots of people experience sexual violence and there are some common experiences that people share after sexual violence. If we look at people who have historically been excluded, oppressed, and marginalized, they have some additional experiences that are less likely to be shared by other survivors.

For people with disabilities, this begins with the prevalence of sexual violence. According to an NPR investigation and information from the Department of Justice, people with intellectual disabilities experience sexual assault at a rate seven times that of people without disabilities. (Shapiro, McEvers and Shapiro, 2018) * **SEVEN TIMES!** We also know that survivors with disabilities have more perpetrators and experience more incidents for a longer period of time. (Schaller and Fieberg, 1998) * We also know that people with disabilities are less likely to access education about healthy relationships and sexual assault. We also know that survivors with disabilities are less likely to access services, supports, and justice. (Smith, 2011) *

The following chapters reflect some of the work that has been done to address these inequities.

Chapter 6

Education

"I never got to go to those classes. They said I didn't need it."
Adult who had been in special ed classes

"The beautiful thing about learning is that no one can take it away from you." B. B. King

Tanya

I first met Tanya when she told me about the person who had sexually assaulted her. She was timid and shy and spoke barely above a whisper. I'm not sure where she found the courage to tell 'his secret' but she did. We began seeing each other on a regular basis to talk about what happened, how she felt about it and what she wanted to happen next. One day, that I will never forget, Tanya was very quiet and looking down at her hands. I knew something important was coming and I waited silently. She slowly looked up and asked with wide eyes,

"I have never said no. Never made a choice. I know nothing about my body. Can you teach me?"

I agreed to help her. I told her she wasn't alone in not knowing these things. I knew Tanya was going to be okay because she was brave enough to tell on someone with more power than her and she was brave enough to ask for help. Looking back, I wish I would have told her that and I wish I would have thanked her for her courage. I thank her now.

I went home that night and could not get Tanya's voice out of my mind. I sat down and wrote a song inspired by her words that day. Several months later, while training volunteers at a local rape crisis center about working with people with disabilities, I met Jill Dixson. This was a serendipity moment! Jill is a talented musician and song writer and agreed to put the words I had written to music. The song is titled "Teach Me". Jill arranged with a professional connection to have the song recorded. When the song was completed, I took the CD to work and offered to play it for Tanya. I told her the song was written for her and I wanted her to hear it. She said she wanted to hear it, so I played it on a boombox. After the song ended, Tanya sat silently for several minutes. She had her head tilted to one side and appeared to be thinking. Finally, in a shocked voice, she spoke, "I'm not the only one this happens to, am I?" No, Tanya, lots of people are sexually assaulted. The important part of this story is that I thought Tanya already knew that she wasn't the only one this happened to. We had talked about it. Two of her friends had been sexually assaulted by the same person who assaulted her, and the three of them had discussed what to do before they came to me, one at a time. The only thing I could figure out was this: music can get inside a person deeper than spoken words. I have been using music to educate and empower and heal ever since Tanya showed me just how important music can be.

Over the years, hundreds of adults with disabilities have told me that they never received any education about bullying, healthy relationships, consent, sexual abuse, or sexuality in school. It's astonishing to me that a community that is sexually assaulted at seven times the rate of people without disabilities, is excluded from prevention education!! Why would this possibly happen? Here are the reasons I have heard from educators and families:

1. Some people believe people with disabilities are unable to learn such complex information. (I disagree!)
2. Some people think if we teach about relationships and sex education, people with disabilities will start having sex. (again, totally disagree)
3. Some people do not believe that anyone would sexually assault someone with a disability. (So wrong here—get educated!)

4. There is a lack of educational materials designed for people with intellectual and developmental disabilities. (Used to be true but isn't any longer)
5. Some teachers are uncomfortable teaching about some of this information. (Sure, but there are others who can do this in most communities. It is also possible to get comfortable.)

Two Important Mentors from Afar

In addition to the many lessons I have learned about risk reduction education from people with intellectual and developmental disabilities, I want to acknowledge two other sources that were important in my learning. I consider Dave Hingsburger as a mentor in my long career. I only met Dave a couple of times but read and listened to everything he created. I believe he was the person who gave me the courage to follow my intuition and taught me to listen closely to persons with disabilities---the true experts in this work. I first 'met' Dave when I read *JUST SAY KNOW!: Understanding and Reducing the Risks of Sexual Victimization* (1995). * His passion and humanity screamed through every page, and I was hooked! As it relates to education, Dave said, and this is a paraphrase, "If you can't say no to carrots at the dinner table, you will never understand that you can say no to a penis!!!" What

186

is the meaning in this statement as it relates to education? People learn by how they are treated. We give people messages every day by the way we act and the words we say. The best way to educate people about reducing the risks of sexual victimization (abuse, violence) is by how we relate to them every day.

Three important points:

1. The long history of oppression and segregation of people with intellectual and developmental disabilities has led to the many risk factors for sexual victimization. Even with new awareness and changes made to eradicate this historical wrongdoing, this pattern of treating people with disabilities as being less capable than people without disabilities continues, which interferes with establishing empowering laws, standards, settings, organizations, etc. that could equalize power and safety.
2. In reality, not many people with intellectual and developmental disabilities are receiving risk reduction training at home or at school, either through routine interactions or through formal education. We need to ensure accessible and available formal education

opportunities for all people with intellectual and developmental disabilities.

3. Education must not stop in the classroom. To be effective, we must provide permission and opportunity for those skills to be used in everyday situations (Like making choices and saying No at the dinner table).

As I was writing this book, Dave Hinsburger's life ended. It was a sad day for many of us who admired him as a person, a teacher, a friend, and a leader. His legacy continues through the thousands of people that he trained and mentored. His words continue to touch lives and be pivotal in creating new ways to honor people with intellectual and developmental disabilities. May you rest in power, Dave.

Another person who contributed to my knowledge and understanding of the intersection of violence and disabilities was Dick Sobsey. In his classic book, *Violence and Abuse in the Lives of People with Disabilities: The End of Silent Acceptance?* (1994), * Dick Sobsey outlines the risk factors for violence in the lives of people with disabilities. Sobsey's integrated ecological model included four categories of risk factors: Potential Victim, Potential Offender, Environment, and

Culture. Each of these categories has a list of risk factors. Sobsey's model makes it very clear that violence in the lives of people with disabilities is a complex issue with lots of aspects that need to be addressed. Risk reduction education of people with intellectual and developmental disabilities typically addresses some of the potential victim risk factors but does not address the risk factors within potential offenders, environments, or cultures. To be effective, we need to address as many risk factors as possible.

Environmental and Cultural Risk Factors

Before I begin discussing these risk factors, I want to clarify that culture in this context is broad and includes the prevailing attitudes within a workplace, a particular setting or institution, or a specific community. After I became familiar with Sobsey's ecological model, I went through each risk factor and tried to decide...can we eliminate or reduce this risk factor? If so, what would that look like? Here is an example: One of the environmental risk factors for violence is 'emphasizes control'. Sexual violence is about power and control, so it makes sense that people who have the least power are at greater risk for experiencing sexual violence. What might you notice if an organization that provides services and supports for people with intellectual and developmental disabilities emphasizes control?

These are some of the responses I have heard from the experts - the people receiving those services:

- The staff are bossy
- I have to eat what is being served
- I have no say in the rules
- I have to go to bed at 9pm
- I can't decide if I take a bath or a shower
- I can't say who helps me with private stuff like bathing
- I want to sleep in on the weekends and that's not allowed
- Other people make my goals
- I'm not allowed to have a bad day without getting written up
- If I'm in the middle of a movie and its bath time, I can't finish the movie. How dumb is that?
- My girlfriend and I have no privacy
- Staff call me selfish if I don't want other people to sit in **my** wheelchair

If we want to reduce or eliminate the risk factor of 'emphasis on control'...what might that look like?

I have consulted with many organizations on creating strategies to equalize power between the organizational employees and the people they work for and with. The strategies have included, but are not limited to:

- People with intellectual and developmental disabilities have an opportunity to join a self-advocacy group
- People with intellectual and developmental disabilities lead their team meetings with support before, during and after as preferred and needed
- People with intellectual and developmental disabilities are part of the hiring team for new employees
- People with intellectual and developmental disabilities are part of the training team for all employees
- People with intellectual and developmental disabilities are involved in the evaluation of employees who work with them
- People with intellectual and developmental disabilities serve on the agency board and on

agency committees AND are active
participants (with support as needed)
- People with intellectual and developmental
disabilities are involved in the development
and revision of agency policies and
procedures
- Policies and procedures are written in plain
language
- Employees who interact with people with
intellectual and developmental disabilities
have performance objectives related to
respectful communication and empowerment

Resources were created and provided to
support these strategies. As you can tell, these
strategies can take time to implement and can also
lead to a positive shift in the organizational culture.

Keep in mind that an emphasis on control can
be involved in family dynamics as well as
organizational dynamics.

In all cases, there is usually a lively discussion
about the dignity of risk and the values of freedom
and safety.

Some of the other environmental/cultural risk factors in Sobsey's model include:
- Devalues/objectifies/dehumanizes victims
- Teaches compliance
- Emphasis on vulnerabilities
- Discourages attachment
- Denies problems/covers up allegations/ discourages solutions
- Attracts abusers/eliminates non-abusers
- Multiple caregivers/transient caregivers
- Isolated from society

Questions for the Reader: (These are best done with a team of people)
1. What strategies can you think of to create an environment that does not teach compliance?
2. How might a family member or a staff member shift from focusing on vulnerabilities to focusing on abilities, talents, dreams and contributions?
3. Discuss your thoughts and feelings when reading the section above about emphasis on control.
4. What would it take for an organization to shift their environment/culture to reduce/eliminate many of these risk factors?

I hope that it is becoming clear that when I talk about education or risk reduction education, I am not simply talking about education of people with intellectual and developmental disabilities. I am also referring to education of family members, employees, managers, and administrators. We all have a role to play in overcoming oppression, segregation, and the common 'power over' relationships which put people with disabilities at high risk for violence.

Potential Victim Risk Factors

As we follow the process of reducing risks for violence in the lives of people with disabilities, let's take a look at potential victim risks. The list below is primarily from Sobsey's work, but two additional risk factors have been added from my many conversations with sexual assault survivors with disabilities (noted with in italics). Each risk factor includes a plain language, first-person description written by Amy Walker.

Potential Victim Risk Factors
- Physical Defenses - I cannot get away or defend myself

- Communication - I may not be able to say no or tell someone
- Lack of Critical Information - no one teaches me about relationships, sex, abuse
- Learned Compliance - I always have to do what I am told to do
- Learned Helplessness - I have learned that I have no power
- Underdeveloped Sense of Personal Space - People are close to me and I get close to them
- Dependency - I depend on others for lots of things
- *Loneliness* - I am lonely and want a boyfriend/girlfriend
- *Reputation* - People don't believe me cause I have lied about something in the past

I think it is important to note that some of these risk factors are inherent within the person, (e.g., physical defenses) and many are a result of how the person has been treated (e.g., compliance). If we want to reduce or eliminate the risk factor of compliance, we have to change how we treat people with disabilities. Again, the environment is of critical importance in reducing risk factors for violence in the lives of people with disabilities. The environment includes home, work, school, community, religious entity, recreational sites, and others.

A quick story. I was asked to meet with a woman who reported being sexually assaulted by a doctor at the emergency room. At the end of our meeting, she said she wanted to report the crime to the police. We met with a detective who said he would investigate. Several days later, we called to check on the status of the investigation. The detective said he had stopped the investigation because a staff member had reported that this woman lied a lot. I convinced the detective to continue the investigation. The next day, the detective called to tell me that the hospital had no record of this woman at the ER on that date. I went to see the woman who had her copy of the papers proving she was seen at the ER on the day she reported. The papers also had the name of the person who had treated her. The investigation continued. This is an example of how a person's reputation can be a risk factor for violence. One person told me. "Everyone has lied in their life. But most people are not watched 24 hours a day with everything they do written down in a chart. We are watched all of the time." I believe that offenders choose their victims based on, among other things, whether they think they can get away with the crime. They oftentimes choose someone who they think won't be believed if they do tell. We reduce this risk factor (reputation) by **believing all people** when they report sexual assault.

Questions for the reader:
1. What ideas do you have to reduce the risk factor of learned helplessness?
2. What ideas do you have to reduce the risk factor of communication?
3. What ideas do you have to reduce the risk factor of underdeveloped sense of personal space? How can family and staff model a sense of personal space?
4. What ideas do you have to address the risk factor of learned compliance?

Providing Critical Information

So, let's spend some time thinking about what critical information people might need to reduce the risks of sexual violence and to know their options to report sexual violence if that does occur. Stop here and think. What do you think is important for people to know and be able to do in order to reduce their risk of sexual assault?

One of the things that Tanya asked me to teach her was to say no. People with disabilities (and many people without disabilities) are often trained to be compliant - to do whatever they are told to do, so saying no is extra difficult. People with disabilities are often trained to be nice and polite. When overcompliance intersects with politeness - a person may not be able to say no except in a soft voice.

We teach people that:

Sometimes we say no nicely.

Sometimes we say no loudly.

Here is another approach: Pam Malin (Disability Rights Wisconsin) teaches people to use their 'POWER VOICE' if their first "no" is ignored. I saw her do this recently with a person she had just met, and the person sat up taller and with a serious face and a loud voice said, "Do not touch me!" They definitely knew what 'Power Voice' meant!

This may seem odd to you, but one of the most important things I teach people with disabilities is how to identify and express their feelings. This is directly linked to expressive communication and safety. When a person can communicate their feelings, these feelings are not building up inside their body. Our feelings hold valuable information. I start by teaching these basic four feelings: happy, sad, mad, scared. Some people, of course, can understand many more than this. If someone is sad after every home visit, there is a reason. They might miss their loved ones. Something hurtful may have happened. We can explore the possibilities. We can use art, music, movement, pictures, story boards, words, pipe cleaners, and gestures in this process. Our job is to help people identify and express their feelings and let them know all feelings are okay. Sometimes, a person is scared because they have been threatened, or exploited or abused. At the same time, understanding what makes us happy helps us to dream about our future. Most humans have the full range of feelings and being able to identify them and express them is critical to live a healthy and safe life. Let's start with that.

Today, in 2022, there are many curricula available for teaching people with intellectual and developmental disabilities and other disabilities about healthy relationships, human sexuality, and prevention of sexual assault. Some of the curricula are available for purchase and some are available at no-cost. I would suggest that as you decide what curriculum to use, you consider the content and the methodology for teaching. While it is easier to use just one, some people customize their approach by selecting more than one curriculum and using the lessons they find best suited to the people that will be in the classes/groups. These are content areas for you to consider as you choose what materials you want to use; feelings, self-esteem, privacy (include body parts, locations, activities, and talk), bullying, rights, respect, boundaries, consent, healthy relationships, dating, sexual violence, human sexuality, sexual orientation and gender identity, safe persons, and reporting.

A sample of the available curriculum is included in the resource section. *

Sexuality is very complicated and no one curriculum includes everything a person might need to know. It is important to have a safe person or resource to contact for additional information and support. A great resource for 'dating with a disability' is a previous colleague Kathy O'Connell, the author of *FIREWALK: Embracing Different Abilities* * and the founder of Radiant Abilities. Kathy's website * includes dating resources, videos, and blogs. She facilitates dating classes and individual consultations/counseling.

If you decide to implement education for people with disabilities, please include some people with disabilities as trainers (more about this in the next chapter). Also, consider advocating for legislation to require sex education for people with disabilities in your state (more about this in Chapter 13 - Washington).

When we provide education about healthy relationships, people in the class will talk about what has already happened to them. Be prepared to receive disclosures in a trauma-informed way. Be prepared to offer support, choices, and referrals for advocacy and counseling (a local sexual assault center can be very helpful). Know your agency's policies and procedures for handling disclosures. Advocate for updating any policies and procedures that are not trauma-informed.

When someone first tells about their sexual assault, it is an opportunity for healing to begin. Sometimes, it is an opportunity for the repeated assaults to stop. Education has been a gift to many people, in many ways. It is my hope that you take the time and effort to provide sexuality and risk reduction training for and with people with disabilities.

Questions for the reader:

1. Consider the information in this chapter, what ideas do you have to reduce the risks of sexual violence in the lives of people with disabilities?
2. What are some ways you can engage with people with disabilities to find out their ideas?
3. What steps can you take to move your ideas to action?
4. Who would need to be involved in implementing some of these changes?

Before We Leave this Chapter

You might be wondering what happened to Tanya. The person who sexually assaulted her was found guilty and went to prison. Tanya learned to use her feelings to make decisions. One time I asked her if she wanted to be part of a videotaping about sexual violence and people with disabilities and she very clearly said, "No." I cheered! Over time, we saw each other less and less. One day she called me to make an appointment. When she arrived, she told me she was engaged and wanted to know how to not have a baby. I showed her pictures and talked about her options. Her decision was none of my business. Today, she is married and shares a home with her spouse. Her family provides some supports, when requested.

Some inquiring minds might also wonder about the woman who was sexually assaulted in the emergency room. When the detective showed the hospital the official papers of her visit to the Emergency Room, the hospital arranged for the detective to meet with the Physician's Assistant later that week. When it came time for the appointment, the hospital told the detective that the Physician's Assistant had disappeared. When the detective checked further, he found the suspect had a pattern of leaving hospital jobs and moving to a new state. Although, the person who hurt her was not found, the hospital made several changes to their emergency room procedures with the intent of keeping patients safe.

Chapter 7

Changing Systems

"The path to big, systemic change is
collective action."
Gloria Feldt

"Systems don't change easily. Systems try to
maintain themselves and seek equilibrium.
To change a system, you need to shake it up,
disrupt the equilibrium. That often requires
conflict." Starhawk

In this chapter, we will explore two different collaborations (teams) designed to address sexual violence in the lives of people with disabilities. WE CAN Stop Abuse was a three-year project creating collaborations between agencies that serve people with intellectual and developmental disabilities and community sexual assault centers. Illinois Imagines was a 13-year project led by a statewide collaboration that included people with a diverse array of disabilities, multiple governmental entities, and statewide not-for-profits organizations (both disability and sexual assault).

WE CAN Stop Abuse

In 2000, the Illinois Violence Prevention Authority awarded Blue Tower Training (where I worked) a small grant to create and implement a sexual abuse prevention curriculum for adults with IDD. Sandy Laesch, a prevention educator at the

207

local rape crisis center and I partnered over a three-year period and worked in five Illinois counties.

When I wrote this grant, I thought it was an opportunity to take what I had learned working with individual survivors with disabilities and expand those lessons to encourage changes at an organizational and community level. I knew that educating self-advocates about sexual abuse prevention and response was important and that it was equally important to educate the employees and change the organizational systems that provided disability services.

Our first task was to decide in what geographic communities to focus our efforts. We sent letters to over 300 agencies serving people with intellectual and developmental disabilities and over 30 Rape Crisis Centers. The letter described the project and expectations for each agency selected to participate. Interested agencies were asked to send us a letter of interest and commitment. We received close to 90 letters. First, we sorted the letters by type of organization and then by geographic region. To be considered, there had to be an interest in the same community by both the rape crisis center and the agency serving people with intellectual and developmental disabilities. The first year, we were able to work in three areas of the state. During year two, we added two more teams in two new areas of the state.

Sandy and I spent two days on-site with each team. The teams included representatives from both the rape crisis center and the agency serving people with intellectual and developmental disabilities. Representatives typically included someone from administration, educators, program staff, and others. I am sorry to say that at this point in my career I was not yet aware of the value of including people with disabilities on the teams. The agenda included:

1. Welcome, introductions and icebreaker
2. Sexual assault in the lives of people with Intellectual and Developmental Disabilities
3. Agency presentations
4. Collaboration tips
5. WE CAN Stop Abuse curriculum
6. Facilitating classes
7. Evaluating learning
8. Environmental checklist and agency goals
9. Expectations and follow-up

The curriculum was evaluated with a 'pre' and 'post' test for each class participant. An environmental checklist was created so that disability agencies could evaluate their current practices related to sexual abuse prevention, response, and intervention from an ecological perspective. Each agency was asked to use their results on the checklist and select one to two areas each year to reduce risk factors and/or increase protective factors within their agency. This aspect of the project related to the fact that people can only learn so much in classes - the living and learning environments must allow and support the skills taught in the classes. For example, teaching someone to say no to unwanted touch has limited value if they are never allowed to say no to anything in their home, work, etc. The agencies seemed open to these ideas and were willing to make the needed changes.

After each site completed the first class and submitted their pre-and post-tests, Sandy and I made another on-site visit. We met with the class trainers and the class participants. We also touched base with an agency administrator about the collaboration, classes, and environmental goals. Following these first three visits, we revised the curriculum and distributed the changes to the three teams.

During year two, Sandy and I created a Peer Training Manual and training to support some class participants to become trainers of the curriculum. We identified and trained persons with intellectual and developmental disabilities to co-train the curriculum. This was implemented in years two and three. More information about this is included later in this chapter in the lessons learned section.

Toward the end of year two, we created and implemented a Review of Individual Skills to evaluate the changes in each class participant immediately after taking the 'WE Can' classes and then again six months after completion. (This tool looked more at a person's behavior in their natural settings over time, vs. their knowledge right after taking the class). This replaced the 'pre' and 'post' test evaluation component of the curriculum.

During the final several months of the project, we conducted workshops across the state and distributed the final version of the curriculum. The workshops targeted disability organizations and rape crisis centers and included information about sexual violence in the lives of people with disabilities and how to use the curriculum. I do not remember the exact number of curricula that we distributed, but I think it was between 50 and 75. I do know that agencies are still using the curriculum today in 2021.

Lessons Learned:

1. **A sexual assault center and a disability agency make a perfect team for prevention education of individuals with disabilities**

It makes sense. Sexual assault centers are the experts on sexual assault - prevention, response, crisis intervention, medical and legal advocacy, and counseling survivors. Disability agencies understand disability and know the people they work with. When we brought these diverse groups together, they learned from each other.

Each collaborative team participated in preliminary training prior to providing classes for people from disability support agencies.

In one community, I received an email from the sexual assault center educators after the first class with this message:

"We had our first class today. There was one man who sat in the corner, and we were told we could not talk with him or engage him in any way. That is not how we treat people. I am sorry, but we cannot continue with this project."

I phoned the educators and connected them with a person at the agency who I thought would be able to help them with this problem. The educators continued the classes and they told me everything was going well. A few weeks later, one of the educators called me to report that they had developed a way to communicate with the man who had been in the corner. He was at the table with everyone else. They communicated with him by hand tapping and a picture book they had created.

A few months later, I learned that the educators from the sexual assault center were conducting training for the employees at the disability agency - not on sexual assault - but on how to communicate with people with disabilities!!

I have discovered that when victim services (sexual assault or domestic violence) spend time in disability organizations, things improve. There tends to be a power shift, at least in one part of the organization. You see, victim services are trained in power dynamics. They understand that violence is all about power and control. They see power imbalances. They are trained to be empowering.

They believe in equal relationships and that equity makes things better. So, when this new set of eyes enter the organizational culture, a positive shift can occur.

2. People with disabilities can be excellent trainers of prevention education with their peers

When the curriculum had been completed with the first group of people in 2000, we drove to that town and met with the class participants. It was just us and the class members in the room. We did not want anyone else present that might unintentionally influence what the participants reported. Here are a few things the women said:

> "It was good to have different classes for the men and the women. It would be hard to talk about this stuff with men there."

> "This was the best class I ever took. Adult stuff, not baby stuff."

> "I never knew the real names for my private parts. I knew other words, but not the right words."

> "Sometimes you say no nicely. Sometimes you say no loudly!"

"I'm glad the men are taking this class too. They need it!"

"I have two safe persons I can go to now if I have a problem."

"Can I take the class again?"

"Keep telling until someone listens. That is good to know."

"I never knew I could say no, but now I can say NO. This changes my life."

I left this meeting knowing that after taking the class, some of the class participants would make excellent trainers of the curriculum. In the years that followed, we had co-trainers in every agency that we worked with. People expressed two concerns when we introduced this idea:

1. Leaders with disabilities may not keep confidentiality of what is discussed in class; and

2. Class participants may tell their peer trainers about sexual abuse and the peer trainers would not know what to do.

The reality is this:

- Everyone needed deeper training about confidentiality. Staff did not always keep confidentiality of the persons in their services and that was already a concern. So, we trained all the class trainers (staff and peer trainers) to uphold confidentiality and checked in regularly for support and to answer questions. We did not have one issue with a peer trainer and confidentiality during the two years we supported this part of the work through the grant.

- People experiencing sexual abuse within these communities were already sharing more information with peers than with staff. It was a great advantage to have the peers trained, supported and ready to respond to a disclosure. In general, we trained peers to respond by listening and not judging or asking lots of questions. We also trained peers to ask the person disclosing abuse about their 'safe person'. (A safe person is someone who is an adult, can help, and can respect your information.) On a couple occasions, the person disclosing the abuse, asked the peer trainer to go with them to talk with their safe person. Professionals at one agency reported that more sexual abuse was being reported than before we began the peer training program. It is GOOD to have more reported

… it does not mean there is more sexual abuse, it means that it is actually getting reported and responded to in a trauma-informed manner.

Based on the data we collected, the peer trainers learned and retained the knowledge and skills taught by the curriculum more than class members who were not peer trainers. It is common sense that we know what we teach. The peer trainers truly became leaders within their agencies and their communities on stopping sexual assault against people with disabilities. Two of the peer trainers have spoken nationally in several states about sexual assault and people with disabilities.

3. **When the living, learning, and working environments support equal relationships, empowerment and safety, ALL people learn about respect, consent, and abuse prevention**

From the beginning of the WE CAN Stop Abuse project, I knew that we could not just use a classroom model to teach people with disabilities to know and understand when and how to say no to unwanted touch; that it was okay to tell on people who have power over them; or that it was okay to set their own boundaries of personal space. The culture of their living and learning environments must allow and support people to speak up for themselves and to say no and to report those who did them harm. So, we worked with agencies to change their culture. For example, it was no longer acceptable to have 'compliance' goals in someone's life plan. We measured how the agency did on their goals to change their organizational culture and we measured how the people who took the classes actually used the skills taught in the class in their environments.

In measuring organizational cultures, we asked questions about policies and procedures, collaboration with community sexual assault centers, employee hiring, training and evaluation processes, relationships between employees and people that were supported, with a focus on respect and power dynamics, as well as representation by people with disabilities on committees, work groups and the board of directors.

4. **When people with disabilities know to tell a safe person when something feels uncomfortable, they report 'grooming behavior', and sexual assault can sometimes be prevented**

WOW!! Really? Yes, at first this one surprised me too. My previous work had focused more on risk reduction and recovery. Can we really prevent sexual assault? This work has demonstrated that sometimes we can! Here is what happened. On one day, two different women came to me, one at a time, and reported the same story: "Joe (staff) asked me if I liked to watch dirty movies. That felt bad so I am telling on him." This sounded like grooming behavior to me. (Grooming is a process an offender uses to gradually gain trust and connection with someone so they can manipulate, exploit, and abuse them. Sometimes the process will gradually cross a boundary to see if the person will tell on them before doing something illegal - it's a testing process). Both women had received training to speak up about their feelings and to tell a safe person if they had feelings that felt bad/uncomfortable. Fortunately, in this case, the agency immediately investigated the situation and fired Joe that very day. During the three years of this project, I heard similar reports. People were reporting things that were not sexual assault but crossed a boundary that made them feel bad. Equally important, there were safe people to listen and believe when these situations were reported. When people have power equity within family and system structures, I believe we are all safer.

One Quick story: The curriculum included a lesson on 'safe persons'. Each participant identified two safe people in their life and gave each one a 'safe person' certificate. One day I received a call from a staff member, the conversation went something like this:

> "I wanted to let you know about something really strange that happened today. One of the women here gave me a 'safe person' certificate, and I was shocked."

> I replied, "You have gotten safe person certificates before, why was this one shocking?"

> He said, "Because, I don't really know this person. I'm thinking they don't really know anybody that 'has their back. Hmmm …. Since they chose me, I'm going to keep an eye out for them and get to know them better. I want to be available if they ever need help."

There it was: a tool for connection and safety.

Things were changing.

Another quick story: At the last class within one agency, the class members each created their own t-shirt. One woman put slogans all over her t-shirt with sayings like:

My Body My Choice

I say who touches me

I have the right to be safe

I Can Say NO

Respect Me

Touch me and I will tell

One day, while working, someone approached her, got too close and called her "Baby". She backed up, pointed to her shirt, and said very firmly,

"Read My Shirt!"

There are many ways to say 'no' and her message was loud and clear.

Questions for the Reader:

1. Students with disabilities are often left out of 'prevention education' classes in school, which includes bullying, healthy relationships,

and sexual abuse. Why do you think that happens? How can this be changed?

2. What stands out for you as an important element of the WE CAN Stop Abuse project?
3. What education have you had about healthy relationships and safe/unsafe touch?
4. Can you think of an example of grooming behavior that you have observed or heard about?
5. What can you do to be a safe person for someone in your life? Do you have a safe person in your life?

Illinois Imagines

"You may say that I'm a dreamer, but I'm not the only one." John Lennon

One of the most meaningful work experiences of my life was working with a statewide team in Illinois designed to address the sexual assault of people with disabilities. This was a Department of Justice federally funded collaboration which began in 2006. While the funding ended in 2019, many of the systems changes that were made continue today and new ones have been created.

In many ways, being a part of Illinois Imagines was a dream come true. It's one of those experiences when you can say, "Well, there's my life *before* Illinois Imagines and my life *after* Illinois Imagines." Before Illinois Imagines, I had been working for many years with individuals with disabilities primarily one-on-one who had been sexually assaulted. I had taken on several different roles depending on the preferences and needs of each person. I had learned to provide crisis response, support during sexual assault examinations, legal advocacy, individual counseling, individual and group education, and family education/counseling. In addition, I facilitated training for disability organizations, sexual assault and domestic violence centers, self-advocacy groups, parent support groups, child advocacy centers, schools, criminal justice organizations, national organizations, and others. It was me flying solo with boots on the ground trying to help one person at a time, and then taking what I learned from each situation to groups of people who could make a difference in their own agencies/communities/states/countries.

In the Beginning

When I stepped into my first statewide Illinois Imagines meeting in the Fall of 2006, I didn't know that my life was about to change. I was excited about the possibilities and a little intimidated by the other folks at the table. I had never been in a meeting with so many state employees and organizational directors/managers. I also noticed that there didn't seem to be representation of any people with disabilities. When I asked about that, I discovered that the group was welcome to that idea and Amy Walker became a member at the next meeting (remember her ABCs poem - this was the meeting). Over the years, several self-advocates (people with disabilities speaking up for themselves and others) had leadership roles at the state and community level. It didn't take long before I realized that this group of powerful people held a perfect mix of expertise and passion that would make positive change across systems to benefit survivors with disabilities.

Imagine.

Twelve years of working in solidarity with people with disabilities!

Twelve years of imagining and dreaming!

Twelve years of making changes that matter!

We needed to imagine what it could be like if we were successful! We had an opportunity to imagine what we wanted to create. From the beginning, the team wanted radical change and came up with the name Illinois Imagines, inspired by the song "Imagine", by John Lennon.

From the beginning, we knew we needed to hear from people with disabilities, as well as employees within disability services and rape crisis centers. We traveled the state. We met with different groups of people. We asked questions. We listened and recorded what the voices said. We analyzed what we learned. **Hundreds of voices informed our work moving forward.** Perhaps this helped to build a foundation of involvement and commitment. Perhaps, but listening to lots of people only matters if you do something with what you learn.

Three Reasons Why I Loved Illinois Imagines

So, what was it that made Illinois Imagines so important? There is not an easy answer to that question. Looking back on that today, here are some of my thoughts:

I was not alone. The team gave me a place and a forum in which to express issues that I had been struggling with for years. The team listened to me and validated my concerns, and I received the incredible opportunity to listen to other people's perspectives and ideas. Most importantly, on many occasions, action was taken to alleviate barriers and to build supportive system responses.

Illinois Imagines was much more than a grant. With the focused and flexible leadership of Teresa Tudor, Illinois Department of Human Services, Bureau of Domestic and Sexual Violence, the project was able to lean into changes that needed to be made. Over time, it became a movement across the state that responded to people with disabilities who experienced sexual assault. A movement to build collaborations and a responsive set of systems that cared about and supported survivors with disabilities in accessing safety, education, health care, healing, empowerment, and justice.

People with disabilities played important roles. People with disabilities were a vital part of the planning and implementation of Illinois Imagines. They served in leadership roles, created resources, conducted training, met with policymakers, analyzed data, supported other team members, generated ideas, and kept the team mission-driven.

Initial Frustrations

It was hard on some of us to not jump right in and get busy making changes. I was one of those people. How long did people need to wait? Hadn't they already waited long enough to access education and support services and justice? Yes - people had waited what seemed like decades for the systems to care enough to include them in prevention education, medical/legal advocacy, counseling, and sexual assault forensic exams. This grant required us to move thoughtfully through a series of steps -create a charter, develop a needs assessment plan, complete a needs assessment, analyze the data, write a needs assessment report, and develop a strategic plan. Many steps required approval from the grant administrator with the Office on Violence Against Women before we could move on to the next step.

Yep, it was frustrating at times. Yes, it took longer than this impatient woman wanted to wait. But, looking back, I think the process was vital to our success! I think the thoughtfulness of each step really made the team come together and improved our outcomes. The process focused us on THE RIGHT WORK IN THE RIGHT WAY! I want to thank everyone on the team who patiently received my rants and frustrations about how long the process took before we actually got down to the business of making changes! A huge thank you goes to Amy Loder, with the Office on Violence Against Women, for her support of our statewide work and true systems change.

Why Our Work Mattered

So, what it is that makes my heart shine and my eyes sparkle when I think about Illinois Imagines? **We made a difference!**

Here are some examples:

1.   It was very clear from our needs assessment that community disability providers and rape crisis centers were isolated from one another. They were silos. They had different funders, different regulations and standards, different philosophies, and different expertise. They made assumptions about each other that kept

them separated. They didn't really understand each other, and therefore did not utilize each other in the best interest of survivors with disabilities. Illinois Imagines put a lot of time and resources into building collaborative teams in every Illinois community that supported a rape crisis center. The membership of the community teams was similar to that of the statewide team: people with disabilities, representatives from area disability and sexual assault agencies, and others whose work intersected with the issue. I provided support to some of these teams, and it was exciting to see the magic happen as people got to know and understand each other.

Imagine this: BEFORE the community teams, if a person at a disability agency reported sexual assault, there was probably a mandated report made. Many times, that was the end of it. The police may be called, and a report may or may not be taken. In rare instances, a referral to a rape crisis center may have been made, and only if that staff member at the disability agency was aware of the center and their services. AFTER the community teams formed and a person disclosed sexual assault to a staff at a disability agency, there was a good chance the person would be offered an advocate from the rape crisis center. This advocate could offer lots of information, support, and choices to the survivor. The advocate could create access to supports where very little existed before, including medical and legal support as well as counseling.

Over time, the community teams identified systems barriers and issues that were experienced by survivors and notified the statewide team so the issues could be addressed. There was a meaningful flow of information from the state team to the community teams and from the community teams to the state team. A flow which supported individual survivors with disabilities as well as the overall movement.

2. Here is an example of a barrier identified at the community level and addressed at the state level. There were survivors who wanted sexual assault exams but could not get them without their guardian consent. When community rape crisis centers reported this barrier to the statewide team, we

took action. We passed legislation that an adult with a guardian who wanted a sexual assault exam could provide their own consent – people with disabilities were now free to access a health care and forensic exam without their guardian knowledge or consent.

This is HUGE! Can you imagine being sexually assaulted and wanting to go to the hospital to make sure you are ok and to have evidence collected in case you want to pursue criminal charges, and being told you could not give permission for your own exam? In the past, this denial of access was very harmful to survivors with disabilities who had guardians. Now, survivors, who had their personal power stripped away from them during an assault, have the power to access a sexual assault exam if they want one. It was finally time: adults with guardians were now treated like other adults in Illinois who wanted a sexual assault examination: with choice, respect, and dignity! I was elated!

3.   The Needs Assessment also identified a lack of resources to address sexual violence in the lives of people with disabilities. The first resource we created was a tool kit that included five modules. Team members

worked on the parts where they had expertise and interest. The entire team was included in the review of each part. When I was involved in creating/revising materials I would intentionally bring into my mind many of the people with disabilities with whom I had worked and all they had taught me. It was a way for me to honor people who had been deeply hurt in efforts that might make life better for others.

The toolkit included an introductory guide complete with an overview of the issues, sample policies and procedures, partner agreements, collaboration tools, and more. We created a guide for Rape Crisis Centers and one for Disability Services providers. We created an educational guide for use with people with disabilities and a multi-media kit with posters and DVDs. One of the DVDs was of self-advocates talking about what they needed from families, disability organizations, and rape crisis centers. We conducted multiple trainings on how to use this toolkit. As the project continued, more resources were added as we learned more about the needs of the community.

Why did this matter? Because now there was one less excuse for not teaching people with disabilities about their rights to be safe from sexual assault and their options if they did experience sexual assault. People with disabilities were now receiving education about healthy relationships and sexual assault. **Things were changing.**

4.   Sometimes an agenda does not cover everything that needs to be discussed during a meeting. Her name is Chelle, and she not only changed the meeting that day, but she also opened and widened the door of empowerment to include a whole new group of people. She asked what we could do about the people in the building where she lived. She said that when someone who lived in the building was too 'handsy', she would tell others, "Stay away from the guy in room ###. Don't even get on the elevator with him." She lived in a multiple story building that rented apartments to people with disabilities. We wondered, how would we reach the folks who lived independently and were not necessarily connected with an organization? We used our imaginations again and after some discussion, we decided to create a Guide for Starting Empowerment Groups that could be utilized in a variety of settings. We trained several

groups of women with disabilities and witnessed their power and pride in speaking up and singing out about rights and recovery, while supporting each other in the process! Thank you, Chelle, for sharing your experiences and expanding our reach!

This I know for sure, if we had followed a rigid meeting schedule with time frames for each agenda item, this would never have happened. The leadership (Teresa Tudor) and the team were flexible and responsive to the voices of self-advocates on the team. Our work was centered around and grounded in these expert voices - the people who were most affected by our work!

5.   I had spent enough time at disability agencies across Illinois (and other states) to know that when someone told their staff that someone touched them sexually without their permission, most staff did not know how to support the person. Everyone knew how and to whom to report abuse and neglect, but it was rare that staff knew how to support the person in a trauma-informed manner. Oftentimes, the staff members response was unintentionally harmful to the person reporting the abuse/assault.

We imagined that when someone told a staff member "I was raped" … or "that has happened to me" the staff would know how to support the person. We created a "Response Card" with 'do's' and 'don'ts' and helpful things to say. Since it is extremely rare that people lie about sexual assault, the response card included ways to believe and support the person and not to judge or criticize them. We included the Response Card in the Resource Tool Kit. We trained the disability agency staff in multiple locations on the use of the Response Card. We also worked with the Division of Developmental Disabilities to include the best practice responses in their Policies and Procedures to enable broader outreach. We also met with the Director of the Office of the Inspector General and reviewed investigative materials and policies and procedures to make them more trauma-informed.

Now when someone reported sexual assault to a staff member at a disability agency, there was a good chance the person would be believed and supported. As I write this, tears are coming down my face – THIS –

this is changing lives and opening the pathway to healing for many survivors.

6.　　We were involved in numerous events that felt magical to me. One that I will share is when we organized a 2-day training event that brought together approximately 30 people with disabilities and 30 educators from various Illinois Rape Crisis Centers. Our goal was to facilitate the engagement of teams to co-train education for people with disabilities in Illinois communities. We supported the audience members to begin co-training on prevention and response to sexual violence. The magic happened as people built relationships, worked in teams, role played parts of the curriculum, and departed with plans to continue to work together and to co-train.

　　At the beginning of the two-day event, Cathy Lynn Saunders, a self-advocate, and poet, asked if she could write a poem inspired by the 2-day event. She was encouraged to do so and was offered the opportunity to close out the event with her spoken words.

　　At the end of the training, Cathy shared her poem and received a standing ovation. We all stood together as catalysts for peace.

A perfect ending to our collective work to make vital information more accessible to people with disabilities with representation of people with disabilities!

A Catalyst of Peace *

By Cathy Lynn Saunders

Empower me.
I want to be a catalyst of peace.
Where there is sexual violence
Let me show sexual liberation
And patience.

Where there is ignorance of knowledge
Let me educate.

I want to be a catalyst of peace.
Bring forth the comrades who will labor with me.

Where there is pain,
Make me a salve to heal the hurt.

Provide my hands with a tender touch,
So that hearts will permeate and know love.

Let me work hard and not tire.
May my word inspire my brothers and sisters
As I labor for an end to sexual violence for
Women with disabilities.

I pray for the day when they see themselves
As they truly are:
Soulful, Beautiful, Sensual, Titillating,
Captivating, Illuminating
Women of Distinction.

A catalyst of peace worthy of royalty
Are you committed or do I stand alone?
How many with me shall stand
To be a catalyst of peace?

Note: In 2019, Cathy published a book of her
poetry. *My Name is Cathy Lynn: A love letter from
me to you,* by Cathy Lynn Saunders * is available
on Amazon. The book has four sections: The early
years, A Poet's Musings, Poems Regarding Sexual
Assault and Other Forms of Violence Against
People with Disabilities, and My Experiences as an
African American Sister, highlighting culture and
family. A Catalyst of Peace is included in her book
and printed here with Cathy's permission.

The Long Arms of Ableism

These are just a few examples of the magnitude of the reach of Illinois Imagines in addressing sexual violence against people with disabilities. Oftentimes, when we found one solution to a barrier, we learned about another related issue that needed our attention. Oppression has lots of tenacles that reach deeply into our systems of supports and services. Forces are present that we may not be able to easily see but they do exist. These forces want to keep the status quo in its place. Most services are created for the typical human. **Ableism has long arms and a wide reach.** The only way to know for sure if we were being successful was to listen to people with disabilities on a regular basis.

A good example of the wide reach of ableism is access to sexual assault exams for people with disabilities.

As I described above, we changed the law so adults with disabilities who had guardians could independently access sexual assault exams. Yes, I was excited about that. But there was another barrier. One survivor reported, "They refused to examine me because they said my legs would not fit in those things." Another survivor said, "I waited at the hospital for hours. No one ever spoke to me. They only spoke to my staff." So here is what happened.

I remember very clearly how it all started. Teresa Tudor, project lead, and I were having one of many deep conversations. We often had these dream talks - a "wouldn't it be great if..." conversation. We were talking about some of the still existing barriers for people with disabilities in accessing sexual assault examinations and one of us said, "Wouldn't it be great if we had a picture guide and worked with the Sexual Assault Nurse Examiner Coordinator to make that happen?" Approximately one week later, I was scheduled to do a presentation about working with people with disabilities for the International Association of Chiefs of Police workshop in Illinois. I entered the training space and took a seat at the back of the room next to another person also scheduled to do a presentation. I introduced myself and you will never guess who was sitting right beside me. Yes, it was Shannon Liew, with the Attorney General's Office, the Sexual Assault Nurse Examiner Coordinator for Illinois. I was so excited and amazed at this gift of serendipity! I told her our idea and she responded. "Yes. Let's do it!" So, the next time she was doing hands on training for sexual assault nurses, I planned to meet her at the hospital. Our goal for the day was to take photographs of each step of the sexual assault exam. She had made arrangements for a 'professional patient' to help with the photographs, and we took the photos during the training breaks and lunch period. The final materials took about a year to complete, but this was the first and very important step in making that resource available. We had the photographs to inform survivors about the steps of the exam and their choices. We had also strengthened our relationship with the state Sexual Assault Nurse Examiner Coordinator. This was a great help to our future work. As the process continued, Shannon helped with the ordering of the steps based on the Illinois protocol at the time, the language for the medical professional version of the guide, and with the Victim Rights Statement.

So many people were involved in developing this resource; victim advocates in Illinois, Kim Day from the International Association of Forensic Nurses, Illinois Coalition Against Sexual Assault staff, people with disabilities, and the entire Illinois Imagines team.

There are three versions of the guide: one for medical professionals, one for victim advocates, and one for people with disabilities (for use in empowerment groups or in decision-making about whether or not to have an exam). We imagined a solution and worked hard to make it unfold as the right partners joined us to make it happen. This resource has been accessed across the nation.

The resource was created in a Power Point format so it could be used on a tablet in hospitals and clinics right in the exam room. This format allows for states to modify the order of the slides based on each state protocol.

The Picture Guide to the Exam Following Sexual Assault * incudes ten different resources related to the sexual assault examination. Please check the resource guide at the end of the book.

Never Underestimate the Power of Dreaming!!

Lessons Learned:

1. It is imperative to listen to the voices and stories of people with disabilities who experience sexual assault. They are the experts on what they need. Without their stories, we may not have included

alternate positions for the exam or provided clear directions on communication.

2. The value of dreaming, idea generation, forward-thinking and believing in possibilities is a value that cannot be overstated. This began with a simple conversation and resulted in creating a doorway to equality and justice for victims of sexual assault who have disabilities.

3. Collaboration is the key to making the right decisions, the right resources, the right training, etc. With attention and intention, collaboration can lead to sustainable change.

4. We have discovered repeatedly, that when we create a tool or resource for people with disabilities, it usually works well for everyone. This resource is valuable for many trauma victims who may have trouble processing information right after an assault.

5. With many of our outcomes, once we really dug in, we discovered some tentacles that also needed changing. As we began implementing this resource in Illinois, we discovered some related issues such as: on the rape kit form, the ordering of steps did not seem survivor-centered; and the consent to treatment form used complicated language. More work needed to be done.

We continued the work, addressing as may issues as we could as they came up. The Illinois rape kit form included complicated language two different areas: 1. where the victim was asked to sign consent for the exam, and 2. the consent for the release of the exam results to law enforcement. Victim Advocates reported the consent areas were difficult for people to understand. The Illinois Imagines team crafted new, easier to understand language for this form. Sean Black from the Illinois Coalition Against Sexual Assault and I met with the person in charge of the rape kit forms with the Illinois State Police. We shared the problem and the possible solution. It was a magical day, because the person took our draft language and said it would be used; when it was time to order new forms they would be updated. What? Sean and I looked at each other and smiled. I believe I did a happy dance on the way home.

Since ableism had long arms and a wide reach, Illinois Imagines needed to do the same. The reach extended across the nation as information was shared at national conferences, and tools were shared with other states and adapted by other grantees.

A Dream Comes True

For many years, I would receive several phone calls or emails from someone I had never met asking for help with getting a counselor for a person with disabilities who had been sexually assaulted. One mother called me and said, "My daughter was sexually abused by the school bus driver, and she is really having a hard time. Do you know someone who can help her?" They lived several hours away, and I was unable to connect them with a Rape Crisis Center because the counselor in their geographic area said, "I would love to help but I don't know how to counsel someone who does not talk. I would never want to cause any harm to someone who has already been hurt." I received calls from agencies too. Here is one example, "Someone we serve has been sexually assaulted. Now they cry, scream, won't eat or bathe. They need help." If the agency was close enough and they could bring the person to me, I would provide the counseling. Otherwise, I would locate and call the Rape Crisis Center in their community. I was not very successful in accessing people who would provide counseling to survivors of sexual assault with disabilities, especially for people whose verbal skills were limited, even in Illinois. I had done some brief training sessions (1.5 hours) at several conferences but that was the limit of my impact. Whenever I thought about this, I was sad and frustrated. I recall one self-advocate whom I had known who would always say, "Never give up on your dreams!" I tried to remember that, but it seemed my time might be running out for this dream.

Until... there was this one meeting when the team voted to create a Guide for Rape Crisis Center Counselors. It was a dream come true! After the resource was developed, approved, and distributed, we held three day-long training events in 2018 for counselors at Illinois rape crisis centers. A person with disabilities co-trained at every event. We began each day with some reflective questions. I am including them here because this part of the day proved to be very revealing and set the stage for sharing and listening.

(1.) What experiences have you had with counseling survivors with intellectual disabilities and/or autism?
(2.) What strategies have you tried?
(3.) What successes have you had?
(4.) What was most difficult?

(5.) How are you feeling about your comfort level in working with survivors with intellectual disabilities and/or autism?
(6.) What do you need to be even more successful?

For question five regarding comfort and confidence in working with people with intellectual disabilities and/or autism, we created a scale which we repeated at the end of the day. The scale was:

0-3   Not very comfortable
4-6   Fairly comfortable but could improve
7-9   Pretty comfortable and confident
10   I could teach this class

At every training, we saw a huge positive change in the counselors' responses between the start of the day and the end of the day - people left feeling much more comfortable and confident in their ability to counsel survivors with disabilities. This was most definitely one of the biggest highlights of my career. Now, people with disabilities who were suffering from the trauma of sexual assault had someone who could help them. I felt myself breathe a sigh of relief at the end of each day. A part of me had been holding my breath for so many years.

The resource for rape crisis center counselors is titled "Counseling Survivors with Intellectual Disabilities and/or Autism". * This would not have been possible without the support of the Illinois Coalition Against Sexual Assault, so here is a big shout out to Carol Corgan and Sean Black for helping to make this happen. In addition, major kudos to the team that worked for months to bring the guide together: Alice Kieft, Maureen Mostacci, Marge Parker, Mary Ratliff, Linda Sandman, Morgan Tudor, and Teresa Tudor. Linda Sandman and I contributed our knowledge and expertise from our many years of counseling survivors with disabilities, and the entire team worked together to develop this important tool for recovery. To all of the survivors who shared their trauma with us and their healing: we are grateful to each of you for your courage in sharing your story and your emotional work to heal the wounds you endured. We are honored to have known you and to have shared such sacred spaces with you.

Information to access the guide is provided in the resource/reference section at the end of this book. I do hope the guide helps counselors at Rape Crisis Centers in other states! Opening the doors of access to counseling for survivors with disabilities is crucial.

Access to Rape Crisis Center Services

As these and other changes were made, due to the amazing work of Illinois Imagines at the community and state level, I could feel sparkles of light moving throughout Illinois. Each time a new door was opened for people with disabilities to access education, advocacy, counseling, safety, health care, justice and compassion, the sparkles of light grew! I could see and feel the light shine! But we have some data about our success too.

The Illinois Coalition Against Sexual Assault measured the number of people who reported having disabilities who received services at their community Rape Crisis Centers. The statewide team monitored the progress. We succeeded in our efforts - more and more people with disabilities received services at rape crisis centers in Illinois. Some of the reasons for this included:

1. Community teams did outreach and engagement activities with people with disabilities.
2. People with disabilities became educated about sexual assault and the resources available to them.

3. Organizations that served people with disabilities were educated about services available at Rape Crisis Centers.
4. Rape Crisis Centers were educated about working with people with disabilities.
5. Counseling services became accessible at Rape Crisis Centers.

For those of you who are interested in data, here are the numbers of people with disabilities receiving services at Illinois rape crisis centers during the grant period.

➢ FY08 – 254
➢ FY10 – 347
➢ FY12 – 585
➢ FY14 – 756
➢ FY17 – 825

What we measure and look at is important…we can see trends and celebrate positive changes. We can make adjustments, if needed; but if we aren't measuring it, none of those things can happen. I was delighted to discover that the numbers of people with disabilities accessing rape crisis centers have continued to grow since the project ended. This is a very strong statement that the work of Illinois Imagines has been sustainable.

- FY18 –1036
- FY19 –1196
- FY20 –1377
- FY21 –1117

I was told I was the only person interested in these numbers and was asked, "Why does this matter so much to you?" It matters because it represents the lives of people with disabilities who are receiving needed trauma-responsive supports when they are sexually assaulted.
It matters - because they matter!!!

Why I Believe Illinois Imagines was Successful

The reason I believe we were able to make these positive changes is because of the team and the fact that there was **no space between our shoulders.**

In the beginning, the Illinois Imagines team was a group of people with different backgrounds, philosophies, regulations, organizational structures, experiences, expectations, and commitments. As I look back on those first meetings, there was this noticeable space between the team members. The original space was filled with different philosophies, different standards, different experiences, different regulations, different priorities, and protective stances. As we grew to know, understand, and respect each other, the space between us became less and less. The voices of people with disabilities diluted that space and brought all of our hearts together into one strong mission to create a statewide system that could seamlessly respond to people with disabilities who experienced sexual assault. Oh, we had disagreements about priorities, strategies, and how to make systems more accessible. Some meetings were threaded with conflict and heavy discussions, but it always came back to doing the right work for the right reasons. People rarely missed the monthly meetings. We were all focused on making systems changes and the more we made, the more we found other issues that needed to be addressed. Over time, this energy became evident to others and people wanted to get involved and join the movement. As the space between team members became smaller and smaller, we became a dedicated force for change.

I know that I have a tendency towards optimism and that I am biased about the work of Illinois Imagines, so I contacted a couple of people who were involved and asked them to reflect back and share their thoughts about the work that was done during this project. I want to share some of their thoughts here:

Mary Hettel, Illinois Self-Advocate said:

> "Sexual abuse among people with disabilities has decreased because the population has learned the tactics that abusers use. Disclosures have increased and legal actions have increased as self-advocates understand that sexual abuse is a crime."

> "Illinois Imagines was my first job after I graduated from college   It was a fun learning experience. It taught me how to be a part of a team. My favorite part of Illinois Imagines was creating materials, trainings, and events. The team collaborated with other businesses to help us create meaningful memories, like creating the video at our conference. We also asked self-advocates who were not on the team to help us, train with us. The skills and knowledge that I learned through Illinois Imagines were a great foundation to start my career. They will stay with me throughout other experiences in my career."

Sean Black, Assistant Director, Illinois Coalition Against Sexual Assault said:

> "In my 20 years of doing this work, I don't know of any other collaborative project at the statewide level that has made this kind of impactful change. We changed legislation! We change policies and procedures! We created resources that are still being used a decade later! **These changes have stood the test of time. In the end, it was a big deal!**"

In summary, when we bring people together with a common mission, amazing things can happen. When we dream and imagine together, the sky is the limit!

Questions for Dreamers:

1. When you think about sexual assault in the lives of people with disabilities, what are your wildest dreams for the future?
2. Can you imagine systems and services that are trauma-informed, responsive, welcoming, accessible, safe, and meaningful for people with disabilities? What steps would be needed to make that happen?

3. Can people with disabilities imagine their lives being safe and free and equal? What would that look like, sound like, feel like?
4. How can we use our collective imaginations and create safe and trauma-informed environments and survivor-centered services and systems for people with disabilities?
5. What do you imagine?

Chapter 8

Words and Labels

"Words are important. If you want to care for something, you call it a "flower"; if you want to kill something, you call it a "weed."
Don Coyhis, Leader of the Native American Wellbriety Movement.

"Assumptions remove mystery and if left unquestioned, replace fact. It is far better to remain curious, to live in a world of mysteries that give way to truth, than to assume you know better." Joseph Smith, Training Coordinator, Photographer, Writer

Words Matter

"Sticks and stones may break my bones, but words will never hurt me." How many times have we heard this? Have we said it? Well, it is a lie! It is a big lie! One person told me, "Words may not break my bones, but they sure can break my heart!" Yes, they sure can. I believe that every human being has been hurt by words at some point in their lives and most of us have been hurt by words multiple times. Let's agree to not say that sticks and stones thing anymore, ok? Good! Let's acknowledge that words can be hurtful and honor that our feelings matter.

Another thing - let's agree that each person knows when their feelings are hurt, and that all feelings are valid. Let's stop telling people not to feel their feelings. I hear folks saying things like "Don't be sad." "Don't cry." "There is no reason for you to be mad, just ignore them." Our feelings are our reality at any given moment. When we have safe spaces to identify and express our feelings, we can learn that our feelings are important. Our feelings help us to figure things out. Our feelings help us to understand ourselves and know what helps us and what hurts us. Our feelings help us to make decisions.

Even when I feel sad, or mad or scared - I try to thank my feelings for helping me. When my body hurts, I know there might be a problem that needs my attention. The same is true for my emotions/feelings. Feelings help us to shine a light on a situation. For example, maybe I am tired and need to rest. Maybe I am in a relationship that is harmful, and I need to talk to someone who can help. Maybe I am saying negative things to myself and need to encourage myself instead. Maybe I am comparing myself to someone else and figure out that I don't need to do that. (Comparison blocks peace of mind!) Our feelings can teach us so much!

Feelings can help us discover our dreams! It is really powerful to ask yourself, "What makes my heart smile?" Feelings of love and joy and excitement can help us identify what kind of job we might want to have, or where we might want to live or go on vacation. Feelings bring meaning to our lives!

From my experience, people with disabilities have frequently not been taught (either through example or education) to identify and express their feelings. When we keep our feelings inside, the result can be depression or aggression. Lots of people, with and without disabilities, are not good at communicating uncomfortable feelings. (I can see you nodding yes as you read that.) I think if humans can learn to do this well, we would prevent lots of problems. We need to attend to these small harms (like minor conflicts) to help prevent the bigger harms (like violence).

Word Choices

We all get to choose what words we say, in whatever way we choose to communicate. (Through our voices, sign language, text, email, communication devices, pictures, etc.) I am not going to provide a lesson on "People first Language" or "Identity First Language" here - you can research that yourself if you want to know what those are. I want to simply encourage the readers to BE AWARE of the words that you use and the messages those words carry. For example, there is a job title often used in the world of disability services that I find offensive and harmful. That job title is "Case Manager". This type of language maintains the historical perception that people with disabilities are "less than" and need "professional experts" to fix them and be in control of their lives. I have heard many people receiving services say, **"I am not a case, and I don't need to be managed."**

Another word that is used frequently is "inappropriate". People with disabilities are frequently told that what they are doing is "inappropriate". First of all, this word is vague and does not provide any specific information to the person. They do not know what is inappropriate or why something is inappropriate or what they could do differently. One year, I asked hundreds of people with disabilities, "what does it mean when someone says you are inappropriate?" and they all said "Bad" or "I am bad". We should not be telling anyone that they are bad…a behavior might be hurtful…but the person is not bad. I believe that the word inappropriate has been passed down and around by employees within organizational cultures. I also believe that this word is never helpful, and that individuals, groups, teams, and entire organizations can make a conscious decision to eliminate this word from their language.

Another word that I think we need to consider is the word "special". 'Special Needs' is often used for people with disabilities. Everyone has needs. Is this language that focuses on differences and keeps people separate? Amy Walker (you may remember her from Chapter 3) once told me, "When someone says the word special, I hear the word segregated. There are special schools, special classes, special recreation, and special buses. All are segregated and they are not at all special!"

Think about the pictures you are painting with your words. Be mindful about words that might be offensive to people in the LGBTQ+ community, people with disabilities, African Americans, Indigenous people, and others. Compare these two examples.

- Imani is a non-verbal, autistic woman with multiple behavior problems
- Imani is an interesting woman who loves nature and art

Which one of these women would you like to spend time with? These are descriptions of the same person! Several years ago, I was asked by a state administration on developmental disabilities to make recommendations for an individual services planning document. I met with several people receiving services, and we discussed what they wanted the document to include. They understood that to receive services with state funds, certain medical labels were necessary. They all said they wanted those labels on the last page at the bottom. They did not want their labels to be on the front page at the top! On the front page, they wanted their personal abilities, talents, preferences (including for supports) and dreams for the future. I recall one person so beautifully saying, "It's not like going to the doctor. **We don't need to be fixed! We need support!**"

I dream about teams in agencies having discussions about what words to avoid, what the service plans should look like, what do people want to be called (most say their name), and the whole topic of words and labels. People receiving services should be on these teams, leading these teams and creating desired outcomes with the teams. Let's focus on shining a light on each person's individual gifts and not their labels.

When words are labels, we have big problems. When we use a label for a person, assumptions are made. For example, when someone hears the label "Down Syndrome" certain assumptions are made. Our brains go to that file in our brains that tell us what that means. This happens automatically and we may not even be aware of it. The label and our assumptions about it, make it harder for us to get to know that particular person!! I want to spend some time exploring some of the labels that have made life more difficult for survivors of sexual assault who have disabilities.

The Myth of Non-Verbal

I am not a big fan of labels. Especially labels that are a part of discrimination and segregation and inequality. People with disabilities experience lots of labels, medical diagnoses and harmful slang words that are used to demean, belittle, and bully. Non-verbal is one of those labels. It seems benign enough. The statement, "My son is non-verbal" means my son does not use his voice to communicate. The statement, "My students are non-verbal" means the students in this class do not form words with their voices to communicate. So, what's the problem with the term 'non-verbal'? There is an assumption beneath the word 'non-verbal' that the person does not communicate at all…and sometimes that the person cannot learn.

So, consider these scenarios about Lou: (Lou's pronouns are they/them)

1. Lou is in a classroom with other 'non-verbal' students. A prevention educator comes to the high school to present information about bullying, respect, healthy relationships, and abuse prevention. The Prevention Educator works in all the regular classrooms but not in the classroom with Lou, because the students in that class are 'non-verbal'. Lou and their classmates do not learn about these important topics.

2. Lou has signs of sexual abuse and the police have been notified. An officer goes to Lou's address, knocks on the door and asks to speak to Lou. The parent says, "Well they can't talk to you. Lou is non-verbal." In most cases, the officer says something like, "Oh, I didn't know that. Thanks for your time." The officer leaves and there is an assumption that Lou is not a credible witness and many times, the investigation stops there.

3. Lou has experienced sexual assault and has become depressed and angry. They are not sleeping well, are losing weight, no longer want to go places in the community, and has times when they cry, and times when they yell

and throw things. Let's think about what might happen to help Lou in this scenario:

➤ They might see the family doctor who orders tests to rule out a medical condition
➤ They might be put on a behavior program. (It could be a behavior program where Lou would have to 'be good' in order to earn the things they like, and/or have these things taken away when they are 'bad')
➤ They might be put on medications for depression, anxiety, or even psychosis

4. A call is made to the local sexual assault center by Lou's mom or social worker at the school. Lou is described as non-verbal. More often than not, Lou cannot access counseling because of the assumptions made about the word "non-verbal".

As you can see in the above scenarios, assumptions about the word 'non-verbal' would put Lou in danger and without support for their traumatic experiences. I had the opportunity to speak with a person one time who had offended several people with developmental disabilities. One of the things he told me was, "I always pick people who can't tell so I won't get in trouble." So, we need strategies that make it possible for people to tell - even if they communicate in non-traditional ways.

Here is what I believe:

1. All people communicate. When we ask parents, "How does your daughter or son let you know when they are happy (or sad, hungry, in pain, etc.) the parents have very concrete answers. When we ask teachers or adult services staff, "How does Miguel let you know what he likes, or dislikes?" the teacher or staff have very concrete answers. **NON-verbal is a myth.**
2. What people are able to say vocally does not equal what they are able to understand when others speak. It is important to communicate with people who do not make words in a traditional, vocal manner. It is important to use total communication - combining sound, facial expression, tone of voice, body language, pictures, sign language, letter boards, gestures, movement, music, and touch within respectful boundaries. It is equally important to observe all of these things when the other person communicates.
3. All people can learn, but not all people can teach. People learn in different ways and at different speeds. If we believe people cannot learn, we do not teach them. When we

provide equal opportunities and allow people to take some chances, they learn. When we believe in people, they learn. When people feel respected, they learn.

4. All people can benefit from education about bullying, boundaries, consent, safe and unsafe touch, healthy relationships, types of abuse, responding to abuse and how to get help. Some adjustments may need to be made to standard curricula. There are now curricula designed for people who may need a variety of learning styles incorporated.

5. It is typically a good practice to check for medical causes when a person's behavior, character, or personality changes. This is especially true for someone who may not be able to easily communicate what the problem is. Someone who suddenly begins slapping the side of their face, may have a tooth ache or trigeminal neuralgia. Sometimes what looks like a trauma response, may be a response to physical pain. Sometimes, there is a physical reason AND a trauma/emotional reason for the observed behavior.

6. From my experience many behavior programs have an element of control by others which only exacerbates the trauma the person is experiencing. For some people, the behavior program punishes the person for their trauma

responses. For example, their behavior program contains an "If you do X, then you cannot have or do Y." I have known people who become upset because they are experiencing a painful memory and then are denied a home visit where they feel safe and loved. Some people have had their music taken away from them because they cried too much, and music was one of the few things that made them feel better. In these situations, the behavior program makes the situation worse. It is also cruel.

7. Many people with disabilities can and do benefit from counseling following sexual assault. This counseling can occur following the assault or it can be years or decades later. I have included a variety of examples and healing strategies in a later section.

8. Many people with disabilities ARE credible witnesses. Many people with disabilities CAN participate fully in the criminal justice process. There is much more information about the criminal justice response in a later section.

Questions for the Reader:

1. Think about the ways that a loved one in your life communicates without using vocal sounds.

How can you tell this person is sad or mad even though they don't say those words?

2. In your opinion, how do our beliefs and attitudes influence our actions? Can you give an example?
3. Can you think of a benefit to using the label 'non-verbal' to describe anyone? What would that benefit be?
4. Are you familiar with the Graham Nash song, "Try to Find Me"? Graham wrote this song for Neil Young who had a 'non-speaking' child. If you have not heard this song before, consider listening to it on YouTube.

Other Things That Get in the Way

In addition to the label of 'non-verbal', I want to discuss some other concepts/words that get in the way of safety and equality: Mental age and Low functioning vs. High functioning.

Mental Age is a term that was originally developed by psychologists to compare a person's functioning level with that of a typically developing person. It is one aspect of a psychological evaluation in order to make a diagnosis of someone with an intellectual disability. This assessment includes things like communication, motor skills, self-care, and other skills necessary for independent living. The assessment typically includes an overall age equivalent. For example, a person may have an overall mental age of 7.6 in their Activities of Daily Living.

What has happened, is that people have been labeled based upon this mental age finding. And our discussions have moved from reporting a mental age on a psychological test to, "She is like a seven-year-old." So, a process designed to understand people and then later, to determine their eligibility for services has transformed into a system that labels citizens as eternal children and denies people with those labels of respect and dignity.

Here is what I believe:

1. A person cannot be an adult, let's say 35 years old, and be like a seven-year-old. Those 35 years of experiences matter. One woman told me, "I am not a kid. People call us 'kids' all the time!"
2. People deserve to be treated individually and based on their chronological ages. One person said, "I am sick of people talking to me like I am a baby! It makes me want to puke!" If you are in human services or criminal justice or any helping profession, you do not want to

make people puke. You want to help them to feel respected.

3. It is very possible to meet state and federal requirements for testing and diagnosis without bringing those labels into a person's life planning. One person said, "When I ran my own meeting, there were no labels; only what I was good at and what I wanted to do with my life. It was about me and what I could do; not what I couldn't do!"

4. Referring to adults as children is degrading. One man in his 50's asked, "Do you think I will ever be treated like an adult? My family and my staff still treat me like I am a child. It hurts my heart."

I am not sure when we began labeling people as 'low-functioning' or 'high-functioning', but I question these terms on a regular basis. It is another way to categorize and judge people as better than or less than. I have heard parents say things like, "Well, at least my child can walk." Or "I'm lucky that my child can talk." And I've heard teachers or adult services staff say things like, "I work with the low functioning people." And I've heard teens and adults say things like, "I have high-functioning autism."

NOTE: I know many people who use these terms without any malice in their hearts. We learn terms and they seem to 'fit' and we keep using them, without question. I do not question the use of these terms to judge others, but to raise awareness.

When we use the terms 'high-functioning' or 'low-functioning', we are adding another label to a person who already has a label that may be judged negatively by society. These labels lead to assumptions about what the person can or cannot do. These labels can cause harm when parents, or teachers/service coordinators, or other professionals assume the person cannot learn, communicate, play a game, learn a skill, be in the community, get a job, have an intimate relationship, etc.

There is another point to be made about the labels of 'high functioning' and 'low functioning'. I believe we all have areas in our lives in which we are 'high functioning' and other areas where we are 'low functioning'. For example, I am 'low functioning' when it comes to changing the oil in my car or lifting heavy objects (and many other things). I don't need a label or a treatment plan for those things, I just need other people to help me out. I am 'high functioning' in organizing a trip or a project and am often called on to help others in those functions. None of us are totally independent. We are interdependent with one another. We need each other and that is okay. We all have gifts, talents, dreams, and contributions to make. And all means ALL.

Words matter. Words can be harmful or helpful. When I asked people with developmental disabilities what they want to be called, 99% of the time the answer was "my name". I think it would be wonderful if we could all stop using the labels 'special', 'non-verbal', 'mental age', 'high functioning', and 'low functioning'. Oh, you ask, what words would I use instead? Here are some examples:

Yolanda uses pictures to communicate.

Juan uses signs and gestures to express his needs and wants.

Bob communicates very clearly, just watch him and you will know what he wants and how he feels!

Lin uses a letter board to spell out words. Write down the letters and you can understand her.

Aaron's superpower is making other people smile!

One of the sayings from the self-advocacy movement is this:

LABEL CANS, NOT PEOPLE.

If we all practice this and become mindful about what words we use to describe someone, I think we could see a shift in relationships, opportunities, and lives. It takes awareness and a conscious choice to think, speak and write differently. Yes, it will take some effort, and I think it is worth the effort to emphasize individual value and make a positive change in the world.

Remember: A diagnosis or label is not the most important or most interesting thing about a person. SEE THE PERSON, not the assumptions you have about a label.

Dangerous Benevolence

The dictionary defines benevolence as 'the quality of being well meaning, kindness; having a desire to do good.' I have seen many people who think they are being kind and seem to have well-meaning intentions. Many people in human services are there to make a difference in people's lives. Not all of us make lives better. Some of us cause harm and do not even know it. There is a difference between intention and impact.

I believe that some organizations, leaders, and employees have good intentions but that their words and actions give dangerous messages about people with disabilities. Here are some examples:

I have seen commercials which make me nauseous. During the Christmas season 2020, there was a commercial about a specific organization which showed pictures of adults with intellectual and developmental disabilities sitting on Santa Claus' lap. I wanted to throw my dinner at the television. This commercial screamed the message: adults with intellectual and developmental disabilities are children. NO! STOP IT! This perpetuates an old myth that people with intellectual and developmental disabilities are eternal children - a myth which has caused so much overprotection and denial of rights that we need to make sure not to allow such messages to exist. And yet, there it was, in my own living room - staring at me from across the room and reminding me that we have so much work to do! Adults with disabilities will not have full lives and freedom in this world if we believe they are eternal children. Please call these things out when you hear or see them. For organizations: When you are preparing any media presentations, consider seriously what messages you are giving about people with disabilities and their families. You have a duty and an obligation to "do no harm" and to respectfully portray the people you support.

Often, when someone says they work with people with disabilities they are told, "Oh, you must be so special. I could never do that kind of work." As advocates for human rights and equality, we must be thoughtful about how we respond. If we say, "Thank you" or "Yes, not everyone can do this work," we are joining them on the bus of bad assumptions. It doesn't take a special person to support other people. It can be fun and meaningful. People with disabilities are more like us than different. Pay attention to the messages you are giving when you talk about your work. An alternative response might be, "It doesn't take someone special to work with other people, it takes someone human." Are you portraying yourself as wonderful for helping 'these poor people'?

Are you portraying people with disabilities as fully human and capable? If not, stop and think about changing the words you are saying. Words matter…they can harm, or they can help. Be sure that your words help.

Another dangerous message is that people with disabilities are suffering and should be pitied. People do not want to be pitied. People want to be respected. Think about some of the stories in this book. Can you recognize the difference between pity and respect? I remember watching TV with a person I was traveling with and someone on the TV said, "suffers with a disability" and my travel partner said very confidently, **"Ummm, NO! I don't suffer from my disability. I suffer from your attitude about my disability."** The distinction here is very important. Be aware. Be open to change. Be respectful.

In her book, *Sitting Pretty: The View from My Ordinary Resilient Disabled Body*, (2021), * Rebekah Taussig has an entire chapter on The Complications of Kindness. It is eloquently written and very much related to what I call Dangerous Benevolence, although much more raw and thought provoking. I highly recommend her book to anyone who wants or needs to learn more about how our words and actions can affect people with disabilities.

Questions for the Reader:

1. If you work with people with disabilities (or other marginalized communities), consider the reasons why you do this work. What are the reasons?
2. Think about the last time you explained your work to someone else. How did you describe the people you work with? How did you describe yourself?
3. What are some examples of dangerous benevolence you have engaged in or witnessed?
4. What can you safely do if you observe or witness an act of dangerous benevolence?

As we end this chapter on words and labels, I encourage all of us, including me, to be aware of the words that we use. It is a choice. None of us are perfect at this. Be open to learning. Be open to apologizing when you make a mistake. Be open to how others feel about certain words. Be open to having difficult conversations about words and labels. It is worth our discomfort to get it right.

In the words of Maya Angelou:

"Do the best you can until you know better. Then when you know better, do better."

That's all any of us can do. I believe that is enough.

Chapter 9

Trauma and Recovery

"To imagine yourself in the future is a radical act of hope."   Suleika Jaoued

"We are not meant to stay wounded. Wounds are the means through which we enter the hearts of other people. They are meant to teach us to become compassionate and wise." Carolyn Myss

The Scoop

In 1973, a woman was given a cold shower when she urinated on herself. No one knew if she had a medical reason for her incontinence. No one knew if she had a trauma history which contributed to her incontinence. She was punished with a cold shower. Punishment is NEVER the answer. The shock of a cold shower can increase physical stress and would rarely be helpful to most medical conditions. If she had a trauma history, the cold shower would be retraumatizing, as being forced to take a cold shower is traumatic in and of itself. In this situation, there was not even a possibility of a trauma-informed response.

In the mid-nineties, a caseworker attended a workshop on violence in the lives of people with disabilities. She heard that elective mutism was an indicator of violence. Elective mutism is when someone can talk, but they do not. She had met with a long-lost family member of a person she was supporting named Laura. The family told her that Laura talked throughout her childhood and as a young adult. Laura had not spoken since beginning services at the agency over 20 years prior. She did what she was told and went along with all routines and instructions…except for one thing. The agency had tried for years to get Laura to eat her meals using utensils. Laura ate with her hands and very quickly. No programs had ever changed the way she ate. Following the training, the caseworker wondered if Laura stopped talking because of a history of violence. The caseworker contacted me and asked if I would meet with Laura.

When I met with Laura, I thanked her for meeting with me. I told her that I helped people who had been hurt. I told her I would like to help her and that if she didn't want to meet with me, that was okay. It was her choice. She stared at me and nodded. I asked her if it was okay if I ask her some questions. She nodded. I said, "I'd like to get to know you. Can you tell me something about yourself?" She nodded. I waited. After a minute of silence, I said, "I know you haven't talked in a long time, and you don't have to talk to me. Your Aunt says that you were very close to your mother. Is that true?" Laura nodded. I said, "I was sorry to hear that your mother died." Laura looked at me and nodded. "What did you call your mother?" Laura moved her eyes from me, put her head down and did not move. I waited. After a bit, Laura said quietly, "Mama." After a few seconds, I thanked Laura for telling me and said, "Do you want to tell me about her?" Laura said, "She loved me."

After that, Laura began telling me about her life. She had been sexually abused on a regular basis by a family member and was threatened that if she told her mom, the man would hurt her mom. Laura had never told anyone. When Laura's mother died, she stopped talking. Her safe person was gone. She grieved the loss of her mother as well as the sexual violations that informed her developmental years. She had learned to "Do as you're told" and "Don't tell". With Laura's permission, we met with her caseworker together and talked about ways that Laura could receive supportive services for her trauma.

I heard from the caseworker two more times after that day. The first call was to inform me that Laura had continued to use her voice to communicate. The caseworker said, "In fact, she talks so much and so fast, she is hard to

understand. I have referred her for speech therapy."
I cannot imagine not talking for over 20 years…but I
do believe that Laura had lots to say once she
found her voice again. The second call from the
caseworker went like this: "You know that Laura has
been on an eating program for many years. We
keep data daily. I was doing her monthly report and
noticed she has eaten with utensils every meal for
the past three weeks. Do you think this is related to
her telling her story and finding her voice?" All I
could honestly say was: "I don't know, but perhaps it
is."

In the early 2000's a woman in her 40's
moved from an institution to a group home in the
community. When I met her, she had no observable
friends. Most people kept their distance from her.
She would occasionally grab the breasts of female
staff members and twist hard. She sometimes put
her clean clothes in a pile on her bedroom floor and
urinated on them. Every night before bed, she
stuffed cotton socks in her vagina. Her primary form
of communication was her actions. The most
common response she received when she did these
things was criticism and yelling. What if the
grabbing of breasts was her way of saying, "This
has happened to me"? What if she urinated on her
clothes to communicate that her clothes had been

soiled by others without her permission? What if the stuffing of socks in her vagina was an act to protect herself at night from further sexual assault? If she had a trauma history, what recovery options were available to her?

I share these stories to express the importance of trauma in the lives of people with disabilities and the need for a new way of thinking about behavior, healing, and counseling.

Over the years, I have received hundreds of phone calls from organizations, support staff, and the family members of people with disabilities who were seeking help for people with trauma histories. So many times, there were no local options. In the past, many professionals did not believe that people with intellectual and developmental disabilities could benefit from counseling. While this has gotten better over the years, it is still a challenge to find competent people who are comfortable and confident in counseling people with intellectual and developmental disabilities.

Let me be clear, not everyone who experiences trauma would choose counseling as an option for recovery, but I believe it should be an available option for survivors of sexual assault and other traumatic events. I believe that rape crisis centers and domestic violence programs that provide counseling to survivors in their communities should serve survivors with disabilities as well. Some of them do. Some of them believe they do. Many times, there are restrictions and barriers. I believe those barriers can be overcome. I am **not** an advocate for having 'specialized" counselors just for people with disabilities. How do we make sure existing counseling resources include the community of people with disabilities? What happens when that "Specialized" person leaves? One woman told me, "I don't want a special counselor. I want a good counselor. I want someone who can help me with my trauma, not my disability."

I spent years providing counseling and recovery services to people with intellectual and developmental disabilities…one person at a time. And together, we created goals and strategies for healing. I worked with families and support staff on being trauma-informed and supporting people in recovery. I learned from every person I worked with. But that did not make it any easier for the masses of people with intellectual and developmental disabilities to access recovery services when they wanted them. So, I channeled my energy into incorporating trauma and recovery into my trainings and consultations. My goal was to share some of the strategies I had learned from survivors and encourage recovery experts to be comfortable and confident in working with everyone, including people with intellectual and developmental disabilities.

From my experience in trying to access community-based recovery services for people with significant disabilities who have experienced violent acts, there are three main barriers that get in the way. One is the general attitude of families and providers that the person with the disability could not benefit from the service. The second barrier is that a non-disability specialist would not know how to work with the person with a disability. The third barrier is that many counselors feel they lack the skills to work with someone who does not express themselves in a traditional manner. I have often been told by deeply passionate counselors, "I would like to help but I would not know what to do. I must first "do no harm" to anyone."

I believe that the most effective way for counselors to feel more comfortable and confident in working with survivors who have disabilities is to have personal contact with people with disabilities. Some engagement activities which have helped with this include:

1. People with disabilities can provide training to staff at victim service organizations on how to work with survivors with disabilities.
2. Educators from victim service organizations can conduct training to people with disabilities and then shares stories about their positive experiences with their colleagues. One educator convinced her co-worker to provide counseling to someone who disclosed after a class saying, "Oh, you can work with Melissa, I know you can!"
3. People with disabilities can help to provide training to victim services counselors and school counselors on what they need for counseling to be beneficial.
4. Counselors can be invited to a self-advocacy group meeting to talk about their services and answer questions.
5. Counselors can visit an empowerment group of women with disabilities to discuss trauma and agency services.
6. A Counselor from a victim services organization could serve on a Human Rights Committee within a disability agency.
7. A victim service organization may recruit people with disabilities to serve as volunteers, trainers, employees, and/or board members with their organization.

8. Representatives from a disability organization, along with persons they support, could provide an Inservice to a victim services organization about their disability services and the referral process.

People with disabilities have a long history of oppression, segregation, institutionalization, marginalization, and discrimination. While we have made progress, this history makes it difficult for the general public to have regular exposure to people with disabilities. Consider what actions you can take to increase your exposure and you will simultaneously increase your comfort and confidence. This recommendation is in no way implying that if you meet one person with a disability, you know and understand all people with disabilities. All people are unique. Expanding your exposure will make your work, and your life, more inclusive and probably more interesting and fun. I believe deeply that being more inclusive is an honorable goal and benefits everyone.

The Space in Between:

I believe that there is an in-between space that survivors experience -

the space between when the violence stops

and the person really feels safe again...

the space between feeling like a victim

and knowing you are a survivor and
even a thriver....

the space between being controlled

and reclaiming your own power...

The work that each of you do is so important during this in-between space - you can make a trauma-informed down payment on a person's future in their healing. You are like a bridge between what has been done through violence - and the life the survivor wants to have. Always remember that what you DO and DON'T DO makes a difference. It can be incredibly helpful, or it can be harmful. Whether you are a family member, a friend, a teacher, a disability professional, a crisis line worker, a police officer taking a report, a nurse or doctor doing a forensic exam, a prosecuting attorney, or someone else in victim services – WHAT YOU DO MATTERS! IT MATTERS EVERY SINGLE TIME!

If you are a survivor living in this in-between space, find someone who will listen and be supportive. You deserve to be safe. You deserve to be listened to and heard. You deserve the opportunity to heal from what has happened. You are more than the harmful things that have happened to you. Know that this space is temporary and that you have the right to make choices that can lead you to a space of safety and healing.

There is a learning curve when we learn to do new things. Be patient with yourself. Know that you do not have to be perfect. I have made mistakes along the way and because I entered the relationship with intention and awareness, I was able to apologize sincerely, repair the situation, and move forward with greater awareness. You can do that too.

The in-between space can be successfully traveled on the road towards surviving and thriving. We may meet one another at any point on this journey, and our shared experience at that time can be life-giving for everyone. I thank the people who want to learn more about how to support people with disabilities who experience sexual violence; your commitment to caring, learning, and doing the right thing is evident if you are taking the time to read this and similar writings, and learning to be humble and sensitive to each person's needs. I thank the people who are currently living in this in-between space; thank you for your courage, your resilience, and your willingness to trust others to walk this road by your side. I thank the people who have made it through this space; your light shines in the distance and reminds us to stay the course, proving that there is indeed life beyond the in-between.

Broken Hearts and Healed Hearts

The people I worked with in response to their sexual violence and other traumas, understood the fact that their hearts had been hurt by the person or people who had harmed them. In communicating about the heart, I would place my hand or fist over my heart whenever I said the word heart. I also used pictures of hearts to expand the communication. Many people did not have language to express their emotions and this 'heart' language was very helpful in supporting that skill. One of the most useful tools I used with lots of people is the heart chart.

My Heart Chart

Things that help

Things that hurt.

One use for the heart chart is for the person in recovery to be able to tell the people in their life what helps and what hurts in terms of their recovery. Several people chose to present their heart chart to family members and/or support staff. One person chose to have their heart chart posted in the kitchen of their group home. When a staff member or housemate did something that hurt their feelings, they would go to their chart and point to the broken heart. Prior to this point in their life, their typical response to having their feelings hurt was to yell, threaten or throw things. When someone did something helpful or made them happy, they would point to the whole heart and thank them. The heart chart gave them an avenue to express their feelings in a clear and constructive manner.

Some people have taken their heart charts to their annual Individual Service Planning meeting. They explained about the hurtful and helpful things and wanted everyone to know how to help them. Some heart charts had words about the hurtful and helpful things and others had pictures. It is a very individualized process and can take more than one session to complete. It is also a fluid tool that can be revised as people learn new things that help and hurt.

I worked with one man for several months. He had built many walls to protect himself from further harm and to claim his power. I respected his pace, his process, and his inner power. When I would have things on the table, he would often point to them and say, "I'm not doing that." I would say, "Okay. I will leave it here. Let me know if you change your mind."

One of the things on the table was a red paper, heart-shaped doily. It was very lacey and fragile. One day, he pointed to the heart and said, "What's that for?" I asked him if I could pick it up and show him. He said "yes." I gently picked it up and said, "This is like your heart. We have to treat it gentle, so it doesn't get hurt. Are you ready to take good care of your heart?" He very carefully took it from my hand and held it against his chest and said, "I can take good care of my heart. Can I take it home?" And I said, "Yes, you can take it home. It is your heart." The next time we met, he told me that he was taking good care of his heart and that he had hidden his heart in his room so no one would find it and tear it. I told him that he could show his heart to safe people when he was ready. Every time we met; he would tell me that he was taking good care of his heart. This was just one part of our work together, but a central one.

NOTE: Heart doilies are on sale at party shops every year after valentine's day.

Mirror Work

Mirror work is a healing process that can be used to help someone strengthen their self-concept and feelings of worthiness. The process involves having a person look into a mirror while saying specific words. I have personally done mirror work in my own recovery, so wondered if it might be valuable for some people that I worked with. I noticed that many of the people I knew with intellectual and developmental disabilities did not seem to look in the mirror very often. I observed people combing their hair without looking in the mirror and found that curious. I had a few theories: perhaps they had not seen other people use mirrors; perhaps they had not been taught to use a mirror; perhaps someone else provides their personal care; perhaps the mirrors in their home are not low enough for someone who uses a wheelchair; and/or perhaps they did not like what they saw when they looked in the mirror. And of course, there can be a combination of reasons and the reasons would vary for different people.

There are three main ways that I incorporated mirrors into my work with survivors with disabilities.

1. This is something I learned from Orieda Horn Anderson. A two-sided mirror compact can be used to explain the counseling process. Before using this, carefully break the mirror on one side. When the compact is open, one side is broken, and one side is whole. The broken side is used to represent how we feel when someone has hurt us, and the intact side is used to represent how we feel when our heart

is healed. I used this on several occasions during an initial session with a survivor of violence. The process goes something like this:

> I would open the compact and hold the broken side up for the person to see and ask them to look in the mirror. I would tell them, "When someone rapes us (hits us, etc.), we feel hurt and broken. Like you see in the mirror." I would provide time and space for the person to process that message and provide support as needed. Clinical judgment is used to determine the timing of the next step.
>
> Then I would turn the mirror around and say, "If you want to, we can work together so you can feel safe again; feel okay again. Like you see in this mirror." I would provide time and space for the person to process the message and then ask if the person wants to work together.

This process provides a pathway to recovery and holds space for healing.

2. Another way I have used mirrors in recovery work is to practice self-awareness and positive identity during our sessions. I have a beautiful, ornate, hand-held, heart-shaped mirror that I used specifically for this purpose. I might hand the mirror to someone and ask them to look at themselves. And then I would ask them, "What do you see?" The answer is very telling. One man immediately said with a confident voice, "UGLY!" But over time, he was able to see his wonderful smile and his beautiful eyes.

For some people I worked with, the answers were concrete, like ugly or pretty. For others, they would mention the pain or the fear in their eyes. As always, the work is flexible and person-centered. One woman I worked with adamantly refused to look in the mirror, which of course, was okay with me. I would have the mirror on my desk face down when we met but never asked her again to look in it. I was honoring her decision. One day she said that when she could look in the mirror, she would know she was doing better. And that day did arrive - in her own time, as it should be.

3. I have introduced mirror work as a homework assignment or as an aspect of someone's treatment or service plan. In that situation, the person would practice stating positive self-statements while looking in the mirror. The statements would be individualized, and the person would help to craft each statement. I have seen much success with this strategy in helping people feel better about themselves. There are so many negative messages for people with disabilities, this practice can help to strengthen the person's immunity toward negative people and systems. NOTE: This is only effective as part of a person's service plan if it is a self-report practice. I hate the idea of staff standing and watching this (unless the person wants them to) and recording it on a service plan data sheet.

Advice From a Yoga Instructor

I was in Washington State one night training Special Education professionals and parents of students who attended Special Education classes. After the session, a mother shared this story with me that reinforces the value of mirror work as a 'protective factor' in the lives of people with disabilities.

"I am a yoga instructor, and my son is on the autism spectrum. I have taught him to look in the mirror every morning and say,

'I am love. I am light. I am peace.

I have a light inside of me that no one can take away.

I am love. I am light. I am peace.'

He does it first thing every morning. I do not have to remind him. It sets the pace for his day."

I want to be clear; this practice was developed as an 'immunization' from harm, not as a treatment after harm has occurred. I love what this mother has done and is doing with her son. This mom also teaches yoga classes for people with disabilities and is excited to share the wonderful responses she has observed. I believe we can all use our gifts, talents, passions, etc. to contribute to others in some meaningful way.

Other Things to Consider

It is important to incorporate a variety of learning and communication modalities into the therapeutic process. This includes pictures, videos, music, words, writing, movement, role playings, tactile exercises, storytelling, symbolism, gestures, facial expression, and others. Combining sensory processes can be very effective with people who use atypical communication. I frequently had pipe cleaners and a slinky available when I met with people. These items add a tactile and a visual element to whatever is being said. More details about this, as well as other strategies are available in the Illinois Imagines *Counseling Survivors with Intellectual Disabilities or Autism Guide.* *

Sandy

Supporting survivors of trauma who have disabilities typically requires support outside of a one-on-one therapeutic relationship. I met Sandy at the request of an organization a few hours away from my home. The organization wanted ideas on how to improve her life and the life of those who worked with her. I was told that Sandy was sexually aggressive with others and that her aggression was sudden and unpredictable. I spent three days at the organization. On day one, I spent the day getting to know Sandy in her work setting. We spent a few hours together and I interviewed the staff who worked closely with her. Later that day, I visited Sandy at her group home. By the time I returned to the hotel, this is what I knew:

1. Sandy expressed herself with gestures, facial expressions, shaking her head yes and no, pointing to pictures, and making sounds, but no words.
2. Sandy had excellent receptive language skills - she understood what was being communicated and was very observant.
3. Day program staff reported that Sandy had no friends or close family members. Staff were frustrated with her aggression and kept their distance, when possible.
4. Staff at her home reported that Sandy always kept the bathroom and bedroom doors open and had no concept of private activities or locations. Sandy liked to be around others but had no close relationships.
5. There was no documentation of trauma in her record.
6. Sandy was responsive to everything I asked her to do; spending time with me, looking at pictures, pointing to choices I presented, laughing when I made a funny mistake, and

she came and found me at the end of her day program to smile and wave goodbye.

The next morning, I met with Sandy again. She came in with a smile and patted my arm. I told her that I help people who had problems. I told her that many people with disabilities have been hurt by others. Her smile disappeared. She looked me right in the eyes and nodded. I told her I had a video about people who have been hurt and asked her if she wanted to see it. She put her head down and was very quiet. I waited silently. And then she patted my arm and pointed to the TV. We positioned ourselves in front of the TV, sitting side by side. I told her part of the video was sad and we could stop it whenever she told me to stop. I showed her the sign for 'stop' and she practiced it. I originally had no intention of showing her the video but noticed it in my bag and followed my instincts. It was not created for people with disabilities, and I had never shown it except in staff training.

You're gonna make it * is a rap music video starring J. Saint and Kelly B; created by the Pennsylvania Coalition Against Rape and now available on you tube.

The song is about sexual assault and the hope for recovery. She watched and listened with total focus and then suddenly began making mournful sounds while pointing at the TV and pointing to herself. Tears streamed down her face. When it was over, she continued to cry and grabbed my hand. She then looked at me and pointed to herself. I said, "Someone hurt you?" and she nodded yes. I told her I was sorry. She looked at me. I told her it was not her fault. She kept looking at me. I told her "You are very brave to tell me." She held my eyes. We sat there for several seconds and then I asked her, "Can I help you?" And then she released my hand and put her arm around my neck. It was a breakthrough moment and not a time to work on boundaries.

Sandy and I spent the day together. We established a way for her to communicate safe and unsafe to me without anyone else knowing. We practiced this with photos and scenarios and then walked through the day program areas. I wanted her to identify anyone who made her feel unsafe or scared. We did a similar practice with the residential staff. We used pictures for the staff who were off that day. After feeling confident that she was safe with the current people in her life, we began working on ways that Sandy could understand and respect boundaries - both her own and others. We used pictures for 'private' from the Mayer-Johnson

Boardmaker picture program. We put a laminated picture for 'private' on her bedroom door and the bathroom door at her home.

During day three, Sandy and I did a cursory assessment of things she enjoyed. I wanted to understand what brought joy into her life. I also wanted our last day together to feel hopeful to her. It appeared that she really enjoyed doing fun things with other people. Sandy and I talked about friendships and together listened to some music about friends. I taught her the sign for 'friend'. She approximated the sign and smiled. I explained to Sandy (with words and gestures) that when she grabbed people's breasts or vulva area - she hurt them…their bodies and their hearts. …like she had been hurt. She looked sad. We used feelings pictures to support her understanding of empathy. She pointed to herself and signed 'friend' and pointed to the happy picture. I told her I wanted her to have more friends. She smiled. I had no idea if this would make any difference to her or not, but I had to plant the seed. The person I had spent three days with did not seem to want to hurt other people.

I worked with her support staff and the clinical supervisor about providing Sandy with a trauma-informed response to her trauma. We worked on some schedule changes and some specific responses to teach privacy, boundaries, and to expand her enjoyable activities and her connections with others. I spent the last few minutes at the organization with Sandy, before I drove back home.

A few weeks later I received an email from Sandy's support staff. I saved the email for many years, but no longer have it. The email said something like this:

> Sandy's life has changed dramatically since you were here. She has had no instances of aggression, she respects her own and other's privacy, and she now has some friends! We are hopeful these positive changes will last.

Following my initial time with Sandy, I occasionally worked at that agency again. As I entered the building and was signing in, Sandy would come around the corner, point to me and say hi with her smile and gestures. Staff assured me they had not told her I was coming. I am not sure how she knew I was there, but one thing I do know for sure is that we shared a lasting connection that had meaning in both of our lives.

Victoria

Victoria lived in a group home with seven other people. In fact, it was one of her housemates that suggested that they call me to see if I could help. I was told, "Victoria gets up during the night and crawls down the hall screaming, crying, and stripping. She wakes up the entire house." Some of the staff believed that Victoria was doing this for attention. The typical response was to tell her to stop. She was called rude and attention-seeking. This occurred several times per month and seemed to be increasing. These situations lasted several minutes. I agreed to see Victoria if they could drive her to the town where I lived.

I remember Victoria as being a quiet and gentle person. We spent some time getting to know each other. I told her that I help people who have been hurt by other people. I saw the pain in her eyes when she spoke about her history of being bullied and of being sexually assaulted. I did not push for details, just listened as she shared what she chose to share.

When asked about sleep, she sat quietly for a while and then said, "I'm sorry I wake them up." She shared that she had nightmares about the people who hurt her, and she tries to get away from them.

We talked about what might help her when this happens. After that, and with Victoria's permission, we met with the support staff and together shared what Victoria wanted to happen when she had these nightmares. Her support staff agreed to the plan and all of the staff were trained to follow this procedure:

> When Victoria wakes at night screaming, crying, or crawling down the hall, a staff member is to quietly bend down and say, "Victoria, this is (name), You are at (name of home). You are safe. I will stay with you and make sure you are ok." Repeat as necessary. If Victoria had exposed her breasts or genital area while she was screaming and crawling down the hall, staff would offer to cover her with a sheet as soon as possible. After Victoria has calmed, staff would gently help her to put her clothes on as needed and offer her a cup of hot tea. They would then sit with her at the dining room table. Victoria would decide when she was ready to return to bed and what she needed to feel safe (night light, soft music, door ajar, etc.).

The staff did an excellent job in following the plan and almost immediately the episodes lasted less than a minute. I saw Victoria a few more times so she had an opportunity to process what happened to her and to build her sense of safety, power, and connection. Together, Victoria and I also developed some 'safe sleep' strategies and soon her nightmares were rare.

The Trust Walk-- Beyond Talk Therapy

Jay had no reason to trust anyone, including himself. He had a lifetime of moving from one place to another, each filled with hurtful experiences. He had learned that taking things from others gave him a false sense of value and that lying reduced negative consequences - well, some of the time. He had learned that his feelings did not matter and that others could hurt him and get away with it. Life went on, day by day like a continuous loop of rerun movies. Some of the movies were boring and mundane; others were of the horror variety. But then, the pause button was pushed when an outstanding staff member at his home discovered he had a history of being sexually assaulted. I had worked with this organization previously and the staff member called to see if I could help. A couple weeks later, this staff member drove Jay to the town where I worked. My practice in this type of situation, was to meet with the person and then to invite the support person to join us. After we finished our work together, I would plan with the person what they wanted to share with their support person. The joint meeting typically focused on what the person wanted and needed to feel better (heal). The person shared what they were safe and comfortable sharing. Their decision.

I saw Jay alone for three or four sessions and I could clearly see and feel his lack of trust in me and in himself. I had made a couple of observations that led me to try something I had never done before (and never did again). I noticed that he was very kinesthetic – he was calmer when he was moving, whether he was walking or tapping his fingers or manipulating pipe cleaners. I also noticed that he was curious about people with visible disabilities like someone who used a wheelchair or someone who was blind. When I would meet him in the waiting area of the building, he would tell me things like, "I saw a blind person in the waiting room. What do you think it is like to be blind?" So, this is what we did, with his permission of course. We went into the hallway, and I pretended I was blind and needed his help to walk through the hallways. I put my hand on his elbow, closed my eyes and he guided me safely through the large rectangular shaped hallways back to the room where we had been meeting. I thanked him for keeping me safe. And then we traded places. He put his hand on my elbow, closed his eyes and I guided him safely through the hallways. Back in the room, we talked about what it was like to let someone keep us safe when we could not see where we were going. I have to be honest with you, as the reader; I had a hard time keeping my eyes closed. These hallways were not empty, and I could hear people walking and talking and just how well did I really know Jay? I resisted the temptation though and kept my eyes closed for him. I wanted him to know he could be trusted.

This 20-minute exercise shifted everything. At the end of our session that day, when his support staff joined us, Jay excitedly told her about our walking experience. He ended with, "I kept Shirley safe. Shirley kept me safe." After that day our work together was a beautiful dance. He learned quickly that he did not have to steal things or lie to be cared for and to feel his value. He began expressing his feelings and exploring things that made his heart smile. He taught his staff what he liked and what he needed to heal and feel whole. And it all started with a walk through the hallways.

Some more things to consider:

In working with people with intellectual and developmental disabilities who have experienced trauma, it is important to consider the little traumas (little t's) as well as the Big Traumas (Big T's). The little t's add up, accumulate, and can affect a person as much or more than a Big T. Some people I have supported have expressed profoundly deep pain about being bullied because of other people's view of their disability. For many people, the name-calling, exclusion, and bullying began in childhood; continued throughout their developmental years and into and throughout their adulthood. These emotional scars can last a lifetime and make additional traumas more complex. Do not assume that the physical and/or sexual violence impacts a person more than bullying and name-calling. For some people, the emotional trauma is worse. One person with a long history of sexual violence and painful neglect, told me being called the 'R word' in front of other people was by far the worst trauma in his life.

Remember: we do not know what another person's inner experience is from a situation unless we find out from them. It is theirs to share, or not share. Two people in the same situation can have very different responses. It is important that we do not make assumptions about other people and their experiences. It is equally important to honor the fact that there are many pathways to healing. Each survivor deserves to be actively involved in what works and does not work for them.

Questions for the Reader:

1. I believe that everyone in a person's life can support their recovery. What role might you play?

2. Have you ever experienced the 'space in-between' something traumatic and feeling ok? What was your experience like? What did you find helpful?

3. In what situation could you use a heart chart in your own life or with someone you care about?

4. What are your thoughts about the benefit of counseling for people who do not use spoken words?

5. What are some therapeutic ways you could use pipe-cleaners as an expressive tool when working with someone who has experienced trauma?

Chapter 10

Post-Traumatic Growth

"If you wanna fly, you got to give up the shit that weighs you down." Toni Morrison

"May the stars carry your sadness away, may the flowers fill your heart with beauty, may hope forever wipe away your tears…." Chief Dan George

Paula

When I was preparing to meet Paula for the first time at her apartment, I was told that she was one of the most difficult people that program had ever supported. When staff went to her apartment, she would slam the door shut on them, spit in their faces, cuss and threaten them, etc. They also said she hoarded everything and that roaches filled the space. She had been evicted from several apartments due to the hoarding and possible fire hazards it created.

I was excited to meet her. I wondered what was behind her anger and hoped she would be open to sharing it with me. I began meeting with Paula and rarely experienced the door slamming and swearing responses that had been described to me. Rather, she shared many other parts of herself. She told me several times that when she died no

321

one would come to her funeral. I promised her that if she died before me; I would be at her funeral. Over time, she began to share parts of her story with me. Her parents had been rich and held status in the community. When they had company, Paula would be locked in the basement. They did not want anyone to know they had a child with a disability. She would cling to the locked door and listen for the sounds of the activities upstairs from which she was excluded. I wondered how that made her feel. When I asked her, she replied, "Sad. Mad really. But I loved my dad."

After I first met Paula, I saw her intermittently over a two to three-year time period. I received a call when she was evicted from her latest apartment and was asked to go and help her accept the situation. It was not her first eviction, and it was never an easy process. It was a traumatic day for her. She had only a few hours to have all her things moved out of that apartment and moved somewhere else. She did not want to part with anything, including old pizza boxes and half emptied food containers. All of her 'stuff' provided Paula with a sense of comfort; comfort that she desperately needed. She spent much of the day crying and screaming. The clock did not allow her an easy process, and yet, her resilience kicked in and she moved to her new place with less than half of the things she had before. The staff did an amazing job of finding her another place to live. I provided what support I could.

The last time Paula was evicted from an apartment … she fired her support agency and moved to a shelter for women and children experiencing homelessness. So, literally, Paula moved out of the business of being a client needing support and into the space of an independent community person participating in a community program that is not specifically for people with disabilities. Like many shelters, this one had a lot of expectations she had to agree to before moving in, and she totally rose to the occasion!!

Paula called me every few weeks to 'check in'. She consistently reported how wonderfully she was doing. One time she told me that she was 'saved' and had been baptized. (Neither the agency nor I had ever known she was interested in spirituality). Another time she told me that she was looking for a job working with children. (We never knew she liked children.) The last time we talked, she said she was very happy and preparing to move out. I had never heard her say she was happy before.

I suggested we go to lunch and celebrate. I was leaving town the next day for work and told her I would call when I got back so we could set up a time to get together. When I returned to town and called her to arrange our lunch celebration, I discovered that it was too late. Paula had unexpectedly passed away.

When I arrived at the funeral home, I was thrilled to see that the room was full of people. I said in my mind, "Paula do you see this? You were so loved!"

Person after person got up and talked about how much Paula had helped them - by watching their children while they went to court…or making them feel comfortable when they moved into the shelter. Story after story shed light on this beautiful woman who had finally risen above her decades of trauma. Her light had shined brightly on the lives of so many! When I first met Paula, she had drawn a thick circle around herself that kept everyone out. I believe that she pushed people away before they had a chance to reject her. When Paula moved to the shelter, love drew a bigger circle that included Paula. She had found her true self, shared her love, and discovered her purpose.

Paula is an example of someone who experienced post-traumatic growth. She had moved beyond the trauma in her life and experienced positive outcomes in the areas of personal strengths, positive relationships and meaning. In Paula's life, it took decades for her to leave behind her childhood trauma and repeated adult traumas...but she got there. I cannot express in words how pleased I am that she spent the last part of her life in a happy and peaceful space where she was truly accepted, appreciated, and loved.

I began this chapter with a bit of Paula's story because I think she is a good example of someone who experienced Post-Traumatic Growth. To my knowledge, there are no studies or written articles about Post-Traumatic Growth in people with disabilities. I hope there will be in the future.

Post-traumatic growth - flourishing - is growth following adversity in three main areas: relationships, personal strength and meaning. I will address each of these and why I believe Paula experienced each one.

Relationships with others:

Trauma teaches us to close our hearts and armor up! Healing teaches us to open our hearts and boundary up! When our trauma is relationship-based - we need to experience positive, safe, and trusting relationships to heal. A person with a history of trauma needs at least one trusting person to help them feel safe enough to go through a healing process…to open their heart…allow the armor to come down…and to develop boundaries to keep them safe. One person to be with them through the process - that can be enough. We can learn to accept support…we can learn to identify and express feelings and use our feelings to establish boundaries…learning to trust our own intuition! We can also learn to have empathy and compassion - we may begin to realize that everyone suffers and to see people in a different light. This is what I believe happened when Paula went to the shelter. I never had the opportunity to discuss this with her, but it fits with what I observed in our phone conversations and with the statements made by others at her funeral. The other women at the shelter and the shelter staff loved and appreciated Paula and I believe that Paula loved and appreciated them. Paula experienced healing from her relationship-based trauma through these new loving, supportive relationships!

Personal Strengths:

When someone realizes that they have survived a trauma or multiple traumas - it can lead to a sense of inner strength - and a knowing that you can do hard things and handle difficult situations. I believe that Paula learned this when she was surrounded by other people with trauma histories and apparent resiliency. I believe that she felt less alone and not like such an outcast. I believe that when she experienced so many relationships of 'equal power', she was empowered to find her own strengths. I believe she felt so loved and accepted that she no longer felt a need to push others away. I believe that she experienced a new appreciation for life and learned to control her emotions and make new and healthier choices in her life.

Meaning:

Before Paula went to the women and children's shelter, her life was just about survival. I often wondered how she found the courage to get up every day and put one foot in front of the other. The weight of her trauma was so heavy, I could feel it when we were together. When it became too heavy, she would yell, spit, throw things, slam doors, and run away. Her pain was transformed through her experiences at the shelter. For many people, a central part of finding meaning and purpose, is spiritual development. Paula had discovered a spiritual path that worked for her - a power greater than herself which she found comforting and healing. Her spirituality allowed her to manage life's ups and downs with a faith that 'things were going to work out'. The mental, spiritual, and emotional shifts she experienced helped her to acquire a sense of hope about her future possibilities, and she gained a sense of compassion for others. This compassion for others opened the door to her love for children which led to her desire to work with children - she found meaning and purpose!

Post-traumatic growth typically refers to growth in a person that exceeds what was present before the trauma and a mental shift that occurs as a potential direct result of surviving a trauma. For many people this mental shift includes an awareness of new possibilities and a new sense of gratitude. For many of the people that I worked with (and myself) the initial traumas occurred at such a young age, there is no way to measure the 'pre-trauma' functioning. I believe it is critically important to include people with early childhood traumas in our study of and belief in post-traumatic growth. If we (the majority 'we' that write policies, administer funding, choose who get resources, etc.) don't think this kind of growth is possible, we won't support people in transforming their lives. We would just leave people stuck in their pain. That has happened for too many years. Let's stop doing that!

So, let's talk a bit about the agency that served Paula for several years before she fired them and went to the shelter. This was a reputable, not-for-profit organization with a mission to support people with disabilities to live full and meaningful lives. There were some areas in which the agency appeared to be successful with Paula - her health care, housing, psychiatric, and financial needs were addressed for many years. All areas in which the service standards are clearly stated and monitored. However, the ball was clearly dropped when it came to her spiritual and trauma-recovery needs. I do not think that this was a 'bad' organization. From my experiences in consulting/training, I would say this happens very frequently in organizations designed to support people with intellectual and developmental disabilities. I have seen some shifts over the years but there is much more work to do!

I want to share a few comments on why I think the ball got dropped in serving Paula in an agency for people with intellectual and developmental disabilities. There are many forces at work to keep systems in status quo. One example is that the funding sources focus on measurable goals and what they consider basic life skills. These are not at all focused on the whole person, or the vital parts of true joy in living that cannot be easily measured by steps and percentages. Another reason is the fact that the long history of oppression against people with disabilities continuously informs the public that people with disabilities are 'not like us'. So, we design services that keep power in the deliverers of service and not in the recipients. This is a major problem.

How can organizations support people with intellectual and developmental disabilities to 'recover' from trauma? How can direct contact staff and individual services coordinators support post-traumatic growth in the persons they support? From my experiences, here are a few of the factors that support growth following trauma.

Growth is supported when the survivor of trauma experiences:

> Access to a trained professional when desired/needed
> Attentive and compassionate listening
> Relationships that nurture and validate

> A sense of hope - things can get better
> Being informed
> Making choices
> Focusing on strengths instead of weaknesses
> Knowing that other people have experienced this, and over time have done well.
> Genuine acceptance from others
> Understanding their triggers and how to cope with them

These are supports that employees/families can provide to people with trauma histories.

Organizations will be better equipped to provide these trauma-informed responses to people with disabilities when:

> policies acknowledge the prevalence of trauma in the lives of people with disabilities and establish clear training and guidelines for employees
> standards of care include promising practices related to trauma and recovery
> people with disabilities are involved in policy development, employee hiring, training, evaluation

➤ people with disabilities are engaged in committees and boards which guide and inform organizational services and supports
➤ recovery services are equally accessible and culturally relevant for all people who experience trauma
➤ funding for disability services includes options for prevention of and recovery from trauma

Just because Paula found meaning and joy in her life, does not mean that the trauma she endured was not destructive. It does not mean that she did not suffer. It does not mean that she could just bounce back. It does not mean that she had a perfect life. Post-traumatic growth does not mean that the trauma experience was erased or was 'worth it' due to the final outcome. Some people do recover, thrive, and integrate their trauma experiences into a life of strength, growth, meaning and connectivity.

In summary:

Post-traumatic growth DOESN'T mean
- You won't get triggered again
- The trauma doesn't matter
- You won't get angry about injustice

- You forget what happened
- You don't want accountability
- You invite your abuser over for pie

Post-traumatic Growth DOES mean
- You feel stronger than before
- You can trust certain people
- You learn how to pay attention to your instincts (trust yourself)
- You appreciate life
- You feel you have something to contribute
- You can regulate your emotions most of the time

Questions for the reader:

1. What feelings did you experience in reading Paula's story?
2. Why do you think there are no studies of Post-Traumatic Growth that include people with disabilities?
3. What actions might you take to support the post-traumatic growth of someone you know?
4. If you work at an organization that provides services and supports to people with

disabilities, what steps can you take to support the post-traumatic growth of people supported by that organization? Are you willing to take these steps?

Rest in peace, Paula. Thank you for showing us that it is never too late to heal.

Chapter 11

Criminal Justice

"They shouldn't be able to abuse us and get away with it!"
Sexual assault survivor with disabilities

"It is not possible to be in favor of justice for some people and not in favor of justice for all people." Martin Luther King, Jr.

She's Not a Credible Witness

The first time a woman with disabilities told me about being sexually assaulted and that she wanted to call the police, she asked me to be with her when the police came. I sat quietly and watched as she poured her heart out. The officer was very kind as he asked questions. After a few minutes of questions and answers, the officer asked me to step out into the hallway for a minute. The conversation went something like this: "I think something happened to her, but there is nothing more I can do here. She is not a credible witness." I was shocked but said, "Okay." We returned to the room where the woman was waiting. The officer thanked the woman and left. I supported the woman the best way I could at the time. And then I became furious! I knew nothing about the criminal justice process, but I knew it had betrayed her because she had a disability. I knew she had no chance at justice. I also felt like I had let her down. I got busy and got educated. The next time I was told someone was not a credible witness, I would be ready. Never again, would having a disability be a justifiable reason not to pursue a criminal case. Not on my watch anyway!

In the Park

Renee took a taxi to and from the workshop that she attended five days a week. The taxi picked her up at home and dropped her off at a well-known agency that provided services to people with disabilities. The taxi then picked her up a few hours later and took her back home. One day, Renee came to see me. She told me that the taxi driver had done something bad to her and then shared the details. After I told her that what he did was against law, she said she wanted to call the police. An officer came to take a report. Renee explained what had happened and that the bad thing had happened in the taxicab at a park. She did not know the name of the park. The officer asked to speak with me alone. In the hall, he told me that he did not think Renee was a credible witness.

I asked the officer, "**What is it that you need that you don't have?**"

He said, "We don't know where this happened. I cannot investigate any further without knowing a location."

I replied, "I don't know the names of all the parks either. I bet she can show us which park it is. Can we take a ride in your car?"

The three of us piled into the car. Renee sat in the front passenger seat, and I sat behind her in the back seat. As we drove around town, Renee had her head lowered and would shake her head no and say 'no' as we arrived at the first couple parks. I watched from the back seat. As we approached the next park, Renee raised her head, sat erect, motioned her arms to the right and excitedly said, "Over here! Over here!" The officer pulled into the park. Renee showed the officer exactly where the taxi driver parked the car. A report was filed.

A few days later, Renee came to see me with two of her friends. They had been talking at lunch and discovered that the same driver had hurt all three of them. With their permission, I spoke with each person individually. The other two women also wanted to file criminal charges, and they did.

So, here is what happened. All three women had been sexually abused by the same person, at the same park, in the same parking spot. As it turned out, that side of the park was across the street from a row of several houses; some of which belonged to retired people who were at home during the day. The detective found several witnesses that identified the taxi at the park on several occasions. Each time, the taxi was parked in the same parking spot that Renee had reported.

This savvy detective was able to get a confession from the man who criminally assaulted these three women. Because of that, the women did not have to testify at the trial. The man was found guilty. The women all testified at the sentencing hearing and supported each other before, during and after the sentencing. The man who took the women to a park and assaulted them went to prison for his crimes. The three women each chose what supports they needed following the assaults and after the court proceedings. One woman requested family support and individual counseling. The counseling aspect of her supports began soon after she reported the assaults and continued over a year after the final court judgment.

Note: I have spoken with several people with developmental disabilities who have been sexually assaulted by taxi drivers. In every situation, the driver had invited the person to sit in the front seat with them. In most situations, it was like this: "sit up here with me, it will be easier for you to get in and out of the car". This was a step in the 'grooming process' the driver used. Another step was the driver putting their arm out when approaching a stop sign and 'accidentally' touching the passenger on or near a genital area over their clothes. This was typically followed by "I want you to be safe." Because of the frequency and similarity of these stories, it seemed important to share these with you.

Questions for the Reader:

1. What general feelings and thoughts did you experience reading this story?
2. What did this story illustrate about perpetrator tactics?

3. How might safety training include information about grooming? What examples might be helpful?
4. If you could say one thing to the three women who were assaulted - what would you say?

A Serial Rapist

There was a serial rapist in my community. Two very brave women had reported him to the police as the person who raped them. One woman went to trial and courageously told what he had done to her. It was a jury trial, and the defense attorney convinced the jury that she had traded sex for drugs and the man was acquitted (set free).

Another one of his victims saw his picture on the news and called the disability agency's crisis line in a panic. "That's him! That's him! That's the man who raped me!"

Go back 18 months. Georgia had attended Sunday night church services and taken the church bus back to her apartment. Several people got off the bus to enter the locked apartment building and an extra person slipped in behind the group. As Georgia approached her door with her key, a man asked if he could use her phone. Georgia said yes and he entered, pretended to use the phone, and then raped her. After he left her apartment, Georgia called the apartment manager who came over along with a police officer. Georgia told them what had happened. According to her, they did not believe her. When she stood up to escort them to her door to leave, they noticed she was bleeding - a lot! An ambulance was called. Following extensive treatment, a full report was taken, and a detective was assigned to the case. Who was this man who harmed her? That was the challenge. It was a scary time for Georgia. Would this dangerous man come back and hurt her again? Was it safe to leave her apartment? Would he find out where she worked? Would he hurt other people she cared about?

Fast forward 18 months. Because Georgia watched the news and saw his face on TV, and told others about that, the investigation could continue. Soon after the call to the crisis line, Georgia and I met with an Assistant State's Attorney. She told him what had been done to her. He asked questions and she answered. A few minutes later, he asked to speak with me alone. The Assistant State's Attorney was concerned that Georgia was not a credible witness. He felt like the defense attorney could easily make her look like a liar. I asked him **what he**

needed that he didn't have? He reported that she was hard to understand sometimes because she talked too fast (because of her anxiety) and that she had difficulty telling what happened in a sequential order. I asked if we could meet with her a little longer and I would observe and try to come up with a possible solution to his concerns. At the end of our meeting, he agreed to continue the investigation and I agreed to work with Georgia. A few days later, criminal charges were filed, and the man who raped Georgia was arrested.

Here are the accommodations that we worked out for the courtroom:

1. When questioning Georgia, the prosecutor (assistant state's attorney) would state part of the story and then ask what happened next? For example: "The strange man made a call using your phone. What happened next?" This would avoid any sequencing issues.
2. The prosecutor would avoid using he, she, and they pronouns as those tended to confuse Georgia and influence her response. In addition, he would point to her when he said the word you.
3. In the courtroom, Georgia would be given a white Styrofoam cup with water and the

prosecutor would have a white Styrofoam cup with water as well. When Georgia began speaking fast, the prosecutor would either ask Georgia if she wanted a drink of water or he would hold up his cup of water. The drink of water helped Georgia to calm down and speak slower.

Before court, Georgia and I worked together on a regular basis to practice 'the white cup of water' to help with her anxiety. From the first time we tried it, whenever she took a drink, she would say out loud to herself, "Calm down."

Whenever Georgia would talk about what happened to her, she would repeatedly say:

"I don't want to go to court. I don't want to see him. I am scared of him. But I got to do this. What if he rapes my mom? What if he rapes my sister? What if he rapes you, Shirley? I got to do this. He will keep hurting people. I got to do this."

I was in awe of her sense of justice and social responsibility. I was in awe of her courage. I still am.

Before going to court, we met again with the prosecutor. We also met with the Victim's Witness Coordinator and a Victim Advocate from the rape crisis center. When the court date was scheduled, Georgia, the prosecutor, the victim advocate, and I met in the courtroom where the trial would take place, prior to the actual date of the trial. Georgia sat in the witness stand. We practiced with the white cups. She learned where the man who hurt her and his lawyer would be sitting. She picked a spot for me to sit during her testimony - a spot away from the man who hurt her. She knew where the Judge would sit and where the jury would be. We answered all of her questions. She told us over and over again, she was doing this to help other women be safe.

Georgia was an incredible witness during her testimony. She was 'herself': the depth of her trauma was visible, and her honesty came shining through as she told what had happened to her.

When the defense attorney began his questioning, it was clear to everyone in the courtroom, except for Georgia, that he wanted to make her look like a liar. He tried the previously successful strategy of 'you wanted drugs and traded them for sex' defense. At one point, the defense attorney said, "excuse me a second" as he looked through some papers. Georgia, leaned forward, looked right at him and said, "It's okay, John. Just calm down."

I want you to picture this. Here is a high-powered defense attorney, trying to make Georgia look like a liar and she extends her heart to him. And how did she remember his name? I glanced at the jury and their faces were in disbelief; a few of them covered their smiles with their hands.

The defense questioning was grueling and difficult. Georgia remained calm and answered the questions confidently. And then we waited.

Georgia had survived the worst day of her life. She then courageously relived that day and told what happened to her as she faced her offender in a court of law. Because of her voice and her bravery, this man was found guilty and sentenced to 60 years in prison.

It was Georgia's decision whether or not to face the man who violently hurt her and testify in court. A team of people worked together to support her during the trail process.

When the verdict came down, the prosecuting attorney drove to Georgia's apartment so he could tell her about the verdict in person. This tough and compassionate man wanted to thank her for her service to our community.

A few weeks later, after the sentencing hearing, the rape crisis center held a celebration and Georgia made the list of people she wanted to invite. The list included two people from the States Attorney's Office: 'my attorney' and 'my investigator'. Georgia was told they would both be invited, but they may not come because they are so busy. Both came and everyone was surprised; well, except for Georgia. They were 'her people' and she knew they would come! We all made a circle and one by one, each person gave Georgia a balloon with a wish for her life: She received safety, peace, joy, connection, hope, love, smiles, gratitude, friendship, and lots of hugs (with consent)! It was a beautiful ceremony honoring a beautiful woman. Thank you, Georgia, for your bravery, your courage and for choosing to keep our community safer.

Questions for the reader:

1. Why do you think the States Attorney's Office decided to pursue justice in this situation?

2. What do you think the key factors may have been in the jury deciding that the person who assaulted Georgia should be found guilty?
3. Do you think that many people with disabilities can be credible witnesses in a court of law? Why or why not?
4. Discuss the use of accommodations in criminal cases.

Another strategy

Not everyone is a credible witness; not everyone with a disability and not everyone without a disability. When the police came to interview Carol, it seemed questionable if she would be able to or would choose to endure the stressful experience of pursuing justice through the court process.   Even though there were many questions here, it was absolutely clear that she deserved a chance for justice. When the officer proclaimed that she was not a credible witness and there was nothing else they could do, I asked him to interview the man who had hurt her. I told him: "If this was your daughter, sister or mother who had been assaulted, I know you would do everything in your power to get justice for them. Carol deserves justice too. Please go interview the man and maybe you will get a confession." It was important that the man who hurt Carol understand that people with disabilities can use their voices and that he should not get away with this crime. As it turns out, the perpetrator confessed and was found guilty. He was sentenced to several years' probation and his name went on the Sex Offender Registry.

Summary of strategies when credibility is questioned:

1. **Ask: "What do you need that you don't have?"** This moves the conversation from a preconceived notion about the person's disability to a specific aspect needed for the investigation to continue. This might be location, date, time, sequencing, understanding the person's communication and other things. Once the need is understood, all parties can work to find a solution.
2. **Personalize the crime.** Let the reporting or investigative entity understand that the victim could be someone that they care about or

love. "If this was your loved one, what would your next step be?"

3. **Suggest interviewing the reported perpetrator.** It is important that the person who hurt this victim not think that it was okay. If we stop here; they get away with an assault. You might suggest to the officer: "I know you are here to 'catch the bad guys'. Can you go and talk with the reported offender to see what he has to say?"

4. **Suggest trying to get a confession.** This can be combined with number three or used alone.

5. **Remember the Americans with Disabilities Act.** I have only used this one time and only after the above strategies did not work. I said something like this: "The Americans with Disabilities Act assures equal access to public services for people with disabilities - that includes the criminal justice response for victims with disabilities. If nothing else is done, this person does not have equal access. I know you don't want to have legal action against the city (or county). Let's talk about what can be done to assure this person's access to your services."

I share these strategies as they have worked. I hope they are helpful in your work to ensure justice for victims of violent crimes who have disabilities. Of course, you can come up with your own strategies.

The important thing is not to give up.

Resources for Law Enforcement and Prosecutors

In 2009, the Illinois Family Violence Coordinating Council received an "Arrest grant" from the United States Department of Justice Office on Violence Against Women. A portion of the budget was targeted to create protocols for law enforcement and prosecutors on working with adults with disabilities who experienced domestic violence. I was asked to facilitate this process. We put together a team of people to work on this big assignment, including representatives from:

- Illinois Family Violence Coordinating Council
- People with disabilities
- Illinois Self-Advocacy Alliance
- Illinois Coalition Against Domestic Violence
- Bureau of Sexual Assault and Domestic Violence

- Adult Protective Services/Department of Aging
- Illinois State Police
- Prosecutors within the State
- Lieutenant from community police department
- Attorney General's Office Disability Services
- Sexual Assault Services Manager
- Illinois Law Enforcement Training and Standards Board
- Illinois Network of Centers for Independent Living
- Blue Tower Training

This team met monthly with the goal of creating statewide protocols for law enforcement and prosecutors in responding to domestic violence against people with disabilities. It was important that we learn about each other's roles within the system as well as learn to trust each other. We had some fascinating discussions. One I want to share with you has stayed vivid in my mind and clearly demonstrates the value of having people with disabilities at the decision-making table. See what you think.

We were discussing evidence collection when the victim of a violent crime has a disability. Several people on the team had lots of detailed experience collecting physical evidence at a crime scene. We were all listening to the 'experts' when Hadley asked this question: "What if there is evidence on my wheelchair?" The experts described a process of collecting evidence and locking up her wheelchair in evidence. Hadley spoke up firmly and clearly, "You will never get my permission to keep my chair. I would be moved to a nursing home. I cannot do anything without my customized power chair. Taking my chair will cause me more harm than a rape. Plus, it cost me $27,000! Let's find another way to collect evidence off a wheelchair." And within a few minutes, with help from the state police, we had a solution which allowed a victim/survivor to keep their adaptive equipment or communication device following evidence collection! I believe if the protocols had been developed without input from people with disabilities, this would not have happened, and the protocols would not be as effective.

Once the protocols where completed, some of the team worked on the training curriculum. We the conducted five "Train the Trainer" sessions across Illinois. The audiences included teams from various parts of the state. The teams included representatives from law enforcement, prosecution, people with disabilities, victim services (sexual assault/domestic violence), Adult Protective

Services, and Centers for Independent Living. The goal was for this team to then be able to train others and customize the protocols for their individual jurisdictions.

The protocols, process for development and implementation, and lessons learned have been shared across the nation. A few years later, the Illinois protocols were updated and combined with the protocols for older adults in Illinois. *

In addition to the protocols, the team developed a sample Law Enforcement Accessibility Review tool. * This is a tool for law enforcement departments to determine how accessible their practices are for people with disabilities. The categories include; Accessibility/Accommodations, First Response, Investigations, Environment/Culture, Training, General Orders, Collaboration, and Trauma-Informed Practices. The tool has been informed by lieutenants and sergeants as well as by people with disabilities.

While we were out field testing the accessibility tool, a Sergeant said, "You know what would be really helpful? If you could provide a sample General Order." We asked, "What is a general order?" and we discovered that a General Order is the language used in law enforcement for their policies and procedures. So, we got a sample of some general orders and then created a sample general order * for use with law enforcement departments. This tool includes things such as training, pre-investigation, response at the scene, working with adults who have guardians, evidence collection, continuing investigation and working with victim services.

Some of the strategies that were included in the protocols and the training for both law enforcement and prosecutors included: undue influence, interview strategies, case examples of accommodations used effectively in court, credible witness and communication considerations, and examples of 'winnable cases'.

For prosecution, <u>vertical prosecution</u> is highly recommended for victims with disabilities. This is a process in which the same prosecutor from the State's Attorney's Office is assigned to the case from beginning to the end. This is helpful not only to the victim but also to the prosecutor. This consistency allows for improved communication, trust-building and overall understanding between both parties. This continuity also means the victim only has to tell their story of victimization to one prosecutor.

Evidence-based prosecution has been very useful in domestic violence cases, and I believe can also be useful in violent crimes against some people with disabilities. Evidence-based prosecution is when the prosecution bases a criminal case on evidence collected that does not include the testimony of the victim/survivor. Evidence-based prosecutions can also result in conviction and can be considered when the victim cannot testify.

Lessons learned:

1. Many, many people with disabilities are credible witnesses.
2. Some people need accommodations to participate fully in the criminal justice system.
3. When given the tools, including the right attitude, law enforcement and prosecutors can work effectively with victims with disabilities.
4. Cases involving victims with disabilities can be won in court.

Brenda Claudio

In 2013, Amy Walker and I were conducting a full day training in a mid-sized midwestern community. It was a mixed audience that included people from local disability agencies, rape crisis centers, and two prosecuting attorneys. This was the day I met Brenda Claudio, an Assistant State's Attorney. Brenda asked a few questions about a person with disabilities that she was representing in a sexual assault case. Over the next several months, we occasionally spoke on the phone about details of the case. What I saw in Brenda was a deep belief that every victim of sexual assault deserved an opportunity for justice. Every victim - not just those who were raped by a stranger or those who could talk and walk like the majority of people…but **every** victim. She has this reverence and respect for victims that burns through her veins. I love that about her!

Brenda described Kim this way: "Kim is so sweet. She had a very innocent look about her. Her eyes were big and looked at everything with a wonder in them. I always wish I knew what she was thinking. She loved hugs. She loved to clean the house and help her mom cook. She needed repetition and that is why school was good for her. She went year-round in her Individualized Education Program until she was 21 and rode the school bus. She was very obedient. She loved church."

The sexual assault was discovered when Kim was experiencing stomach pain and her mom took her to the doctor. Kim was pregnant. Before that day, only Kim knew that their family friend, landlord and church deacon had been coercing/forcing himself on her sexually. Most of the assaults occurred in the basement of the family home. As the landlord, he would enter the home through the basement and reduce the chance of his presence being known. As a trusted friend and church deacon, if seen and questioned, he could easily claim that he was there to check on something. He was believed. Some assaults took place in the church. Another place where he was highly respected and trusted. And believed.

Like so many of us, Kim had been taught to listen and obey her elders and people in authority. Kim was threatened by the man who hurt her and told her not to tell anyone. Perpetrators of this kind of violence are experts at getting people to trust them; experts at not getting caught; and experts at getting away with their crimes. Brenda understands this and has spent her career discovering ways to bring light to these 'secret' maneuvers in the courtroom.

In this legal case, the state had to prove that this man had performed sexual acts with a person who did not have the capacity to consent due to their disability. The charges were 2 counts of aggravated criminal sexual assault 720 ILCS 5/12-14 (renumbered ad 11-1.30 (a)(2)) alleging acts of sexual penetration on a victim that is 1. unable to understand the nature of the act or 2. is unable to give knowing consent and causing bodily harm - pregnancy.

One of the first things that Brenda did was file a motion for an interpreter for Kim. Most people had difficulty understanding Kim when she spoke, so someone was needed during the trial to help the court members understand Kim's communication. Kim's mother and brother were able to understand her very well. Kim's mother would be the outcry witness as she was the first person that Kim told about the sexual assault. Kim's brother was recommended as the interpreter during the court proceedings. The defense attorney challenged having a family member serving as an interpreter, because of potential bias. Brenda's motion for the brother to be the interpreter was denied.

Then Brenda found someone at a local disability service agency to serve as interpreter for

Kim in court. The court paid this interpreter to spend time with Kim and learn her communication style. The interpreter's job was to help with Kim's communication during the court proceedings - they did not do trial preparation, as that was Brenda's job. In the meantime, it was discovered that in the past, Kim had sometimes used an assistive communication device. It was referred to as a 'box' and was reintroduced as another way that Kim could communicate. Kim would push a specific picture and the 'box' would speak the word or words she chose. Some pictures were added to the box so that Kim could tell what happened to her, such as locations, body parts, etc. Kim already knew these words; they were simply added so that she could express them in a way that others could understand. Brenda met with Kim on a regular basis to increase their comfort and confidence with each other. Brenda needed to know how Kim thought and communicated and Kim needed to trust Brenda.

In the end, the 'interpreter' was not used during the trail. She would only be able to testify about the 'box' and how it helped Kim communicate versus being able to 'translate' what Kim was saying. The judge stated that it would be for the jury to figure out what Kim was saying. When Kim verbally responded, Brenda repeated what she thought Kim said and Kim would confirm or deny. When Brenda couldn't figure out what Kim said, she would either point to an exhibit or have Kim use her 'box', and that was audible to the jury. Kim's 'box' also allowed her to type something out and the 'box' would say it audibly. Brenda also used anatomically correct models for Kim to demonstrate how the defendant had sexually assaulted her.

Brenda interviewed and secured witness testimonies from two school social workers, Kim's teacher at school, the doctor who delivered Kim's baby and Kim's mom. Each of these witnesses would testify and paint a clear picture of Kim's abilities, personality, learning difficulties, communication style, and life experiences. By the time Kim took the stand, the jury had a clear picture of her as a person including her abilities and limitations. Kim was the last to testify and Brenda utilized pictures, anatomically correct models, and concrete items to supplement the 'box' communication device. The testimony included a demonstration of Kim's lack of understanding of concrete concepts such as the alphabet, coins, and locations. The State also demonstrated that Kim did not know that it was okay to say 'no' to requests or actions from others and Kim did not know where babies came from.

Following the State's case, and before the defense began the presentation of their case, the defense attorney requested a mistrial because of an illness and indicated they might never practice law again. The Judge ordered a mistrial. The defendant would need a new attorney and the process would begin again. This was a huge disappointment and frustration, especially when the original defense attorney was back working two weeks later.

It was a long and winding road to justice. Kim's child was four years old when the man who methodically and intentionally sexually assaulted her was found guilty. The State asked for a 20-year sentence due to the circumstances and the resulting pregnancy. The offender received a nine-year prison sentence.

Did Kim get the justice she deserved? That is hard to measure. Many people were disappointed that the sentence was not longer.

Let's look at the victories here:

✓ Kim had the opportunity to speak about what happened to her in court.
✓ She was believed by the jury.
✓ There was a conviction.
✓ There was a prison sentence.

363

✓ The conviction was later upheld by the Appellate court.

✓ While the offender is in prison, the community is safer.

There is a strong message, at least in this community, that "Just because we have disabilities doesn't mean you can abuse us and get away with it."

It had been five years since this conviction when I spoke with Brenda in 2020, she had this to say:

"Kim had three safe places: home, church and school. He invaded two of those places. I am still angry that he (the offender) did this! We have to be their voice. We gave her a voice with that box and the way we prepared her. You cannot let something like that go. You have to put in the time. You have to be passionate and see beyond the challenges."

Kim's child was nine when I recently spoke with Kim's mother, Mrs. Jones, on the phone. Mrs. Jones felt that this is an important story to share with other parents. She wants other parents to know that a person you trust can cause extreme harm to one of your loved ones. Mrs. Jones was heartbroken that her daughter was sexually assaulted. She was deeply hurt and angry that the person who caused this harm was a family friend and elder in the family church. As often occurs when a family member or close friend is the offender, people take sides. Some people believed Kim and some people believed the offender. Mrs. Jones reported that, "Everybody wanted to take matters into their own hands. Some people were hateful to us." This kind of reaction serves to revictimize the victim and their loved ones.

Mrs. Jones had these tips for other parents.

- Always believe your children over everyone else!
- Teach your children to let you know when someone is at the door and always have an adult answer the door.
- DO NOT teach your children to do whatever elders/adults tell them to do.
- DO NOT allow 'friends' to drop in whenever they want. Set some boundaries.

It is vital that support is present and available to people as they navigate the difficult roads of litigation and personal healing.

Kim found support when her mother believed her.

Kim and her mother both found support from the criminal justice system, especially from the members of the States Attorney's Office; they carefully took the time get to know Kim and to design a case which presented her experience of the crimes committed against her with clarity, compassion, and effectiveness.

Mrs. Jones found support when she told the Pastor, who believed her. The Pastor immediately stripped the offender of all church-related duties.

Lesson learned:

- Brenda reminded me that when someone in the criminal justice system passionately seeks justice for someone with a disability, they may not need a protocol or specialized training. THEY NEED PASSION FOR JUSTICE, TIME, CREATIVITY, AND DETERMINATION.
- Brenda followed the concept of **Disability Humility** in this situation. Disability humility means that as professionals, we do not have to be an expert on disabilities...we do need to

have humility - to be open, receptive, respectful, and creative while we LEARN FROM THE EXPERT - the person with a disability.

- In jury trials, it's not always about the evidence. Sometimes, it's about how much value the jury places on the defendant vs. the victim. Now that is a barrier! Brenda and her trial partner, Carol Costello, strategically presented witness testimony in an order that allowed the jury to get to know the victim very well before they met her. The last person to testify for the state was Kim. The Appellate Court stated that "The personality and limitations of [the victim] virtually leap out of the pages of this record." It is imperative to paint a clear and undeniable picture of the victim with disabilities in court cases to counteract the historical view held by society that people with disabilities have 'less value' than people without disabilities (the defendant, in this case).

Questions for the reader:

1. What role do you have in the criminal justice response when a crime is committed against a person with a disability?
2. What are your thoughts about disability humility? Is this an approach you are comfortable with?
3. If you had not had much exposure to people with disabilities, what could you do to increase your comfort and confidence in working with survivors with disabilities?
4. What accommodations have you requested on behalf of a victim? How would you find out if someone needed an accommodation to testify in court?
5. Are you open to looking at your own behavior with children and others as it relates to the messages your behavior communicates? For example, do you provide choices for children about touches with people in their life?

Thank you for all you do to assure justice for people with disabilities who experience violent crimes!

Chapter 12

Life as a Trainer

"The world changes according to the way people see it, and if you can alter, even by a millimeter, the way people look at reality, then you can change the world." James Baldwin

"Education is for improving the lives of others and for leaving your community and world better than you found it."
Marian Wright Edelman

My Thoughts on Training

I have always loved training and have been honored to have had the opportunity to do work that I love. When I began training outside of the organizations where I was employed, it was important to me that I continued to have regular, ongoing contact with people with disabilities. I wanted to be authentic and to speak from lived experiences. It was important that the messages I conveyed were centered in the realities of people with disabilities and that strategies that I shared were practice-based as much as evidence-based. I also wanted to be known as a trainer that did not just lecture but utilized creative activities and techniques that understood and respected the adult learning styles of the audience. One strategy I always incorporated into my training was storytelling. I believe strongly that we can learn from other's experiences. I also believe that shifts in perception occur through the art of storytelling. I love James Baldwin's quote at the beginning of this chapter, because if I can help to shift someone's perception of people with disabilities, maybe the world can be changed for all of us - one person at a time, one audience at a time, one organization at a time, one community at a time.

I could not do this - change anyone really - if my ego was 'front and center'. Trainers must have some content expertise to share and if we are not careful, getting up in front of groups can be an ego trip. When I began my training journey, I had a lot more healing to do from my multiple traumas. But there I was standing in front of people and sharing knowledge and expertise and boosting my own ego at the same time...because you know, I didn't feel all that good about myself. Yes, I had some good information to share but I wanted the audience to like me, and I needed to feel worthy! I craved excellent evaluations. I had some good and excellent evaluations, but I remember one training where a couple of brave audience members called me on my stuff, and I had to take a good look at myself. Well, first, I had a pity party. Luckily, I had learned through a 12-step group that pity parties only lead to a ring around your butt. So, the pity party didn't last too long. Afterwards, I took an honest look at myself - humbled myself -admitted I needed to work on myself (healing) and I created a practice of being what I call mission-centered. This meant that my focus in training was on:

#1. the reason I do the work I do (equality, safety, justice, respect, healing, etc. for people with disabilities); and

#2. the audience members understanding, growth and actions based on our time together.

This can be a tricky dance, because I had to use myself to accomplish these goals and it was important that I was prepared and skilled and authentic, but I was not the priority. It was not really about me anymore. It was about the audience. It was about the mission.

I remember co-training with someone and as we were preparing to leave at the end of the day, this person said, "Don't you want to see the evaluations before we leave?" and I said, "No. They will probably send them to us. It's only important if there is something we need to change or consider." The co-trainer could not believe it was not that important to me. I remember early on, if I had 100 people in the audience and one less than excellent/good evaluation, I would be devastated focusing on that one less than excellent evaluation and ignoring the 99 good ones. As a trainer, you have to be able to sort out what is yours to own. I am responsible for the material I select to use, the presentation materials and their accessibility, the words I use when I speak and how I respond to each audience member. I am responsible for being on time and taking care to get enough sleep and nutrition. I am responsible for keeping my word and following up on things I promised. I am not responsible for changing the mind of someone who disagrees with me. I am not responsible for someone else having a bad day. I am not responsible for the date that the host/sponsor chose to have the training. I am not responsible for the temperature in the room (although I will try and assist if I can). The room set up may be a shared responsibility depending on the situation. Know what is 'yours' and own that. Be open to input that makes your training better.

Learning From My Mistakes

I remember co-training in Michigan several years ago. I know the topic was sexual violence and people with disabilities. I know I was training with Jacqulyn Thomas, super trainer. I know it was a full-days training, but I don't recall the name of the town or the specific audience. What I do remember very well is being called out about my language! Yep. At the first break, a person approached me and said they were concerned about my use of the word 'crazy' as many people she worked with found that word insulting. I listened to her and then thanked her for her comments. I assured her that I would not use that word again in my presentation. I spent a few minutes in silence to get myself grounded. After the break, this happened:

> "At break, someone shared with me that when I used the word 'crazy' to describe a situation, it was a hurtful word to use. I am grateful for the feedback, and I want to apologize to all of you. I will not be using that word again. It is an offensive word, especially to people with mental health concerns. This demonstrates what I strongly believe: We are all teachers and students."

It is important that we are open to learning and apologizing and changing. We do not know everything and that is okay...if we are open to learning.

Questions for the Trainers:

1. How do you view your role as a trainer?

2. As a trainer, what steps can you take to separate your ego from your job as a trainer?
3. What role do training evaluations play in your role as a trainer?
4. When I was 'called out' in Michigan, do you think I should have just kept this feedback to myself? What are the pros and cons of publicly sharing this with the audience?

Communities that Have Been Excluded

When we work in communities with a history of oppression and discrimination, we must be open to learning from the people who are most impacted by our work. We must respect that those with lived experiences are the experts. We can apologize when called out, be opened to learn to do things differently, be bold enough to speak the truth as we learn it and be responsible for our own learning. People with disabilities are a part of every community and every group that has been excluded and viewed as "less than" by society. We must be willing to learning beyond the disability community…for we are everywhere and a part of every community. In conversation one day, a woman asked me this question: "I am Black,

Lesbian, Disabled, and a rape victim. Who is going to help me?" This is a perfect example of how social identities can overlap and the importance of working from an intersectional lens. This can deepen our understanding and broaden our perspectives as we do this work.

As a trainer, an important practice that I cultivated, was to focus on each audience as I prepared the training materials. I asked myself: Have I learned anything new that needs to be incorporated? What important perspective needs to be brought into this training? It felt unethical to me to present the same training I had already done without first reviewing it carefully and making needed updates. Some things stayed - some things were deleted - some things were revised - some new things came in. This was a process that honored the people I had learned from and recognized and respected the new audience I was responsible to for sharing the best information and strategies possible for them.

After learning from a parent in Washington State about respectfully including people with disabilities who identify as LGBTQ+, this intersection was included in many of the trainings I facilitated, and I was often approached after a training by someone who thanked me for including the LGBTQ+ community into my sessions. The truth is that you just do not know what you do not know! Suggestions like the one from this parent not only opened my eyes and deepened my understanding, but also invited me to share their wisdom and experience with countless others.

I believe that it is important to have training which respects all of the intersections a person may experience. In addition to what I already mentioned, I would ask myself these questions as I prepared a presentation:

- What tools am I going to use with this audience? How can I make these tools accessible?
- Do I need an icebreaker? I typically used an icebreaker for any training that was 3-hours or longer. I tried to find an ice breaker that was connected to the training topic.
- What accommodations are needed? It is best practice that audiences have an opportunity to request reasonable accommodations. The host needs to be prepared to made handouts in Braille, Large Print, and to provide closed captioning, American Sign Language interpreters, Communication Access Realtime

Translation services, different types of chairs, etc.

- If using a Power Point presentation, is it accessible? I studied and used universal design and was open to continue to learn what worked for various audience members. I was not perfect at this but was able to learn and adapt.
- Do the visuals within the Power Point presentation reflect diverse communities? Representation in photographs from a variety of communities is one way to honor and include people who may not typically be included.
- Are the words on the Power Point easy to understand by most people?
- Are the use of pronouns and/or gender/sexuality labels respectful of the LGBTQ+ community?
- Is there any language which is potentially disrespectful to any culture, religion, race, age, size, diagnosis, job title, etc.?
- Do I need a content or trigger warning? Given the nature of many of my presentations, I always included a slide on creating a safe learning environment. A trigger warning was a part of this. I also learned to ask the audience

members, what made them feel safe in a training session/meeting.

- Are the group activities respectful of adult learning styles? Do I need to make any adjustments for people with disabilities e.g., if someone is there who cannot see, what accommodations will this activity require?
- Do I need a microphone? I learned that it was best practices to use a microphone and to ask each audience member to use one as well (even those who said they didn't need one). This is respectful of audience members. A person who is hard of hearing should not have to announce that because someone refuses to use a microphone.
- How should I adjust the pace of my speaking so American Sign Language interpreters can follow the flow? Would it be helpful to provide handouts or other materials to the interpreters ahead of time?
- Am I prepared to verbally describe any visual images on the slide presentation for audience members who may not be able to see them?
- Will there be audience members with chemical sensitivities? I never wear fragrances and typically ask sponsors of events about this issue. People with chemical

sensitivities can become very ill from perfumes, hairsprays, carpet cleaning chemicals and other fragrances. This can be discussed and proactively addressed when preparing for a training event/group meeting.

• The room size and set up is typically the responsibility of the person who hires the trainers. It is, however, a good practice to discuss the set up with the organizers. For example, there needs to be at least 36 inches between chairs when pulled out for people who use wheelchairs to easily move through the room.

Questions for the Trainer:

1. As a trainer, what strategies or practices do you have to keep your ego in check?
2. What do you do to keep your trainings current and fresh?
3. What can you do to assure that each audience member is able to fully participate and has complete access to all the information presented?
4. What education do you need about universal design?

Bloopers:

1. I was scheduled to train a large group of professionals from a disability services organization. It was a 2-hour drive from home and when I went to leave that morning, my garage door opener would not work. My skill set did not include opening garage doors without an electronic opener, so I called someone who came over and opened the door for me. I got on the road as quickly as I could but was worried about being late and already stressed when I entered the building to prepare to train.

   During the training, we were discussing ways to enhance the criminal justice response to victims with disabilities. I was providing information about the criteria for someone to be a credible witness in a court of law. I was making a point that a person did not have to have an advanced degree or large vocabulary to be a credible witness and I said,

   "You don't have to be able to <u>smell</u> Chlamydia to be a credible witness. I mean **spell** Chlamydia."

The audience went wild with laughter, and I joined them. An embarrassing blooper, indeed.

2. I was co-training with Linda Sandman in Washington State about trauma in the lives of people with disabilities to a mixed audience. We both had a headpiece with a microphone that we put close to our mouth when we spoke. We each had to remember to turn it off when the other person spoke. We were doing really well at this until mid-afternoon when it was my turn to speak and a person in the audience said they couldn't hear me. My hands went to my waist to turn on the volume and it was already on. I touched my ears and mouth and found no microphone. I began patting myself and looking all around and then someone pointed at me…I looked down and the headpiece microphone was hanging down between my legs around my knees. Oh my. I can only imagine what that looked like. I wish I had a photo to share with you. This was planned to be my last time training before I retired. Perhaps I had waited too long.

A Trainer's Dream

I loved being a trainer! To be face to face with a group of people who are mutually interested in an important topic and to experience minds expanding and energy growing, is one of the best experiences a trainer can have. I have had some training experiences that were only average and at least one that was pretty bad, but there were lots and lots of wonderful hours and days where the information and inspiration flowed back and forth in celebration of the possibilities of making lives more meaningful, safe, and free. Over the years, I began to ask audiences to share ideas of actions they would take when they returned to their workplaces. Sometimes, I offered a free educational resource for people who took an action within a week and emailed me about what they did.

Oftentimes, after a training…on the plane ride back home or during the drive to the next place, I wondered…. did our time together lead to any lasting changes? Was there something more I could have done? I cherished the times when I would get a follow-up email telling me what changes a person or organization, or system had made because of our time together. On a few occasions, the dream of making a difference was evident. I'd like to share some of those with you now.

GUAM

The first time I worked in Guam it was at the invitation of the Guam Coalition Against Sexual Assault and Family Violence. Teresa Tudor and I had the opportunity to train a cross-section of the entire island. The Coalition did an amazing job of outreach and engagement for this training event. All organizations that intersected with violence in the lives of people with disabilities had representatives present. We co-trained for two days on the topic of sexual violence in the lives of people with disabilities. The audience included people with disabilities, family members of people with disabilities, victim services organizations, disability organizations, law enforcement, prosecution, child welfare, educators, health care professionals, and government allies.

Several noteworthy things occurred, and I want to mention two of them. On the second day in the early afternoon, we divided the room into 'islands'. There was a law enforcement island, a parent island, a victim services island, etc., etc.

People systematically visited other islands and offered information and support based on their expertise. Towards the end of the activity while people were sharing what they learned from each other, a high-ranking law enforcement officer stood up in front of everyone and said, "We've been doing this all wrong. This mom who has a child with autism taught us the best way to interact with a person on the autism spectrum and from now on, we will be doing this differently. She is going to come and train all of us the right way to communicate with someone on the spectrum." And there it was. The coalition had created the time and space and conditions for people to learn from each other. All the expertise they needed was right there in the room!

The second note-worthy happening was the time that was carved out for future planning. Before the event closed, we did some action planning. What actions would be taken to respond to survivors with disabilities in Guam? Who would be responsible for taking what steps to assure that survivors with disabilities had access to a trauma-informed response to their experiences of violence? What steps would be taken to increase offender accountability when the victim has a disability? These questions were an intentional part of the 2-

day event and the answers would guide the next steps for the audience members. When there is an action plan, people are more likely to take action.

This powerful and unique gathering was possible because of Cynthia Cabot, Executive Director of the Guam Coalition Against Sexual Assault and Family Violence. Her leadership and intentionality created this opportunity to make Guam a safer place for people with disabilities and all people.

Guam - An Unexpected Gift

While I am expressing gratitude, there is a story I want to share. I never would have made it to Guam if it had not been for this experience.

I received a call one day from the South Side of Chicago. Five people with developmental disabilities wanted to come spend a few hours with me to tour an agency and learn about services in my part of the state. It was a delightful experience to watch disability advocates interview executive staff about their services, funding, and decision-making. Over lunch, each person shared stories about their current life experiences and frustrations with the system that was supposed to support their individual needs, hopes and lives. One person shared that the staff had put her on a diet and that she did not get to choose her own foods. Another person shared that before moving to a new area, she was not allowed to go to her boyfriends' birthday party. Another person shared that everyone in her home had to have mustard on their burgers whether they liked mustard or not. There was a central theme in the stories; one of being disrespected and treated as 'less than'; common themes of being denied access to desired activities and people.

After a few stories had been shared, one person asked what was happening in my life. I asked if they would help me make a hard decision. They nodded yes and I went on...

> "I've been invited to speak in Guam about sexual violence in the lives of people with disabilities. I'd really like to go but getting there takes more than 24 hours. You all know I have trouble walking and lots of pain after sitting too long, so am not sure I should do this. What if the pain is so bad, I can't stand up to get off the plane? I'm not sure what to do."

They all listened closely and when I finished explaining my dilemma, every one of them said something to the effect of,

"You have to go."

"Take some Advil with you."

"You may never have this chance again."

"I would say YES!"

They assured me that I could plan ahead and take my cane and take Advil and make sure I got up and moved on the plane. I had just heard several stories about how they wanted to say "Yes" to life and how they were denied the chance to take risks. They were right of course. How could I pass up a once in a lifetime opportunity?

Right after lunch, I accepted the invitation to speak in Guam. Yes, it was a long trip and yes, I experienced a lot of pain, but you know what? The adventure was worth it!!

Iceland

I met Svava at an Institute on Violence, Abuse and Trauma Conference in San Diego in 2006. She attended a session I conducted on sexual assault in the lives of people with disabilities. After the session, she stayed behind and introduced herself. She told me about the organization where she worked in Iceland and said they needed to hear my message.

A few months later, I was invited to a conference in Reykjavik sponsored by Blatt Afram. Blatt Afram was founded in 2004 in Iceland as a non-governmental organization dedicated to the prevention of child sexual abuse. Blatt Afram provides primary and secondary prevention education for adults, teens, and children. Over the years, they have received multiple awards for their work to prevent and respond to child sexual abuse. They have provided an array of written materials and books, ad campaigns, and a variety of educational sessions.

Blatt Afram was the brainchild of Svava and her sister Sigga…both survivors of childhood sexual violence…and was created in order to establish a platform for discussion of and remedies to end child sexual abuse. The sisters wanted to use their difficult experiences for good and to help prevent other children from similar trauma experiences. They wanted to communicate and educate people about the consequences of sexual violence on children and to find ways that could possibly prevent children from experiencing such violence. I was honored to work with both sisters and to participate in their nation-wide conferences in both 2007 and 2008.

Svava and Sigga were very intentional about scheduling a full-day island tour before the conference began. This allowed time for the speakers to get to know each other and for Svava and/or Sigga to spend more time with the presenters. An entire day of casual conversations about each presenter's work served to enhance relationships and deepen understanding with the leaders of Blatt Afram. The presenters had time to learn about the culture of Iceland and the work of Svava and Sigga. They also took the time to pre-schedule the conference speakers for additional presentations and meetings in Iceland. For example, I met with the president of the Iceland family support group (family members of people with disabilities). They really maximized the time and expertise of every presenter.

As we traveled across the unique landscape of Iceland, I became acutely aware of the connection that we all have as human beings. The brilliant contrast of climate, geography, and culture that exists there, combined with the mission of preventing child sexual abuse, came together in my spirit, screaming: WE ALL WANT TO BE SAFE…WE ALL WANT TO BELONG…WE ALL WANT TO BE LOVED. No matter where we are from, no matter what our life experiences are … we are all connected in this way, in this basic desire.

Government officials were invited to the two-day conference. The conference was structured for strategic planning to occur after all the sessions were completed. The government officials, with input from others, issued a policy statement on a child-friendly society and the promotion of prevention of sexual violence. The actions outlined included increased services and supports for Deaf children and children with disabilities. The leadership of Blatt Afram and the nation of Iceland was evident in this intentional and impactful process and outcome.

In 2019, Blatt Afram joined forces with a bigger organization, Barnaheill –Save The Children in Iceland.

Washington State

   Betty Schwieterman, with Disability Rights Washington, first contacted me about speaking at a criminal justice conference in Bellevue, Washington in 2006. As our phone conversations continued, Betty arranged for me to speak to some other groups while I was in the area. I told her, "If you'd like me to speak directly with people with disabilities and/or their family members, I am happy to do evening workshops while I am there. Please use me." By the time of my departure, she had scheduled several speaking engagements across several towns with a variety of audiences, including day and evening engagements. My only request to make this happen, was that someone drive me to each location and back to my hotel at the end of the day.

   I was used to speaking with a variety of audiences including people with disabilities, family members of people with disabilities, sexual assault centers, disability service providers, statewide disability administrators, special education teachers and administrators, law enforcement, prosecutors, health care professionals, adult protective services, and disability advocates. However, this was the first time that I would speak with three different audiences in the same day, multiple days in a row and in different towns! I recently asked Betty if she knew what year I first came to Washington and worked with her and she stated, "The time I ran you ragged and forgot to leave any time for you to eat? Still apologizing…that was so amazing though. It was 2006."

Between Betty and her colleague, Andrea Kadlec, one or both attended every session I presented. I remember Andrea was driving me from one presentation in one part of the state to a different town for an evening presentation when she remembered they had not scheduled a time for dinner. She stopped somewhere and got me something to eat in the car. It was fine because I was nourished by her kindness and her passion to make a positive difference in the lives of people with intellectual and developmental disabilities. I was also nourished by the energy of each audience. And I was elated at the circle that was being created in the State of Washington to support people with intellectual and developmental disabilities who had experienced sexual assault or who might in the future.

Over the next twelve years, I returned to Washington State on several occasions, often traveling with and presenting with people with disabilities.   Sometimes I worked in Washington when Betty or Andrea made arrangement for multiple presentations with multiple audiences in multiple towns, and sometimes I worked there when others invited me. When I included the work in Washington State under "A Trainer's Dream" it was because of the impact I saw developing over the years. Here are some examples:

1. After training Special Education teachers about sexual abuse and the WE CAN Stop Abuse curriculum, the school initiated the following measures to keep students informed and safe: screening tool for risk factors of sexual abuse; inclusion of protective factors in each student Individualized Education Program; and classroom training of the WE CAN Stop Abuse curriculum.
2. In another school district, a teacher implemented the WE CAN Stop Abuse curriculum with the transition students (ages 18-21) at the school where she taught. Years later, this same teacher is partnering with People First of Washington and Special Olympics to teach sex education to prevent sexual abuse in sports.

3. During an evening session with one district's Special Education parents, teachers, and administrators, one parent asked what the Special Education district was going to do about including sexual abuse prevention education within the special education classes. Within a few minutes, the Superintendent stated a commitment to begin those classes the very next Fall. Since the FLASH (Family Life and Sexual Health) Curriculum * was created in King County Washington and is cost-free, the selection of a curriculum was not a barrier. The families were thrilled at this fast decision and commitment.

4. I do believe that we are all teachers AND students. I often learn from audience members and workshop hosts and sponsors. This time, I learned something very powerful from a person behind the registration desk for one of my workshops. The lesson arrived a few weeks after the workshop in an email meant for someone else. I do not have the original email, but it said something like this:

> I understand that you will be teaching the We Can Stop Abuse curriculum next month in my son's classroom. I wanted

to make sure that if you are teaching about private body parts, that you do not refer to male bodies and female bodies as this would cause my son a lot of distress. If body parts are included in the curriculum, please use language like this: 'people have different kinds of bodies. Some bodies have a penis, and some do not. Some bodies have a vulva, etc. I need you to take care of my son's emotional health during these classes.' I am happy to discuss this with you if you have any questions.

This wonderful mother and I had a phone conversation later that day. I explained that I was not teaching the class but was one of the creators of the curriculum. She was generous in sharing her ideas about safe approaches to teaching sexual abuse prevention for diverse audiences. She and her son were my first teachers about using respectful, gender-neutral language in teaching people with disabilities about their bodies. Later I would learn to expand this respectful, inclusive approach to trainings and resource development with all audiences. On the day I spoke with the mom, we changed language in the curriculum and contacted those we could find, who had purchased the curriculum with an urgent message and instructions to be added to the class on private body parts.

5. Sharing legislation - It was Andrea who shared with me the Washington State legislation that required public schools to teach disability history and awareness, as mentioned earlier in the section about Amy Walker. We shared this idea with self-advocates in Illinois and many were excited about trying to pass a similar law here. We met with Representative Bob Flider and discussed the need for this, and he said he would champion the legislation. He met with some of his colleagues, while groups of people in various locations who spoke with their legislators and others to try and build momentum for the legislation.

When we learned that the bill may not pass because it was an "unfunded mandate", meaning it required education with no money to make it happen, Andrea helped us find several no cost resources for implementing the required training within the education system

Andrea also shared with us a disability history and awareness bingo game that she developed, and we made copies and distributed them to self-advocates and some agencies in Illinois. We did a session at the Speak Up Speak Out Conference so people would know how to use it in their communities. We made and distributed nearly 100 copies of the Disability History Bingo game: planting the seeds of information in several communities.

Later, we were happy to share the new Illinois sex education bill with Andrea and Betty. In 2020, healthy relationships and sex education were included in the State of Washington waiver and could be paid for through Specialized Habilitation Services. * These services can help individuals create healthy relationships, adapt to challenges, and improve overall quality-of-life.

If you have relationships with people in other states who care about equality and justice for people with disabilities, consider sharing legislative ideas for systems change. It can prove to be very meaningful.

6. Being intentional about 'passing the torch' as I planned for retirement was on my radar for

several years. Connecting someone to the folks in Washington State occurred in 2018, when Linda Sandman and I spent 3 days training and consulting about trauma in the lives of people with disabilities. We worked for the Washington State Developmental Disabilities Administration in three different locations. Our host for the three days was Joseph (Joe) Smith, Region 2 Training and Technical Assistance Coordinator. During the first full day of training, a participant asked about access to counseling services for people with intellectual and developmental disabilities who experienced sexual assault. Joe indicated that there were counselors available and that if anyone had any difficulties with this, to contact him for assistance. To be honest, I was shocked and pleasantly surprised. From my experiences, there was a huge gap in counseling services for survivors of sexual assault who have intellectual and developmental disabilities. Perhaps it was not a service gap in Washington State.

A few weeks later, I heard that the assumption of easy access to counseling services was incorrect. I was in awe that Joe had done follow-up on this issue. This is what he discovered: The process needed to access funding for such services requires the survivor to contact every provider on the list for their geographic area, share what their need is and after they are repeatedly denied, a process would begin to secure state funding for the needed counseling services to address the trauma. In some areas of the state, the list may include 12 counselors while other areas could have 200 or more providers on the list. When I spoke with Joe about this he said, "As I figured out this process, my jaw was literally hitting the floor and the rest of my face with it. I always felt that Washington State was very progressive in meeting people's needs. I was shocked to discover we were not able to fund therapeutic services for survivors of sexual assault. For a trauma survivor, the process is not at all feasible. Most people would give up after the first call." We explored some ways that a trauma-informed system of accessing counseling services might be created. Follow-up phone calls with Betty and Andrea occurred about increasing the system's capacity to support healing and recovery for people with intellectual and developmental disabilities who experience sexual assault.

Systems change takes time and I am confident that Washington State will continue to push for the needed resources so that survivors of sexual assault with intellectual and developmental disabilities can access the therapeutic services they choose and need.

Fun Fact: For many years, I would sing Willie Nelson's song, "On the Road Again" as I traveled from my home to an airport or the next worksite. Even today, there are times when I am in the car, and I start singing that song. I wonder, what do you bring to your work to make it more fun?

A Closing Gratitude

In closing this chapter, I want to thank Maryam Mostoufi for teaching me about professional training. When I first met Maryam, she was the training director for the Illinois Division of Developmental Disabilities. Maryam taught me many things and here are a couple that still stand out today - several decades later. Maryam taught me the key to developing effective training is to consider what you want the audience **to not only**

know, but **more importantly, be able to do** at the end of the training. She taught me to think from the end. To outline the desired behaviors/outcomes. I have remembered this and shared it with many other people over the years.

Maryam also taught me the value of generosity and connections. When Robert Perske came to Illinois to train, Maryam arranged for me to have an afternoon with Bob at her home. If you are not aware of Bob's work to free innocent, but convicted, people with intellectual and developmental disabilities from prison, check out his legacy. * This was an afternoon I will never forget…a real gift!

Maryam also added to my experiences of sisterhood in healing from trauma and in traveling safely along life's journey. Thank you, Maryam, for teaching me what I needed to know in those early days!

Questions for the reader:

1. After you attend a training, what can you do to make sure you use new information/skills in your workplace?

2. If you are a person who trains others, what strategies can you use to encourage audience members to use the information/skills you are training?

3. If you are a supervisor or manager, what creative ideas do you have for employees to share and use what they learn at training?

4. Seeing the powerful impact of including a wide variety of persons/representatives in an audience, think of people beyond your field of expertise who would benefit from hearing of the things you have learned.

Chapter 13

Thinking Outside the Field

"The greatest enemy of knowledge is not
ignorance; it is the illusion of knowledge."
Stephen Hawking

"Silo builds the wall in people's minds and
creates the barrier in organizations' hearts."
Pearl Zhu

I think it is important to look outside the fences that are built around our individual fields of work to find other models and practices that can enhance our individual and collective work. I want to share some examples that have positively impacted my work with people with intellectual and developmental disabilities and the organizations that support them.

Recovery Capital

My brother, William White aka "Bill", is a well-known addictions expert, with a focus on long-term recovery. I occasionally read his professional writings (there are many) and his blog. One that really caught my attention was an article he wrote with William Cloud in 2008 about recovery capital. *

So, what is recovery capital?

According to the article, recovery capital is "the breadth and depth of internal and external resources that can be drawn upon to initiate and sustain recovery…". The entire article is focused on recovery from alcohol and other drugs but as I read it, I wondered…does this make sense for recovery from trauma in the lives of people with disabilities who experience bullying, sexual and/or domestic violence, neglect, and exploitation at alarming rates? Hmm…

The article describes three kinds of recovery capital as well as early scientific findings and implications for clinical practice. There are two things in the article that really caught my attention.

One was the idea of evaluating our effectiveness based on <u>what has been added to the lives of people and families with whom we work</u>. For many people with disabilities who have been labeled with terms like 'maladaptive behavior', we have traditionally measured success by looking only at what has been subtracted. For example, "John will not exhibit aggressive behavior 90% of the time for three months." Please don't get caught up in evaluating the objective written here and focus instead on the idea of taking something away. We focus on subtracting aggressive behavior from John and we may take things from John to teach him not to be aggressive. We may even take away some of his rights to do this. What if instead we focus on adding some resources into John's life? Not candy or pop, but some real and sustainable resources. Examples might include helping John pursue a dream or life passion; helping John learn a new coping skill that he wants; supporting John to participate in a self-advocacy group, if he desires; exploring with John songs with strong self-esteem messages; or helping John to access counseling with a community provider. The possibilities are endless, the important thing is to 'allow for the possibility' that when you focus on adding to John's life rather than subtracting. John's life can be better...and you will have been a part of making that happen!

The second key element of the article that I love are the types of recovery capital and pondering the applications to the lives of people with disabilities. I think this can provide a <u>framework for service planning</u> which is much broader and richer than the ones that have been used in the past. In addition, a review of community recovery can funnel ideas into the organizational strategic planning activities. So, let's look at the elements of recovery capital.

The three types of recovery capital include: personal recovery capital; family/social recovery capital; and community recovery capital which includes cultural capital. I will explain each of these and provide examples for people with intellectual and developmental disabilities.

Personal recovery capital includes both physical and human capital. Physical capital includes physical health, health insurance, financial assets, access to transportation, food, clothing, and shelter that is safe and recovery-enhancing. Human capital includes a person's self-esteem, self-awareness, self-confidence, education, work skills, personal values, and knowledge.

In order to recover from trauma, a person must feel safe. Having your basic needs met is crucial to this sense of safety. Many disability-specific organizations focus on physical recovery capital when they support people to access health care, transportation, housing, and personal assistants to help with daily needs. While there has been a focus on work skills for people with disabilities, from my experiences, there has been less emphasis on assessing human capital and creating supports for enhancing self-esteem, self-confidence, self-awareness, and personal values. The people I know who support people with disabilities with a trauma history have done amazing work to address these human capital issues. Karyn Harvey's Happiness Assessment * comes to mind, as well as the 'relationships with self' sessions in the healthy relationships curriculum developed by Disability Rights Wisconsin (in process) and the work by Kathy O'Connell with Radiant Abilities. I encourage organizations, self-advocacy groups, parent groups, special ed programs, and others to consider adding these components to their current service options. How we feel and think about ourselves, and our beliefs and values help to define our lives and growth following trauma.

Family/social recovery capital includes family relationships (family, as defined by the person) which are supportive of the person's recovery from trauma, as well as other relationships who are willing to support the person's recovery. In order to make this happen, we must take sexual assault against people with disabilities out of the darkness. We can shine a light on this crucial issue. We must educate family members and others about the prevalence of sexual assault and other violent crimes against people with disabilities and what trauma-informed support looks like and feels like. One resource for working with parents and family members around issues of sexual assault is the Parent Guide developed by Illinois Imagines. *

When someone is in recovery from trauma, things change and those changes impact family members. If family members do not understand what is happening, it can cause chaos within the family unit and it can make recovery more difficult for the survivor. It is important to work with families so they understand the impact of trauma and what recovery might look like for their loved one. Service providers can provide education and support to family members that increase the probability that the person in recovery is supported by their family members. One way to do this is to collaborate with sexual assault and domestic violence organizations in your communities. These agencies can support people with disabilities, as well as family members and support staff with education, medical and legal advocacy, and healing services.

From my experience, peer support is crucial, and educating people with disabilities about how to support a friend needs to be a part of any recovery capital initiative. Some resources for this include the Empowerment Guide lessons created by Illinois Imagines* and the Healthy and Safe Relationships curriculum developed by Disability Rights Wisconsin (in process). *

Community recovery capital encompasses community attitudes, policies, and resources that support recovery from trauma in the lives of people with disabilities. Some things to consider when thinking about community recovery include; stigma, continuum of treatment resources, accessible diverse human services resources, and access to recovery community organizations. Community recovery actions help to get rid of silos which lead to fear and mistreatment of people we do not know. Cultural capital denotes the availability of culturally prescribed pathways of recovery that honor the intersections within the person's identity and preferred recovery journey. For example, an indigenous person may prefer indigenous ceremonies, such as sweat lodges, as a tool for recovery from trauma.

Let's explore community recovery capital within the context of trauma in the lives of people with disabilities. I think it is important to point out that many disability organizations are fairly closed systems - attempting to meet all of the needs of the individuals they serve within their organizational structure. For example, many disability service providers 'do it all' - they may bring in barbers/hair stylists to do hair, reading tutors to teach reading skills, art teachers to run art classes, parks within the organization's property and on and on and on. All things which can be done within the larger community. For community recovery capital to be effective, the entire community needs to be considered. For example, we cannot address stigma and discrimination within the closed walls of any institution or organization; in fact, isolation and exclusion only reinforce stigma.

To truly enhance community recovery capital for people with disabilities, community resources and the community at large need to be accessed on an ongoing basis, both by people with disabilities and by service agencies who provide disability-specific supports. When the goal is recovery from trauma, it is important to consider partnering with community victim service organizations, i.e., domestic, and sexual violence agencies. These agencies are an amazing resource for education, advocacy and healing services for people who experience trauma. Yes, for ALL people who experience violence...even those with labels of disabilities. Any disability agency can reach out to one of these organizations and begin to share information and resources. In the early 90s, I made an appointment with the local rape crisis center in the town where I lived. I was looking for educational materials to use with people with intellectual and developmental disabilities related to sexual abuse prevention. Over the next several years, the following activities took place:

1. The sexual assault center provided training for agency staff on sexual assault and their services.
2. The disability agency provided training for the sexual assault center employees on working with people with disabilities.
3. The sexual assault center provided education to self-advocates on bullying, consent, healthy relationships, abuse, body safety, and more.
4. The disability agency participated in Take Back the Night annual events, and survivors with disabilities have spoken.
5. The sexual assault center Executive Director served on the disability agency's Human Rights Committee for several years.
6. The sexual assault center facilitated a survivor support group at the disability agency.
7. The disability agency trained volunteers of the sexual assault center on working with people with disabilities.
8. A counselor at the Rape Crisis Center provided counseling services on-site at the disability agency when transportation was a barrier.

These activities have made a huge difference for all people within organization. While I consider this partnership a promising practice from a trauma-informed perspective, I believe this practice is much bigger than that. This is an example of people who historically have had all of their needs met within a silo (disability agency) shifting to having their needs met within the broader community - like everyone else!

Other things to consider under Community Recovery Capital include access to support groups within the community (such as NA, AA and ALANON), mental health supports (such as through the mental health center), religious practices (access to churches, mosques, or synagogues of the person's choice), spiritual recovery practices (access to spiritual retreats and practices), and culturally specific groups (access to Black Lives Matter, LGBTQ+, Pacific-Islanders groups, Indigenous groups, etc.). I know this list might make some readers very uncomfortable. We tend to think in silos and only focus on the disability needs of people…but people are more than one thing. We must look at the whole person and all of the intersections within their identities, affiliations, histories, cultures, and preferences for healing and living a meaningful life.

For readers who are responsible for service planning with people who have intellectual and developmental disabilities, consider how you can incorporate these concepts into your conversations with people as they plan for their team meetings. Consider how you can engage community members in outreach, education, and engagement so that more community services can become viable options for the people you support.

For administrators and managers of disability-specific organizations, consider having a 'Disability, Equity and Inclusion' work group that includes program participants and members of the community at large. Consider how you can engage the community in anti-stigma activities. Meet with people, their families, and staff to identify barriers to community recovery and gather input on ways to overcome these challenges. Consider putting 'Community Recovery Capital' into your program evaluation and strategic planning processes.

I hope the readers are as excited as I am about this new way of looking at service planning and organizational operations.

For those of you who want to learn more about Recovery Capital and a broader concept of "community recovery" - the idea that whole communities may have been wounded and require a conscious recovery process, I am including some articles for you to check out. *

I am thankful for the work of William White and William Cloud for opening my mind to some new ways of looking at recovery from trauma in the lives of people with disabilities.

Questions for the Reader:

1. Have you had conversations about safety with the people in your life? At work and at home? Do you know what makes others feel safe? What makes you feel safe?
2. What are some ways that we can support families to understand about the recovery process for their loved one and options for their own support?
3. What are some ideas you have to decrease the stigma of people with disabilities in your community? How could an organization work to decrease community stigma?
4. What ideas do you have to increase access to community recovery options for people with disabilities in your community?

Historical Trauma

Historical trauma refers to the complex and collective trauma experienced over time and across generations of people who share an identity, affiliation, or circumstance...and includes communities that share a history of oppression, victimization, and massive group trauma exposure. (Mohatt, NM, et al 2014). *   Maria Yellowhorse describes historical trauma as "cumulative emotional and psychological wounding over the lifespan and across generations, emanating from massive group trauma." (1985-1988)

Typically, when someone refers to historical trauma, it focuses on a group with a long history of oppression, marginalization, segregation, discrimination, colonization, and forced relocation. This trauma is held and carried within individuals and is transmitted across generations. Lots of communities struggle with historical trauma and carry the pain of their ancestors pain with them, sometimes having no idea what this pain is or where it comes from. Examples include generational survivors of: the persecution and attempted annihilation of Jewish people during Nazi Germany; African Americans being stolen from their native lands, being enslaved, abused, murdered, raped, incarcerated and denied basic human rights; Native Americans being exterminated and displaced from their land, mass murders, high rates of rape, violence and victimization, and denied basic human rights; the internment of Japanese Americans during WWII being forced to relocate and incarcerated into concentration camps with armed guards to prevent their resistance and release.

As I became more and more familiar with the effects of historical trauma in groups of marginalized people, I wondered....do people with disabilities experience historical trauma? Can someone experience historical trauma and not be aware of the history of victimization against people who are like them? These questions seemed to float around in my mind and would occasionally surface for consideration.

So, why did I wonder about historical trauma in the lives of people with disabilities? Since disability history is rarely a part of the history curricula in schools, let me explain. People with disabilities have a long history of oppression, segregation, marginalization, discrimination, mass murders, forced sterilization, rape, institutionalization, medical experimentation, abuse, neglect, and exploitation. The first people targeted

420

in Nazi Germany were people with disabilities. As I write this in 2021, there are still lots of people with disabilities who live in institutions and parents with disabilities who lose custody of their children at birth only because they (the parents) have a disability. It was confusing in my mind because the person with the disability may be the only person in their family with a lifelong disability, so it felt different than the historical trauma effects for a person whose entire family identifies with a culture that has been traumatized for centuries. And yet, my gut kept telling me there was something there.

I was speaking at a conference in Guam several years ago and one of the other speakers worked with Pacific Islanders who experienced domestic violence. She was an expert on historical trauma. I had an opportunity to speak with her briefly outside of the elevator where she was waiting to head home. I told her I worked with people with disabilities and asked her my burning question. "Can people with disabilities experience historical trauma when they are unaware of the horrific treatment of people like them throughout history?" She looked me in the eyes and took a moment to study me. Then she replied, "You know the answer to your question. **Remember, we were all outside when the poison came down.**" Her comment caught in my throat. The elevator door opened, and I told her "Thank you" as she entered the elevator and left. So, we were all outside when the poison came down. WOW! Think about that! Everyone was and continues to be affected by the poison of racism, colonization, oppression, and ableism, all the systemic and individual hatred against 'others'. The poison was in the air and permeated every space across the globe. People were divided into groups. 'Good enough' and 'not good enough'. 'We' vs. 'Them'. 'Valued' and 'not valued'. And the list goes on and on. As for people with disabilities, even if a person with a disability has no details about their history and continues to be treated as 'other', they are affected by the history. So, it seems that the 'isms' are in the air we breathe. My friend Amy Walker wrote a poem about feeling hated. These feelings emerged by how she has been treated. I wonder. Is this poison still in the air today? What poison are we breathing today? Are we even aware of it?

So, how does understanding historical trauma help us support survivors of trauma with disabilities? Remember that historical trauma is not only about traumas in past generations, but also about what is happening today in the lives of people with disabilities. Bullying and discrimination of people with disabilities today has a direct link to the way people with disabilities have been treated throughout history. When we understand our history, we can acknowledge that we are not alone. We can acknowledge our resilience as a people. We can share our stories. We can find strength in numbers. We can find solidarity with others who are standing up against oppression. We can understand our inherent value as humans. We can fight to make sure that the horrific acts within our history are not repeated. We can work with others in the disability community and take direct action to make changes. Many of these actions can and do have a healing component.

Sometimes when we think outside the field, we find a treasure. As I was in the final stages of finishing this book, I once again googled historical trauma in people with disabilities and for the first time, I found a scholarly article on this topic. I was so excited! Andrea Lou Zuber wrote *Implications for Healing, Transformation and Prosperity: Historical and Cultural Trauma and People with Intellectual and Developmental Disabilities* * as part of her master's degree at the University of Minnesota (December 2018).

This groundbreaking work makes the case that people with intellectual and developmental disabilities meet the criteria of experiencing historical trauma. Zuber clearly describes the components of historical trauma, how historical trauma is transmitted, communities who have experienced historical trauma and the parallels within the intellectual and developmental disabilities community. Zuber states, "They are not necessarily genetically connected to each other but having an intellectual and developmental disability automatically connects one with a community who has suffered from trauma of all kinds." Please be clear that she is talking about the direct suffering people experience because of the trauma inflicted from oppression - not suffering because they have a disability. This distinction is extremely important.

The article describes grief as the underlying result of historical trauma - grief over what has been lost (freedom, equality, family, safety), over what harm continues today, and over the outlook for the future. Perhaps my favorite part of this thesis are the implications for hope and healing. Zuber refers to healing of the body and soul on an individual level as well as the healing that needs to occur within our families, communities, and society.

This article is the beginning of some cutting-edge work that I hope others will continue.

I encourage clinicians and researchers to look closer at historical trauma in the lives of people with intellectual and developmental disabilities and their families. Share your ideas, practices, and results so others working in this field can benefit from your work. Looking at healing within other communities that have been historically excluded would be a great place to start these conversations and practices and studies. Go for it!

Questions for the Reader?

1. Are you familiar with the concept of historical trauma?
2. Do you believe that people with disabilities experience historical trauma? Explain your response.
3. What might the value be in educating people with disabilities about their history of trauma? What supports would need to be available when this occurs?
4. What can we learn about healing from historical trauma from other communities who experience historical trauma?

Components of Well-being

In his 2011 book, *Flourish: A New Understanding of Happiness and Well-Being – and How to Achieve Them,* * Martin Seligman describes five elements that human beings need in order to flourish in life. Seligman is a researcher, a scientist, and a psychologist. When I read his book in 2012, I grabbed onto the five elements of well-being that he described and never really let go. Why? Because I have been working with people with intellectual and developmental disabilities (and other disabilities) and wanting them to have better lives. I had written, read, and heard about thousands of individual's plans (goals) and most were pretty boring and insignificant. What if we helped people with disabilities and their families and their service providers learn about these five elements of well-being? What if individualized educational plans and services and support plans focused on happiness and well-being? I get goose bumps just thinking about that.

The five elements are:

<u>Positive emotion</u>: having a pleasant life...doing things that you enjoy and make you feel good. Asking, what experiences lead to happiness and life satisfaction? For some people, this would mean

exposing them to a variety of experiences and observing their responses. When we have experiences that make us smile and laugh, life is fun! What activities might bring pleasure to this person?

Engagement: being in the flow...thoughts and feelings are usually absent while in the flow state...great conversations, music, weaving, running, writing, etc. When we can take a break from our thoughts and feelings, it reduces our stress and increases our health. What engagement activities might the person want to try?

Meaning: belonging to and serving something you believe is bigger than yourself. Examples might include delivering meals on wheels, volunteering at a pet shelter, joining a self-advocacy group, serving as an usher at church, being a member of a women's group at a spiritual center, working at a childcare center, etc. What might bring purpose and meaning into the person's life?

Accomplishment or achievement: achieving something for its own sake (can be monetary or not) ...maybe joining a group of interest, taking a dream vacation, writing a book, finishing a difficult task, meeting an exercise goal, learning a new skill, etc.

What opportunities for accomplishment can the person explore?

Positive Relationships: enjoying time with other people. Other people make us feel better. Most of our high points take place with other people. What opportunities would the person like to deepen their relationships?

You can read more about these five elements in Seligman's book. If you have a plan for your own life, consider these five elements. If you are a parent, consider these elements as you make decisions for and with your children. If you work with others who need supports, consider these elements in your conversations and planning activities. If you gather teams together to plan for a person you help to support, what areas are you already including and what areas might be missing? I have rarely seen a person's plan that includes 'meaning'. And yet, I have known and met hundreds of people with intellectual and developmental disabilities who get meaning and purpose through their self-advocacy work.

I believe that when we focus on well-being and happiness, whether in our own lives or others, we see less 'behavioral' concerns and less trauma-based responses in our everyday lives. When people feel whole and valued, their lives are happier.

Flourish was written for people. It does not focus on people with disabilities. It focuses on well-being and happiness for all people. People are people.

When I began sharing these ideas with people with disabilities and with disability professionals, so many great discussions began to happen. Many professionals who facilitated the planning of services shared that they had not really taken most of these five elements into account in working with people or in developing their support plans. Just consider how different a support plan might be that included most or all of these five components. A plan that brings more joy, achievement, positive relationships and meaning into your life sounds pretty good to me!! This is an opportunity to stretch your thinking and to shake up the status quo and most importantly, learn about what really matters to people and set about making those things a reality!! For those of you who are already using these elements, KUDOS TO YOU! You are creating pathways to a whole and meaningful life!

Questions for the Reader:

1. How would you rate each of these five elements in your own life? What changes might you choose to make?
2. Who might you have discussions with about what brings a person meaning in their life…what makes their heart smile…what dreams do they have?
3. Why do you think that many plans for children and adults with disabilities focus on subtracting things from their lives?
4. What barriers do you identify in adding these elements to plans that are required for people with disabilities who receive formal services? What ideas do you have to reduce or eliminate those barriers?

Chapter 14

Figuring Out Retirement

"Tell me, what is it you plan to do with your
one wild and precious life?"
Mary Oliver

"Ends are not bad things; they just mean that
something else is about to begin."
C. JoyBell

Can I Really Retire?

The older I got, the more I recognized the many opportunities that I had to be of service. I was grateful for the many people I had the opportunity to work with and for the changes that I witnessed which improved the lives of people with disabilities. I also became more aware of two things. One was the fact that as much as I loved the work, the work was hard on my body. I had been in some pain since 2001 and the travel made the pain so much worse. Secondly, I discovered that there were other people doing the type of work that I was doing. When I started addressing violence in the lives of people with disabilities, I didn't know anyone else who did that work. Now I know several. So, maybe I could slow down…maybe I could retire. The question that haunted me was this: If I really cared about survivors of violence with disabilities, how could I possibly stop? I had been with survivors in emergency rooms and during sexual assault exams; during court proceedings speaking about what happened to them; and in counseling sharing their trauma and raw emotions. They didn't give up. They didn't stop trying to do what needed to be done. They kept going, so, shouldn't I? So, what to do?

My brother gave me this advice: As long as you are filling up this space, it does not leave room for others to come behind you or beside you to take up that space. Who are you mentoring to fill those spaces you will leave open?

I had begun some mentoring over the years, but this made me realize I needed to do so much more. I put a plan in place and gradually began mentoring others to do parts of the work I had been doing. I began looking at my role in a new way. In 2016, I retired from my full-time position at a community not-for-profit organization and co-founded Blue Tower Solutions, Inc. with three colleagues. Blue Tower Solutions, Inc. * is a not-for-profit organization based in Illinois designed to continue our collective work of the past many years. Leanne Mull, Krescene Beck and Linda Sandman were the other Co-Directors. Each brought different areas of expertise and passion. I gradually 'retired' from some of my ongoing partnerships and transitioned the partners to some of my previous roles.

Parents with Disabilities

For years, I had practiced this way of thinking about my work. If I was interested in doing something, I would write a grant proposal, submit a Request for Presentation, let someone know I'd like to participate in a project, or spend time dreaming what it might be like. I would 'put it out in the universe' and keep moving forward with my daily work. I did not worry about it or put any extra energy into it at all. IF the work came back to me, it was mine to do. Over time, I found myself, walking through life saying "Thank You" as opportunities came to me. Sometimes, work came to me that I had never even imagined before the opportunity greeted me. This was one of those situations as I moved towards a space in my life to retire.

In 2016, the first time I kinda retired, I had an opportunity to be an Infant/Early Childhood Mental Health Consultant in my hometown. No airports. No hours of driving to different destinations. No hotels. My body needed the rest. I was gifted with the opportunity to work with home visiting programs that served families who had infants and toddlers, as well as six preschool classrooms that included children who were high risk for school failure. The consulting focused on the social-emotional development of the children, ways to support the families, and supporting the direct contact staff who provided these valuable services. The work done by these child development specialists, teachers, and assistants, is extremely important and often challenging. One home visitor I worked with supported a pregnant teen who had no family or friends. The home visitor showed the mom how to begin bonding with her baby during the pregnancy, supported the mom during childbirth, and supported the mom while the child was an infant and a toddler. This mom learned about child development, brain development, nutrition, social and emotional development, and so much more. Mom and child thrived. How might this story had been different if the home visitor was not part of this woman's life? Their work is life-changing and community enhancing. When we support mothers during pregnancy and their early years of parenting, they can flourish, and their children can develop physically, cognitively, emotionally, and socially. I personally wish that every parent could have a child development specialist during the first three to five years of their child's life. I want to acknowledge Delreen Schmidt-Lenz and Linda Delimata for their amazing support of my development and work, and

Sue Ripley, Kelsi Barney and Cristine Coleman for their leadership and commitment to children and families in our community.

In addition to supporting the classrooms and home visiting programs, I was asked to create a statewide training program for the birth to five home visiting programs in Illinois on working with parents with disabilities. This was one of those invitations that unexpectedly came into my life which met my long-term desire to support parents with disabilities. I knew about working with people with disabilities but was pretty new at supporting moms and dads to be great parents - and another gift arrived to complete the package. Tammy Livingston and Lynn Liston, seasoned Infant Mental Health Consultants, joined me in developing and implementing the curriculum, titled "I Can Parent, Too!" Life brought all of the pieces together beautifully!

Here is the issue: The right to be a parent is one of our basic human rights. We are assumed competent to parent until we do something that indicates abuse or neglect of a child. This basic right has not always been assumed for parents who have disabilities. Based on data from 2012, there are 4 to 6 million parents in the United States who have disabilities. According to *Rocking the Cradle:*

437

Ensuring the Rights of Parents with disabilities and Their Children, * forty to eighty percent of parents with intellectual disabilities lose custody of their children. Many times, babies are taken away before the parents are even given a chance to parent; taken away at the hospital after birth. There has been a lack of resources for parents with disabilities as well as for professionals who work with parents.

Here are some facts that were discussed in every training session:

> Many parents need support and resources during pregnancy and after birth. This includes parents with and without disabilities.

> Parenting is hard.

> Not everyone with a disability is/can be a good parent.

> Not everyone without a disability is/can be a good parent.

> Services and supports for parents should be inclusive.

During the roll out phase of "I Can Parent, Too!", we provided two identical full days of training to approximately 150 people. Those same people were invited to log their experiences over a six-month period of time and return for a four-hour follow-up gathering. At the follow up events, participants had the opportunity to reflect together on their experiences, and they heard a presentation by a parent with disabilities and had the opportunity to ask the parent questions. The audience members also learned some additional access tools, strategies, and resources, and had an ongoing opportunity to share with one another and receive new resources via monthly email connection. This unusual opportunity for follow-up, additional training, ongoing resources, and consultation was provided due to the generosity and understanding by the Illinois Department of Human Services Maternal Infant Early Childhood Home Visiting program. Following this initial roll out, the Ounce of Prevention Fund incorporated this training into an annual event within their training roster, so it is regularly available to practitioners and advocates for early childhood education. (Note: The Ounce of Prevention Fund has since changed their name to Start Early.) Adaptations had to be made during the pandemic, including shortened trainings via webinars. In September 2021, Tammy Livingston and Leanne Mull also worked with the Rapid Response Virtual Home Visiting Team and members of Brazelton Touchpoints Team. During that work, participants from all over the world viewed a one-hour recording with Start Early prior to the live webinar facilitated by Tammy and Leanne.

I am thrilled that this initiative has become a routine part of training for child development specialists in Illinois. Parents with disabilities who have a child development specialist/home visitor now have better support in navigating parenthood and a greater chance of maintaining custody and at having someone advocate with them when issues of stigma and discrimination occur. And yet, I know this is not enough to change all of the inequities in a society where many people believe a person with a disability cannot parent, simply because they have a disability. I know this is not enough to change possible discriminatory practices within the child welfare system. I encourage those reading this who are interested and/or have influence, to create some additional solutions and to challenge attitudes they observe related to parents with disabilities.

Questions for the Reader:

1. What are your assumptions about people with disabilities being parents?
2. Do you believe that most parents need support with parenting? Why or why not?
3. What resources are available in your community or state to support the rights of

parents with disabilities? What needs to be developed or expanded?

4. Do you have suggestions on how early childhood programs and disability agencies could collaborate and learn more about each other?

Listening to My Body

By the end of 2018, I 'retired' from Blue Tower Solutions and all work in preparation for a surgery I had postponed for many years. I knew I couldn't travel like I had in the past, so I was making peace with the fact that my body needed me to stay close to home. I was still recovering from surgery when I was asked to do some national consulting. I told the person I could only work from home, and they kindly said, "We will take whatever we can get." And thus began my 'from home' consulting. My spirit was happy to contribute in some small way - to not give up completely. By the end of 2019, I had accepted another consulting job that would mostly be from home with occasional travel by car.

Along this journey to figure out what retirement means for me and to figure out how I want to navigate this last phase of my life, I have learned to pay more attention to my heart, body,

441

mind, spirit, and the universe. Here is an example of a situation that led me to consider retiring from travel.

One of my disabilities is low vision. I had not driven at night for many years and was able to negotiate my schedule and support so that I was never in a situation to drive at night. When I worked in multiple cities back-to-back, I made sure I had time to drive from 'City A' to 'City B' before dark. This worked for me! Well, it worked until it didn't. I completed training in Rockford, IL in plenty of time for me to drive to Joliet for the next day's training. It would have been plenty of time if there hadn't been a vehicle collision involving a semi-trailer truck along my way. The East side of the interstate was shut down for over two hours. I sat in my car and watched the sun go down wondering what I was going to do. By the time the cars began moving, it was totally dark, and I noticed lightning in the sky. I could see car lights but could not tell which lane they were in. I stayed in the right lane and prayed for safety. Luckily, I only had 25 minutes' drive to the hotel, and it was right off the interstate. When I arrived and parked my car, I put my head on the windshield and cried. I knew at that moment, I had to make some different decisions around travel and work. It broke my heart, but I had to listen. I could not put myself or others in danger.

Another consideration that I had been paying attention to is my cognitive capacity. Training takes lots of energy, passion, memory, and quick responses. I started noticing anything that might indicate I needed to back down because of a change in the quality of my presentations and/or consultations. One afternoon, I was consulting with a program supervisor when suddenly, and without warning, the words that came out of my mouth did not make any sense. I knew what I wanted to say, but the words were a jumbled-up mess. I tried again, but the problem was still there. This astute supervisor, Sue Ripley, guided me through a stroke screening, face – arm - etc. which I passed. In a few moments, I was able to speak normally. Before I left, Sue very kindly offered to give me a ride home, which I turned down. I immediately stopped all out-of-town work travel and scheduled an appointment with a neurologist. Over the next several months, I had a series of tests performed, mostly on my brain and everything turned out normal. I have had no repeats of the speech problems. Perhaps this was the invitation I needed to make a decision to stay closer to home.

Late in 2019, Lois Moorman, Director of Adult Protective Services in Illinois, invited me to speak at a statewide conference. I respected Lois a lot for her work to make Adult Protective Services inclusive of people with disabilities who lived in the community. I accepted the invitation as long as another person with disabilities would be a co-trainer. Cathy Saunders accepted, and we created two sessions for the conference. Both sessions were well-received, but I noticed that I had difficulty finding a word when explaining the mass persecution of people with disabilities during Nazi Germany...a situation I had explained hundreds of times in the past. A 'normal' lapse in memory or an indicator to stop training? Not an easy question to answer. I continue to monitor my abilities and limitations as I write this.

Mexico

What I figured out...and maybe I am still figuring it out, is this: Retirement is a label. Maybe I don't need to define with a label how I want to spend this phase of my life. My wife has reminded me more than once that I can decide each time an offer comes my way whether or not to say yes. This has been great advice. I can take the time to check in with my body, mind, heart, and spirit about each possibility. This has been working for me really well. Because of my privilege (and Social Security), I can also decide if I want to do something on a voluntary basis. I have slowed down and keep my schedule flexible so that I can be supportive to my family members and community members. I continue to contribute to the inclusivity of and equality for people with disabilities. It fulfills my calling and uses my talents.

In 2020, I received an email from an international consultant looking for someone to help an agency in Mexico support a youth with disabilities who had been trafficked. When a bilingual counselor I knew was unavailable, I agreed to work with Deborah Garcia, Residential Director of Eternal Anchor in the Baja Area of Mexico at no cost. We meet on a regular basis over Zoom and the relationship has grown over time. Deborah is energetic and dedicated to the children and adults in her care. When I share a resource, she has it translated into Spanish and has had great success in learning about recovery from trauma. I am in awe of her enthusiasm and her capacity to support healing in the youth and adults that she supports.

Eternal Anchor * was originally formed by two friends, Deborah Garcia, and Austin Robinson, in order to save a child's life. They are located in an area of Mexico where there are no children's homes that accept children with disabilities - with the nearest home accepting children with disabilities almost three hours away. Prior to Eternal Anchor, there were no adequate placement options for children with disabilities experiencing abuse or neglect. Seven years later, they have grown into a comprehensive services organization that includes a special education school with over 50 students and 20 local teachers; a safe and loving residential program (providing small homes to 12 people); adult disability services (16 people); early intervention; horse therapy; a mobility equipment workshop, and community outreach. They continue to save lives and receive very little government funding.

Final thoughts

As I navigate this phase of my life, I am more and more aware of the quote by Mary Oliver: "Tell me, what is it you plan to do with your one wild and precious life?" I've known this quote for years and liked it, but it has had more meaning to me as I become very aware that I have no power over how much life I have left on this earth. I think about what I want to accomplish but equally important, I think about family, enjoyment, contributions to others, being present, relaxing, and spiritual growth. Life is very generous and as I have slowed down my work life, new doors have opened to expand my joy. Some of the doors reignited previous passions like writing poetry, gardening, and going to hermitages. Some of the doors opened up new avenues of joy, like drawing and small acts of service within my own community. Where work was a central component of my life for many years, now my wife, children and grandchild are my top priority. As I work less and open space for other things, new adventures and opportunities show up. The possibilities are unlimited. I will continue to shine a light on inequality and violence in whatever ways I am called to do so.

I used to think that I wanted to complete a list of activities before I died and not have anything left on my list, but my mind has changed on that due to a life-altering experience with my mom as her life came to an end. When my mom was placed on Hospice, I spent time with her daily. She always had a list of things she wanted to accomplish. Each day, I took notes of what she wanted me to do for her. The list included things like locating someone she had lost track of over the years so she could send them a letter or sending a card to someone who was having a difficult time. Every day she had more tasks for me to do. Every day, I worked on her lists. And one day, she was no longer able to tell me what else she wanted done. The family gathered to surround her with love and to say goodbye to this amazing woman. After she passed, I felt bad about her list of 'unfinished' tasks. I thought, I want to finish my list and then just relax before I die. I sat with that for a long time and then changed my mind. I think it is wonderful to be alive and full of dreams and things to do until the very last moment of life. Like my mom, I want to live my one wild and precious life every day and have it full to the brim with joy and service until that very last breath.

Questions for the Reader:

1. What does retirement mean to you?
2. Are there any volunteer opportunities that you might be interested in now or when you retire?
3. Are there people that you want to thank? Are there relationships that have unresolved conflict that you want to heal?
4. What do you plan to do with your one wild and precious life?

Chapter 15

The Next Chapter

"We are here not only to transform the world
but also to be transformed."
Parker Palmer

"Life is generous." Catherine Adelman

What I Know

I know that this is not a comprehensive book on sexual violence in the lives of people with disabilities. I have made mistakes and stumbled along the way. I do not know everything there is to know on this subject. This is what I do know:

- I do know that when the voices and lives of people with disabilities inform our work, the work has meaning and validity.
- I do know that sexual violence exists within a context of power and control differences. People with little power, are at high risk to experience sexual violence. People with disabilities deserve to have more power in their lives.
- I do know that I have learned a lot from my decades of working side by side people with disabilities - many of them who were/are survivors of sexual assault.

- I do know that I have witnessed intense courage and strength within people with disabilities who have survived sexual violence in addition to surviving their years of oppression.
- I do know that the strategies and resources in this book have been helpful to many people.
- I do know that I have an obligation to share what has been helpful so that others who are hurting can find solutions.
- I do know that supports for survivors will continue to grow and change…long after I leave this earth.
- I do not know what happens next or who will be doing this work, however, I trust that the work for equality, safety, healing, justice, and inclusion will continue. I am holding hope for each of you.
- I also know that progress can stop and move in reverse if we are not careful. The thousands of people with disabilities and their allies who are working for equality must continue to be vigilant in the movement to end violence. We must not forget the horrors of the past and they must not be repeated.

Gratitude

As I look back on my life's journey, it is very clear to me now that life has given me all that I needed to find and follow my passion. I am grateful for those first work experiences in 1973 working with people with disabilities which grabbed my heart and held on tight. I am grateful for the many invitations that arose during the past decades that provided chances for me to make a difference in people's lives.

I am in awe of the many people who shared their lives with me and the many opportunities that unfolded as we, together, sought safety, freedom, equality, justice, inclusion, and meaning. You were my greatest teachers and I carry you in my heart each day.

Today, I am grateful to be present with this day at this moment.

What gives me hope

I do have a lot of hope for the future. Here are some of the reasons:

There are a lot of people and organizations doing great work to create equality and justice for people with disabilities and to address the violence they experience. Nearly 50 years ago, when I started this work, I did not know of anyone else doing the work. Today we have self-advocacy groups across the United States working for equality and violence prevention and response. We have Vera's Center on Victimization and Safety * to "enhance efforts to prevent and address interpersonal violence and related crimes." We have the National Center on Criminal Justice and Disability, * directed by Leigh Ann Davis, serving as a bridge between the criminal justice and disability communities. Several national organizations now include people with disabilities in their conferences every year. There are several people and organizations addressing human sexuality of and sexual assault against people with disabilities.

There are several curricula and related resources now available on healthy relationships and sexual assault prevention. There are resources for advocates and counselors for working with survivors with disabilities. There are resources to support the work of criminal justice professionals in their work to increase accountability of offenders against people with disabilities. New resources are being developed every year. New people are joining the movement to end violence against people with disabilities. The federal government Department of Justice Office on Violence Against Women provides needed support in funding for adults with disabilities as well as other "Underserved Populations" who experience violence. This density of people and resources gives me hope, lots of hope.

In 1963, Martin Luther King, Jr said, "Injustice anywhere is a threat to justice everywhere. We are caught in an inescapable network of mutuality, tied in a single garment of destiny. Whatever affects one directly, affects all indirectly." Martin Luther King Jr. knew that we must not think of ourselves as separate from others - that what we do affects others. People can have several identities and important characteristics - some of which may result in discrimination. I believe that the scarcity thinking that surrounds us can lead to minority groups competing for resources. There can be a push-and-pull for grants, scholarships, training opportunities, jobs, etc. It pains my heart to see the separation between groups when we have so much in common and the goal is justice for ALL.

An intersectional approach takes into account all of a person's identities and the systemic discrimination based on ability, sexual orientation, gender and gender identity, race, economic status, immigration status, and others, which can lead to a lack of access and opportunity. **Intersectional practices are the hope for the future!!** I have begun to observe a shift to intersectional considerations and practices during the past few years. It doesn't appear to be common yet, but there is an evident shift. For example, there is at least one, and possibly more, Black Lives Matter groups that are welcoming, affirming and inclusive of people with disabilities, people in the LGBTQ+ community, Indigenous people, and other people of color. This gives me hope.

Another thing that gives me hope is the increased inclusion and representation of people with disabilities. For decades, when politicians were running for office and talking about their positions on certain issues, I always listened for their positions on working with and for people with disabilities. Historically, the mention of 'disabilities' as an issue to address was mostly non-existent. It is still not common. However, there has been a shift and I occasionally hear the word disabilities mentioned and we celebrate those occurrences! We have definitely seen an increase in the representation of people with disabilities in public workplaces, on television, in print materials, in sports, and in the community at large. We still have much work to do, but I am encouraged by the current expansion.

Another thing which gives me hope for the future safety and justice of people with disabilities is the redefining of justice that is occurring. I do not know a lot about transformative justice, but I am excited about the possibilities. According to the Sexual Assault Centre of Edmonton, "Transformative Justice is a political framework and approach for responding to violence, harm and abuse. At it's most basic, it seeks to respond to violence without creating more violence and/or engaging in harm reduction to lessen the violence." From what I have gathered, the process of transformative justice is survivor-focused, trauma-informed, and accountable at the community level. If all people effected by violence had opportunities for long-term safety and healing, it might actually curb the incidence of violence. We know that our current system of criminal justice does not seem to be working. Lengthy incarcerations do not seem to curb violence. I do not know the answers but am inspired by the fact that some new alternatives are being developed and tried.

These are a few of the things that give me hope.

I wonder, what gives you hope?

Life is Generous

Life is generous. I have not always felt that way. Trauma can color the many gifts that surround us. Over the years, I have learned to be grateful for the doors that closed – they were an invitation to learn something about life and myself. Each door that closed led to new open doors that I could not see until that one door closed! My recovery journey has been long and jumbled and ongoing…and mine. My recovery from trauma included a 12-step program, counseling at a sexual assault center, other therapies, Native ceremonies, spiritual support, and supportive friends. My life and my recovery have been interconnected with the lives of people with disabilities who helped me to recognize that we all have gifts and talents and contributions to make; who taught me to never give up; and who taught me to love myself and to forgive others. Reciprocal (equal) relationships can do that. Yes, relationships can save your life. Finding my calling and my purpose when I did was lifesaving. When I turned my pain into passion…and my wounds into wisdom…and my hurt into helping…I changed, and my life changed. I continue to learn and grow and heal…and I believe those are life-long opportunities for each of us, available to all of us.

Some dreams for the future

I am a dreamer. I know many of you are too. So, I want to share some of my dreams related to equality for people with disabilities. I hope it leads to action and that some of these dreams come true. I also hope that it inspires you to have your own dreams.

Dream # 1: American Sign Language (ASL) qualifies as a foreign language requirement in hundreds of colleges and universities.

I first had this dream in the 1970's when I attended the University of Illinois. In 2019, I met with some college students to discuss this for the university they attended. The dream continues. Maybe you can help make this happen. Wouldn't it be awesome if more of us knew American Sign Language and could communicate with others who use American Sign Language as their main way to communicate?

Dream #2: Broader representation of people with disabilities from television and movies to the Supreme Court.

Broader representation of people with disabilities is needed for two important reasons. The first reason is so that people with all kinds of disabilities know that they are a part of the world - that they belong and can have dreams for their futures. The second reason is so that we can all have opportunities for engagement and connections with people with disabilities; providing all of us chances to learn from the talents and skills of people who have historically been excluded.

Dream #3: All of the communities that have historically been excluded due to oppression would come together in solidarity to fight for equality and justice.

People with disabilities are part of every community. We are not separate from each other. We have a lot in common. Let's join forces and create systems that work for all of us. There should and can be an unlimited supply of justice. I know this is a huge dream. One step moving in that direction is my next dream

Dream #4: Local, state, national and international conferences include training at the intersections of all oppressed communities.

Let me explain. I have been at many conferences and there are sessions that address working with the Black community, Indigenous community, the LGBTQ+ community, people with disabilities, people who experience mental health concerns, Muslim community, immigrants, etc. I am happy to see so many communities being represented. However, where are the sessions that address all of us together? People are not just one thing. Remember the woman who asked: "I am Black, Lesbian, Disabled, and I was raped. Who is going to help me?" Let's find a way to integrate the commonalities and still honor the uniqueness of each community.

Dream #5: People are safe to be who they are.

This is a beautiful dream and I hope we can get there someday. It is sad that not everyone feels safe being who they are. I have seen children and adults pretending to be someone they are not because they are afraid of being made fun of or being judged as wrong or broken. Heck. I have done that before too, and it is such a relief to be able to be myself. I am very concerned about

461

people in the LGBTQ+ community in relation to this issue. This year, several states have passed laws that are anti-trans...others have tried to get legislation passed. I believe that people have a right to be who they are. In many places today, it is not safe to be so. This is a dream that is going to take active resistance to these legislative proposals. These laws can make a person consider suicide. We must stop the hate. We can and must do better. If you want to learn more, about how you can help, check out the National Center for Transgender Equality *

Dream #6: All people will be safe from sexual assault and other forms of violence.

This is another huge dream. I believe that we can. What would this take? I certainly don't know all of the answers, but I have a few thoughts. What if we actively teach our children, starting at a young age about consent, boundaries, and their personal power? What if we make conversations about feelings and safety common within our families and organizations? I believe that those two things would lead to less abuse and earlier reporting of abuse. If we discover abuse and violence early, we can help people heal sooner...hopefully before they hurt other people. Intermixed within these teachings and conversations are peaceful means of conflict resolution. Another aspect of this is creating a society that works for everyone. When ALL people have equal access to resources, and ALL people have equal power, I think we would have a lot less violence. There are people and resources available right now to make this a reality. How do we reach the masses? How do we create a mass movement focused on creating an equal and peaceful world? I wonder, what ideas do you have to eliminate violence?

These are just a few of the dreams that I carry with me.

I wonder, what dreams do you have for our future?

Closing

Today I welcome the next chapter. I have hope for the future. I see things changing. I know I will not be as actively involved as I have been in the past. I widely receive the gifts that life offers me today. I hold hope for each of you who choose to work for access, inclusion, equality, safety, healing, and justice for people who have historically been excluded. I believe the world is ready for more equity. The doors are opening, so let's step across the threshold and keep moving toward our goal.

As I was writing this final chapter, I had a delightful conversation with my second cousin, Kayleigh. She currently works for Nebraska Appleseed, a nonprofit organization that fights for justice and opportunity for all Nebraskans. However, I remember an experience we shared a few years ago in Denver, Colorado, while I was traveling for work and Kayleigh was an AmeriCorps VISTA member working with veterans experiencing homelessness. We met up for dinner and began walking together afterwards, back towards the hotel where I was staying. The next thing I knew, we were at a local eatery buying dinner for a person who had been standing on a corner asking for money. I was in awe of her kindness and authenticity. While we waited for the person's food to be made, Kayleigh asked them about their story and brainstormed with them about what local resources could be helpful. It was stunning to see how during a short interaction, she was able to build a genuine connection. She has a passion and a calling, so it is exciting to engage her in conversations about the world. I am sharing this because of something she said last night:

"One of the biggest barriers I find in discussions around equity and social justice issues, is the belief many people have: 'things are what they are, and they cannot change.' But, that kind of attitude ignores the many things that **have** changed for the better thanks to various movements, and it hinders future positive changes and growth. I remind them, and sometimes myself, 'Things don't have to be this way!'"

And there it is...those of us who believe that things can change, that we can have a world where everyone's basic needs are met:

- we are the changemakers,
- we are the dreamers and visionaries,
- we are the light for those who live in the darkness.

I invite everyone who is reading this to hop on the hope train for a better, more equal, more compassionate, more just world.

First, we must imagine it, see it, feel it. Only then can we create it.

In closing, I want to share one more story, in honor of a woman I will call Sarah.

We were the first to arrive at the funeral home and when the man asked, "Are you family?" we had to reply, "Sarah has no family." The fact is Sarah had very little history that could be captured in writing or through pictures or through stories told by family or friends. Sadly, Sarah had a made-up birthday because there was no known record of her birth.

Sarah had lived in a large institution for many decades. During the 'deinstitutionalization movement', a pathway was created for Sarah to move into a new town. She moved to a home in a residential neighborhood and lived with three other people. She participated in a day program a few days each week. She made friends and appreciated her new life and opportunities. When her medical needs became too great to care for her in the group home, Sarah moved to a nursing home a few hours away. When Sarah died, we brought her back to town and held a funeral so her friends could tell her goodbye.

A few weeks later, an ironic twist of fate put Sarah's gravesite on the front page of the local newspaper. An exceptionally cold winter for

466

gravediggers was the topic of the article. There in the picture was Sarah's tombstone for the entire community to see. For those of us who knew her it seemed to ring out: "I do have a history. I did exist."

Rest in peace, Sarah. We remember you.

Creating Pathways – a poem

So many things are buried
     deep in our horrific history
          so many ways that inequality
               haunts and hurts us
continuing still today
     for those who are different
          than those who are in power.

We must shine a light
   on our lives
      on our stories
         on the many ways
            people are being excluded and hurt

We must shine a light
   on the souls
      who live on the edges
         who are excluded and not easily seen

Show our humanity
     show our value
          show our wholeness

We must create pathways
        to equity
            to safety
                to healing
                    and to justice

There are many pathways
        only a few are shown here

            YOU ARE NEEDED

        to create new pathways
            to keep the movement
                going forward

and the past...need   never   be   repeated

What part will you play?

Resources/ References

Chapter 3

Disabled Persons Protective Commission

www.mass.gov/orgs/disabled-persons-protective-commission.

(The website is Welcome to Massachusetts: Mass.gov >> go to search engine in the center of the page, type: disabled-persons-protective-commission)

"*Real Choice*" by Karen Donovan
Recorded at Speak Up Speak Out; November 5, 2009
Available on YouTube:
https://youtu.be/q2yC1inCy7Y

Lives Worth Living

YouTube: *Lives Worth Living, Full Documentary*

https://youtu.be/zS6qsGRqdhs

Chapter 5

The Start by Believing Campaign

www.startbybelieving.org

Paceley, Megan S., et. al, *Beyond a shared experience: Queer and trans youth navigating COVID-19*. November 2020. Sage Journals. Qualitative Social Work.   Retrieved from https://journals.sagepub.com/doi/full/10.1177/14733 25020973329

(Go to: https://journals.sagepub.com > search for Paceley and select the article)

Shapiro, A., McEvers, K. & Shapiro, J (2018, January 8). *Abused and Betrayed*. Retrieved from https://www.npr.org/series/575502633/abused-and-betrayed

(go to https://www.npr.org > search for abused and betrayed)

J. Schaller and J.L. Fieberg, "*Issues of abuse for women with disabilities and implications for rehabilitation counseling*," Journal of Applied Rehabilitation Counseling 29 no. 2 (1998): 9-17.

Smith, N. Forging New Collaborations, *A Guide for Rape Crisis, Domestic Violence, and Disability Organizations*, VERA Institute on Justice, April 2011

Chapter 6

Hingsburger, Dave, *JUST SAY KNOW!: Understanding and Reducing the Risks of Sexual Victimization* ,(1995)

Sobsey, Dick, *Violence and Abuse in the Lives of People with Disabilities: The End of Silent Acceptance?* (1994)

A sample of the available curriculum include:

Sexuality Education for People with Developmental Disabilities (Katherine McLaughlin)

Women with Disabilities and Sexual Violence Education Guide (Illinois Imagines)

Picture Supplement Guide for use with Women with Disabilities and Sexual Violence Education Guide (Illinois Imagines)

Family Life and Sexual Health—FLASH (King County, Washington State)

Dating and Friendships—Alaska

Sexuality for all abilities (high school and transition ages) -Minnesota

****

O'Connell, Kathy, *FIREWALK: Embracing Different Abilities*, (2012)

Kathy O'Connell, the founder of *Radiant Abilities*

(www.radiant abilities.com)

Chapter 7

A Catalyst to Peace, Cathy Saunders

https://icasa.org/resources/illinois-imagines/imagines-resources

(Website: www.icasa.org >> go to Resources >> select Illinois Imagines >> Select Resources >> a download link for this poem is the first item listed)

Saunders, Cathy Lynn, My *Name is Cathy Lynn: A love letter from me to you,* (2019)

The *Picture Guide to the Exam Following Sexual Assault* incudes ten different resources related to the sexual assault examination. Please select the one that is most relevant to your situation. You can begin here:

https://icasa.org/resources/illinois-imagines/materials-toolkit-and-other-material

(Website: www.icasa.org >> go to Resources >> select Illinois Imagines >>Select Materials – Toolkit and other Material >> scroll down to down to SANE Picture Guides >>Select the one most relevant to your situation)

Counseling Survivors with Intellectual Disabilities and/or Autism

https://icasa.org/uploads/documents/illinois-imagines/Counseling-Guide-3-18-mini.pdf

(Website: www.icasa.org >> go to Resources >> select Illinois Imagines >>Select Materials – Toolkit and other Material >> Counseling and Advocate Guides >> select Select Counseling People with Developmental Disabilities and/or Autism)

Chapter 8

Taussig, Rebekah, *Sitting Pretty: The View from My Ordinary Resilient Disabled Body*, (2021)

Chapter 9

Counseling Survivors with Intellectual Disabilities or Autism Guide.

https://icasa.org/uploads/documents/illinois-imagines/Counseling-Guide-3-18-mini.pdf

(Website: www.icasa.org >> go to Resources >> select Illinois Imagines >>Select Materials, scroll down to Counseling and Advocate Guides, >>Select Counseling People with Intellectual Disabilities and/or Autism)

You're gonna make it

Rap music video starring J. Saint and Kelly B; created by the Pennsylvania Coalition Against Rape

https://youtu.be/Y4tbcCdpTkl

Chapter 11

The protocols for law enforcement and prosecution are available at this link under Model Protocols:

http://www.icjia.state.il.us/ifvcc/projects

(Website is Illinois Criminal Justice Information Authority www.icjia.illinois.gov >>go to Partner Sites >>Select: Illinois Family Violence Coordinating Councils>>Select: Projects)

Both the law enforcement accessibility review and the sample general order are available at the same link as the protocols.

http://www.icjia.state.il.us/ifvcc/projects

(Website is Illinois Criminal Justice Information Authority www.icjia.illinois.gov >>go to Partner Sites >>Select: Illinois Family Violence Coordinating Councils>>Select: Projects)

Chapter 12

FLASH (Family Life and Sexual Health) Curriculum

https://kingcounty.gov/depts/health/locations/family-planning/education/FLASH.aspx

(Website is www.kingcounty.gov >>> enter FLASH into the search engine)

Specialized Habilitation Services

https://www.dshs.wa.gov/sites/default/files/DDA/dda/documents/featured/Specialized%20Habilitation%20External.pdf

(Website www.dshs.wa.gov >>> Type Specialized Habilitation in the search engine >>> select 2. Featured Services >>> select Specialized Habilitation)

Robert Perske

www.robertperske.com

Chapter 13

2008 article about recovery capital written by William White and William Cloud

(http://www.williamwhitepapers.com/pr/2008Recove ryCapitalPrimer.pdf).

(Website: www.williamwhitepapers.com >>Select Papers>>Scroll down to papers written in 2008, select Recovery Capital Primer)

Karyn Harvey's Happiness Assessment

https://karynharvey.org/uploads/1/2/2/1/122160508/ happiness_assessment_and_procedure_for_staff.p df

(Website: Karynharvey.org >>> Select: About >>> scroll down and select Happiness Assessment and procedure for staff and Happiness Assessment revised)

Kathy O'Connell with Radiant Abilities

www.radiantabilities.com

Parent Guide developed by Illinois Imagines
https://icasa.org/docs/illinois%20imagines/soft%20c
over%20guide%20for%20parents%20and%20guard
ians%20module%204.2.pdf

(Website: www.icasa.org >> go to Resources >>
select Illinois Imagines >>Select Materials >> Select
Toolkit Module 5: Guide for Parents and Guardians)

Empowerment Guide lessons created by Illinois
Imagines
https://icasa.org/docs/illinois%20imagines/empower
ment%20guide%201-15.pdf

(Website: www.icasa.org >> go to Resources >>
select Illinois Imagines >>Select Materials >> Select
Toolkit Module 7: Guide to starting Empowerment
Groups)

Disability Rights Wisconsin: Healthy and Safe
relationships curriculum (in process)

(For information contact: Disability Rights Wisconsin
– Victim Advocacy Program info@drwi.org
608-267-0214   Healthy and Safe Relationships
Curriculum funded through Office of Violence
Against Women Underserved Grant – Pam Malin,
Project Coordinator)

Articles about Recovery Capital and Community
Recovery

http://www.williamwhitepapers.com/blog/2014/03/re
covery-landscapes.html

(Website: www.williamwhitepapers.com >>Select
Blog/New Postings on the main page>>Scroll down
to Monthly Archives >> Select March 2014 >>
Select Recovery Landscapes)

http://www.williamwhitepapers.com/blog/2020/10/recovery-people-places-and-time.html

(Website: www.williamwhitepapers.com >>Select Blog/New Postings on the main page>>Scroll down to Monthly Archives >> Select October 2020 >> Select Recovery: People, Places, and Time)

http://www.williamwhitepapers.com/pr/dlm_uploads/2013-Community-as-Patient-Recovery-focused-Community-Mobilization.pdf

(Website: www.williamwhitepapers.com >>Select Papers>>Scroll down to papers written in 2013, select Community as Patient Recovery-Focused-Community-Mobilization)

Historical Trauma

Mohatt, N. V., Thompson, A. B., Thai, N. D., &
Tebes, J. K. (2014). *Historical trauma as public
narrative: A conceptual review of how history
impacts present-day health. Social Science &
Medicine, 106,* 128–136.
https://doi.org/10.1016/j.socscimed.2014.01.043

(Website: sciencedirect.com >>> write 'historical
trauma' in the keywords section of the advanced
search >>>scroll down to article)

Zuber, Andrea Lou, *Implications for Healing,
Transformation and Prosperity: Historical and
Cultural Trauma and People with Intellectual and
Developmental Disabilities, (December 2018)*
https://conservancy.umn.edu/bitstream/handle/1129
9/201570/Zuber%20MLS%20Final%20Project.pdf?s
equence=1&isAllowed=y

(Go to https://conservancy.umn.edu/ do a search
for Zuber, scroll down to article)

Seligman, Martin, *Flourish: A New Understanding of
Happiness and Well-Being – and How to Achieve
Them,* (2011)

Chapter 14

Blue Tower Solutions, Inc.

https://www.bluetowersolutions.org

Rocking the Cradle: Ensuring the Rights of Parents with Disabilities and Their Children

https://www.ncd.gov/publications/2012/Sep272012

(Website: www.ncd.gov >>>Select: Publications >>>Select: 2012 >>>Scroll to *Rocking the Cradle: Ensuring the Rights of Parents with Disabilities and their Children*)

Eternal Anchor

www.eternalanchor.org

Chapter 15

Vera Center on Victimization and Safety

https://www.vera.org/centers/victimization-and-safety

National Center on Criminal Justice and Disability

https://www.thearcofil.org/arc-national-center-on-criminal-justice-disability/

National Center for Transgender Equality

https://transequality.org/

Acknowledgments and Appreciations

In gratitude to people who co-trained with me the past several years. Thank you for sharing your stories, talents, hope and light with others.

Alice Kieft	Amy Walker
Ann Ford	Barb Pritchard
Barry Portman	Billy Clymo
Brenda Henson	Caitlin Rae Botcher
Carl Nave	Cathy Lynn Saunders
Charlotte Earving	Chelle Galasi
Cindy Bentley	Courtland Booker
Cristein Seiders	Eric C. Arnold
Erica Jones	Evettte Parks
Florence Wilson	Hadley Ravencroft
Jacqulyn Thomas	Jenn Knapp
Joanne Archambault	Karen Randolph
Kim Lonsway	Kim Smith
Krescene Beck	Leanne Mull

Leslie Pearce

Linda Heath

Lisa Burns

Lynn Liston

Mary Hettel

Mary Suggs

Megan Paceley

Michelle Staples

Nancy Smith

Pam Malin

Ravell McDonald

Sandy Laesch

Scott Palm

Shweta Sawant

Tammy Livingston

Tiffany McFadden

Varsha N.

Will Speirs

Lester Pritchard

Linda Sandman

Lorraine Cotton

Marge Parker

Mary Mathis

Maryam Mostoufi

Melissa Holder

Maureen Mostacci

Orieda Horn Anderson

Randy Planthaber

Rosie Kuhlman

Sean Black

Shelley Karl

Stephanie Campbell

Teresa Tudor

Tony Richards

Vickie Smith

I am forever grateful to my mother whose bravery, honesty, love, compassion, sense of adventure, and service to others informed many of my life choices. I celebrate you always, Mom.

I have been honored to know many people who allowed me into their hearts and lives as we shared sacred spaces of trauma and healing. Each pathway was unique. Some spaces included sexual assault exams; some facing offenders in court hearings; some in hours of therapy; some in collaborative team meetings; and some traveling and training others about violence prevention, response, and healing. You have blessed my life tremendously. May you always remember how brave and whole you are.

Families are always impacted by our work life. I am very appreciative of my two children, Meg and Jon, who are amazing people making positive contributions to the world. You both make my heart smile every day. I also appreciate my grandchild, who shows me daily how to embrace power, joy, love, laughter, and all human feelings! I am a better person because of you!

A big thanks to my sister, Carol Tatum, for always supporting my work and for traveling with me to some of the cool places I was honored to visit!! We shared many 'ooh la la' moments, as well as tragic ones. My life would not be the same without you!

Another big thank you to Kay Scrogin, who believed in my vision and allowed me the opportunity to create a training/consulting division within the organization that she led. And thanks to Dreux Lewandowski, for his continued support when Kay passed him the organizational torch.

I want to formally acknowledge the influence that Teresa Tudor has had on my work life. Together, we co-created trainings, resources, articles, and lots of fun! Thanks for accompanying me on my first trip to Guam. I could not have survived a 27-hour flight schedule without your physical and emotional assistance! Thank you for rescuing me on the escalator incident in Atlanta! You always ask the best questions to expand my thinking and that is a real gift! This journey was much more fun (and safer) with you by my side on so many occasions.

I also want to acknowledge Amy Walker, Karen Randolph, Krescene Beck, Brenda Henson, Leanne Mull, Mary Suggs, Stephanie Campbell, Cathy Lynn Saunders, Linda Sandman, and Teresa Tudor for their wonderful commitment over the years to create and sustain training to prevent and respond to sexual assault against people with disabilities.

I am so grateful to have so many people to thank, including:

♥   The core members of the Illinois Imagines statewide team for being such great colleagues and friends for so many years: Teresa Tudor, Sean Black, Mary Hettel, Carol Corgan, Amy Walker, Alice Keift, Marge Parker, Krescene Beck, Linda Sandman, Chelle Galassi, Lora Thomas, Lois Moorman, Vernie Breuhler, Mary Scanlan Ratliff-Babcock, Pam Myo, Lacy Pollack, Ovelia Smith-Barton, Susy Woods, and others who made contributions at the policy level or in creating resources: Amber Buckley, Lyn Schollet, Maureen Mostacci, Theresa Parks, Cheryl Jansen, Morgan Tudor, and Julie Boland.
♥   Betty Schwieterman and Andrea Kadlac from Disability Rights Washington for their years of support and their dedication to the safety and equality of people with disabilities. You have both impacted my work and my life in many positive ways.
♥   My brother, Bill White, for reviewing and commenting on the entire book before it was finalized.

♥ Teresa Tudor, Leanne Mull, Krescene Beck, Amy Walker, Barbara Pritchard, and Brenda Henson for your early reviews of specific chapters. Thanks also to Linda Sandman and Alisha White for their ideas on a title and/or book cover.

♥ Leigh Ann Davis and James Meadours for their thoughtful review of this book. I am so grateful for my relationship with Leigh Ann and the many ways we have supported each other's work and for her contributions through the ARC of the US and the National Center on Criminal Justice and Disability. I am grateful to James for his courage, labor, energy, and heartfelt work to speak up about sexual violence and people with disabilities. You are both making positive changes in this world!

♥ Amy Loder with the Office on Violence Against Women for our outstanding conversations, including some disagreements, over the years and the great dinners we shared when I worked in DC.

♥ Nancy Smith, Sandra Harrell, Amy Judy, and Leslie Myers with the Center on Victimization and Safety for their work to end violence against people with disabilities. I am grateful for the many spaces and work that we shared over the years.

♥ The ALSO (Alliance of Local Service Organizations) Team - for the opportunity to work from home as I navigated the journey of semi-retirement. I appreciated learning from the Department of Justice's Underserved Grantees technical assistance team: Cristina Damiani, Zarena Leblanc, Lisa Gilmore, Quenette Walton, and Topher Williamson. You all opened my mind and filled my heart on many occasions.

♥ Pam Malin for the opportunity to work together on a Safe and Healthy Relationships project in Wisconsin. I will always remember that we dedicated as much attention to "relationship with self" as we did to "relationships with others". It was a joy to work with you and the team creating something that will help so many to live safe and healthy lives.

♥ End Violence Against Women International (EVAWI) for the opportunity to be of service, for the many lessons I learned through our relationships and for the Start by Believing Campaign.

♥ Joseph Shapiro from National Public Radio for his decades of work focused on unequal systems of justice.

And...a lifetime of gratitude to my spouse, Cate Adelman, who has supported my work for many years. Without your editing, writing, and publishing skills, this book would not be the quality that it is today. Most importantly, without your love and generosity, my life would not be as full and fun! Thank you for always supporting me to be my best.

About the Author

Shirley Paceley has dedicated a lifetime to the transformation of lives; individually, collectively, and organizationally. She began her work with people with disabilities in the early 1970s, and quickly became aware of rampant abuse and neglect. Her career commenced into a personal mission that expanded into international impact as she worked tirelessly towards equal access to justice, prevention, and healing for survivors with disabilities. Shirley is a visionary: a disability rights activist, consultant, counselor, international trainer, and published author. Her work has not only impacted the lives of thousands of individuals but has also supported systemic change on all levels. Shirley served on the Board of Directors of End Violence Against Women International, the Editorial Board of *Sexual Assault Report* and as Project Advisor to the National Center on Criminal Justice and Disability. Examples of her work include leading a team that developed model protocols for law enforcement and prosecutors; developing training for Sexual Assault Nurse Examiners; and co-creating a manual for sexual assault counselors. Paceley has trained thousands of people on effective strategies for trauma-informed responses that support survivors with disabilities and hold offenders accountable. Shirley received a 2021 Professional Impact award from EVAWI (End Violence Against Women International) for her lifetime of professional achievements.

Feel Free to contact Shirley at
shirleypaceley@gmail.com